RIGHTS AND THE CITY

RIGHTS AND THE CITY

PROBLEMS, PROGRESS, AND PRACTICE

EDITED BY SANDEEP AGRAWAL

 UNIVERSITY *of* ALBERTA PRESS

Published by

University of Alberta Press
1–16 Rutherford Library South
11204 89 Avenue NW
Edmonton, Alberta, Canada T6G 2J4
amiskwaciwâskahikan | Treaty 6 | Métis Territory
uap.ualberta.ca | uapress@ualberta.ca

Copyright © 2022 University of Alberta Press

LIBRARY AND ARCHIVES CANADA
CATALOGUING IN PUBLICATION

Title: Rights and the city : problems, progress, and practice / edited by Sandeep Agrawal.
Names: Agrawal, Sandeep, editor.
Description: Includes bibliographical references.
Identifiers: Canadiana (print) 20220259968 | Canadiana (ebook) 2022026001X |
ISBN 9781772126266 (softcover) |
ISBN 9781772126709 (EPUB) |
ISBN 9781772126716 (PDF)
Subjects: LCSH: Urban policy. | LCSH: City planning—Social aspects. | LCSH: City dwellers—Civil rights. | LCSH: Sociology, Urban.
Classification: LCC HT166 .R54 2022 | DDC 307.1/216—dc23

First edition, first printing, 2022.
First printed and bound in Canada by Houghton Boston Printers, Saskatoon Saskatchewan.
Copyediting by Angela Wingfield.
Proofreading by Kay Rollans.

This publication is licensed under a Creative Commons licence, Attribution–Noncommercial–No Derivative Works 4.0 International: see www.creativecommons.org. The text may be reproduced for noncommercial purposes, provided that credit is given to the original author. To obtain permission for uses beyond those outlined in the Creative Commons licence, please contact the University of Alberta Press.

University of Alberta Press supports copyright. Copyright fuels creativity, encourages diverse voices, promotes free speech, and creates a vibrant culture. Thank you for buying an authorized edition of this book and for complying with the copyright laws by not reproducing, scanning, or distributing any part of it in any form without permission. You are supporting writers and allowing University of Alberta Press to continue to publish books for every reader.

This book has been published with the help of a grant from the Canadian Federation for the Humanities and Social Sciences, through the Awards to Scholarly Publications Program, using funds provided by the Social Sciences and Humanities Research Council of Canada.

University of Alberta Press gratefully acknowledges the support received for its publishing program from the Government of Canada, the Canada Council for the Arts, and the Government of Alberta through the Alberta Media Fund.

CONTENTS

Acknowledgments VII
Introduction IX
SANDEEP AGRAWAL

I THE RIGHT TO THE CITY

1 | Whose Right to What City? 1
Indigenous Rights amidst Claims for Constitutionally Empowered Cities
ALEXANDRA FLYNN

2 | The Right to the City as an Emerging Norm 27
Codification and Cultural Institutions
JENNIFER A. ORANGE

II RIGHTS IN THE CITY

3 | Human Rights and the City in the Pre-*Charter* Era 53
SANDEEP AGRAWAL

4 | Group Rights and Collective Rights 79
What Are They and How Do They Affect Urban Issues?
SANDEEP AGRAWAL & ERAN S. KAPLINSKY

5 | Human Rights and Canadian Municipalities 105
SANDEEP AGRAWAL

6 | Becoming a Human Rights City 133
Lessons from Edmonton
RENÉE VAUGEOIS

III OTHER RIGHTS IN THE CITY

7 | The Right to Adequate Housing Around the Globe 159
Analysis and Evaluation of National Constitutions
MICHELLE L. OREN & RACHELLE ALTERMAN

8 | Property Rights and the Canadian City 187
ERAN S. KAPLINSKY

9 | The Dangers of Allowing "Othering" Speech in a City's Public Spaces 209
OLA P. MALIK & SASHA BEST

Afterword 235
After Rights?
BENJAMIN DAVY

Contributors 241

ACKNOWLEDGMENTS
—

THIS WORK is supported by the Social Sciences and Humanities Research Council of Canada. Thanks go to several research assistants who worked diligently on the project. Jahaan Premji, Fiona McGill, Jill Lang, Julie Edney, Hayley Wasylycia, and Pradeep Sangapala are notable among them.

The project benefited immensely from Donna-Lee Wybert's meticulous manuscript editing and eye for detail. At University of Alberta Press, it was a pleasure to work with Mat Buntin, who remained enthusiastically supportive throughout the project. Two anonymous reviews that he solicited helped improve the manuscript significantly.

At its core this book has the collective spirit of collaboration and is a result of the patience, perseverance, and passion of the contributing authors. It demonstrates our insights, efforts, and commitment to promote and protect rights and freedoms for all.

INTRODUCTION

SANDEEP AGRAWAL
—

RIGHTS AND THE CITY takes stock of rights struggles and their progress, with a primary focus on Canadian cities. It explores the meaning of people's experiences for the realization of human and other related forms of rights—locally, nationally, and globally. In addition, the project aims to examine the legal, conceptual, and philosophical aspects of rights, including the various forms of rights—human, Indigenous, housing, property, and various others embedded in or encompassing these. This book is unique in its use of empirical evidence and examples to explain rights and to translate the philosophical and legal aspects of rights into more practical terms and applications, such as the application and practice of rights to and in the city.

The compilation elicits the constraints and ambiguities that municipal governments face, and some of the progress made when they attempt to combat discriminatory practices, while advancing a human rights agenda. This edited volume has one implicit question that unites all its parts: *What is (and what ought to be) the role of municipal governments and planners in regulating, implementing, and advocating rights' claims?* It answers the question empirically via legal research or analysis of statutory and case law, or it relies on qualitative case studies. This exploration presents a nuanced understanding, which sometimes encompasses multiple perspectives, of the ethical or moral dilemmas and compromises that local governments endure to enforce human rights.

In Canada, and elsewhere in the world, urban issues are increasingly being contested on rights grounds. Notable among these issues are those involving squatters, tent cities, greenfield development, "single-family" zones, and the siting of places of worship, emergency shelters, and residential care facilities. The scholarly literature on rights at the city level is dominated by a discussion of property rights (such as Alterman, 2010; Davy, 2012; Needham, 2006; Webster & Lai, 2003) at the expense of other rights to and in the city. Hence, this collection brings together national and international planning and legal scholars and practitioners, as well as local human rights advocates, to engage vigorously in this debate. Collectively, the contributors bring a wealth of experience and insight to a topic that is gaining momentum in the national policy arena but which has received relatively little scholarly attention to date at the municipal level. Thus, the publication of this book is topical and timely.

Although this work was conceptualized and much of it written before the rise of the Black Lives Matter protests and marches across the United States (and around the world) against police brutality, the essays debate many of the issues that align with the undercurrent of this widespread unrest. The issues are diverse: a continued violation of the right to the city, including the right to protest in public spaces; a complete disregard for human rights and freedoms, including freedom of expression and the right to equality, life, and liberty; the right to housing; and the right to private property. The recent protests have demonstrated a collective cry for a right to the city, along with solidarity to uphold the human rights and freedoms of the citizens who occupy it.

Concomitantly, the pandemic that is unfolding in real time provides a surreal but live backdrop to this project. It has exposed the long-standing systemic and structural inequalities in Canadian society and elsewhere in the world. In particular, racialized minorities, the poor, and women who live in Canadian cities experience the more adverse effects and discriminatory impacts of COVID-19 (Public Health Ontario, 2020; Statistics

Canada, 2020). They face greater risk because they often work in frontline jobs, live in smaller and more crowded homes, and encounter barriers when accessing health information. Concurrently, homelessness is on the rise in Canadian cities, as witnessed in the dramatic emergence of tent cities since the beginning of the pandemic. Although the *Canadian Charter of Rights and Freedoms* (the *Charter*) and human rights legislation prohibit any form of discrimination in employment, housing, or health care, these legal tools do not offer any specific social and economic rights, such as the rights to housing, health care, social assistance, or work that are guaranteed in the *International Covenant on Economic, Social and Cultural Rights* (ICESCR). However, Canada, as a state, offers a comprehensive social protection and assistance framework in the form of unemployment benefits, social assistance, and health care to every Canadian. Unfortunately, each of these social programs has experienced steady funding cuts and reduction in assistance over the years.

This volume adds might to the voices of people who are most affected by today's structural inequality and systemic discrimination, and who are sometimes subject to state violence. It explains how planning instruments were and still are complicit in creating a divisive, segregated city. At the same time, it describes the efforts and progress made, albeit slowly, with some hiccups along the way. In sum, this book is a call to reclaim and rebuild our cities so that they are equitable, diverse, and inclusive.

Rights and Freedoms

While no one definition of rights exists, *rights* are generally understood to be the fundamental normative rules in a given society for what its people are allowed to do or what they are owed by others, including governing bodies. These rules may be defined by a legal system, social conventions, or ethical theory. By one definition adopted here, rights are institutionally defined rules specifying how people can act with one another; they are upheld by enduring legal protections granted to individual citizens by the liberal-democratic state. They encapsulate two moral and political claims (Donnelly, 2013)—rectitude (righteousness or the right thing to do) and entitlement (having a right, or a right that is owed to someone). Among these categories are the right to vote, the right to property, and the right to information. Of course, there are others.

Freedom also has multiple philosophical, political, and constitutional conceptions. Garvey (1981) offers one definition, stating that "a freedom protects from state-imposed constraint individual choices to perform or not to perform certain actions, and to pursue or not to pursue certain conditions of character" (p. 1757). Thus, freedom of expression protects both the choice to speak and the choice to be silent. Garvey highlights two key differences between freedoms and rights: (a) the consequences of securing rights are much more predictable than those of securing freedoms; and (b) freedoms may carry different values for different individuals (such as a child or a cognitively disabled person), unlike rights, whose values remain constant regardless of individual differences.

Freedom is a necessary precondition to enjoying rights (Howie, 2018). For example, freedom of speech, together with other freedoms—like freedom of assembly and association—is crucial for the effective exercise of the right to vote (UN Human Rights Committee, 1996, para. 12). Freedoms, however, are not absolute. States can limit them under certain circumstances, to respect the rights of others or in the interest of national security, public health, or morals. An illustration here is that laws against hate propaganda or child pornography may limit freedom of expression but are warranted because they prevent harm to individuals and/or groups.

The book builds on two broad concepts of rights: the right *to* the city, and rights *in* the city. The *right to the city* calls for all inhabitants to be able to fully enjoy, contribute to, and participate in city life, with all that it offers. However, *rights in the city*, as a concept, focuses on how human rights are implemented in cities, using international treaties and conventions, including the *Universal Declaration of Human Rights* (UDHR), and in some states, using constitutionally guaranteed human rights (Reuter, 2019). Rights to housing and the right to own property are included in the UDHR, but they are not specified as human rights in the Canadian context or clearly included as the right to the city. Freedom of expression, while included in the Canadian context, is not absolute. Hence, these diverse rights are included as the "other rights and freedoms in the city" in this volume. The following few sections will unpack the two concepts, drawing into focus the differences and commonalities between the two.

Right to the City

A rights-based discourse on urban policies first surfaced in the 1960s as part of wider social protests against capitalism as a result of the urban crisis in Paris and elsewhere. Henry Lefebvre's radical and highly influential work *Le droit à la ville* (Right to the city, 1968) and his subsequent book *The Production of Space* (1992) have led to the idea of a right to the city, informing an urban social movement. Both texts depart from the idea that "old classical humanism ended long ago and badly" (Lefebvre, 1996, p. 149); instead, they emphasize the need for the participation of all urban dwellers in urban planning.

Lefebvre's right-to-the-city concept encompasses two interrelated principal ideas:

- The city is an oeuvre, in which all its citizens participate and make decisions that contribute to the production of urban space.
- Spaces are produced by their inhabitants physically appropriating them—accessing, occupying, and using them in everyday life.

Notably, this right to the city resists the power of capital and the state by calling city inhabitants to engage in direct struggle and urban politics in order to achieve access to and occupancy in urban spaces.

Lefebvre's right to the city conceptualizes the city as essentially a social organization built by city dwellers' intense involvement in shaping it. It has also become the locus classicus in an ever-growing body of scholarship on Harvey's (2013) "rebel cities," Fainstein's (2011) "just cities," and Holston's (2008) "insurgent citizenship." This scholarship emphasizes the urban potential and obligation to bring prosperity, participation, and equal treatment to all inhabitants. It thus adds to the revolutionary and transformational works related to rights and cities (Fainstein, 2011; Harvey, 1973, 2013).

Many planning scholars who resist the prevailing neoliberal tendencies in planning, like Harvey (2013), Fainstein (2011), Miraftab (2012a, 2012b), Mitchell (2003), and Sandercock (2003), have embraced Lefebvre's concept of the right to the city. However, others, like Purcell (2002) and Qadeer and Agrawal (2011), point to the gaps and disconnects within Lefebvre's ideas, as well as between his concept and human rights. For instance, Lefebvre's concept critically overlooks practical guidance on what this right to the city entails or how it informs relations between urban dwellers and the state. Some argue that the concept is effective to resist significantly the privatization and homogeneity of public space, but that it is frankly more useful as a rhetorical or theoretical device than as a policy-making or legal instrument (Marcuse, 2009; Purcell, 2002). In other words, the concept remains vague, with undefined terminology: What is a "right"? What is meant by "the city"?

The concept can still be adopted, however, by relying on current institutional frameworks and invoking moral and legislative policy (Fainstein, 2011) that affects people and their surroundings, as Brazil and Ecuador have done. The judiciary can facilitate and enforce this orientation by applying human rights in state policies and practices. In fact, recent scholarship (Huchzermeyer, 2018; Purcell, 2002) interprets Lefebvre's later writing as potentially encouraging transformation within existing legal rights frameworks. Mitchell (2003) also advocates inscribing rights in law and policy, to provide institutional support for disrupting the destruction of differentiated spaces that urban inhabitants produce.

Rights in the City

Human Rights

The idea of rights in the city focuses on the implementation of a bundle of human rights. They are primarily a Western liberal concept, tend to be secular in nature, and are better achieved in liberal democracies (Agrawal, 2020). Political philosophers such as Donnelly (2013), Sandel (1998), and others argue that the historical roots of human rights lie in John Locke's idea of the divine notion of rights.[1] Donnelly attributes the modern secular conception of human rights, including the UDHR of 1948, to Kant's idea of humans as rational beings governed by objective moral law. Human rights, as Donnelly further explains, arise from the inherent dignity of the human being and are needed for a life worthy of a human being. Thus, we all possess them by virtue of being human, based on our inherent dignity and equal worth *as* human beings. These are the highest moral rights because they regulate the fundamental structures and practices of political life; in ordinary circumstances they take priority over other moral, legal, and political claims. Human rights thus arise from human action and are not given to people by God or nature. The liberal commitment to individual rights,[2] which limits the democratic commitment to widespread empowerment, makes liberal democracies receptive to human rights successes.

The UDHR is the foundation of human rights law, inspiring extensive and legally binding human rights laws. As many scholars have pointed out, the issue with human rights when they are not codified is that they are often vague, abstract, too hard to enforce, and not adaptable to the cultural context (Donnelly, 2013; Goodale, 2009; Hopgood, 2013; Merry, Levitt, Servan Rosen, & Yoon, 2010; Oomen, 2016). Concomitantly, codified human rights suffer from several inherent contradictions. For instance, they suffer from the "Kantian imperfect obligations"[3] (Sen, 2004, p. 319) and "public reasoning"[4] (Sen, 2005, p. 160), which may not be covered in the law. A contemporary example of this might be the decision to not deport illegal residents of a country or to provide affordable housing to all, which the human rights law may not allow.

Although not originally conceived in these terms, modern states—because of their political dominance in the contemporary world—have emerged as the essential institutional forms for effective implementation and enforcement of human rights, as well as being the principal threat to the enjoyment of these rights (Donnelly, 2013). While almost all nation-states have ratified the UDHR, the domestic instruments of implementation vary considerably from one country to another because the implementation of human rights is largely political.

Several countries, especially Western liberal democracies (including Canada, the United States, and many European nations), in concert with the United Nations, have long championed the human rights agenda at home and abroad. In Canada both the *Charter* and federal, provincial, and territorial human rights statutes provide rights to individual Canadians, supported by a basic mechanism and legal framework to protect their rights. The humane development of inclusive cities depends on these constitutional and quasi-constitutional guarantees and their inherent values and on judicial enforcement.

While the discussion of rights, justice, and space is plentiful, academic literature on the nexus of human rights and space is limited, as is attention to human rights as it applies to cities. Reuter (2019) attributes this deficit to the fact that human rights do not take into account the spatial dimension of urban problems. There is, however, an emerging literature on human rights and the city (Agrawal, 2014, 2017, 2020). As discussed earlier, the two concepts—right to the city and rights in the city—have unique ideological origins and have evolved through different processes. What is common between the two is that both have been embraced as possible responses to cities' growing intolerance—with highly surveilled public spaces and ever-increasing segregation by land use, income, and race. Nevertheless, the local application of human rights is recent. Both movements embody the "collective right [of urban dwellers] to reshape the process of urbanization" (Mahmud, 2010, p. 70).

Lately, the two ideas have been increasingly approaching each other: they are often used together, interchangeably, or nested, one within the other. Significant instances that exemplify this trend are recent UN documents, such as the *New Urban Agenda*, a resolution adopted by the UN General Assembly (2017), and an earlier policy paper for this agenda (2016). The UN policy paper states: "The right to the city encompasses all civil, political, economic, social, cultural, and environmental rights as enshrined in existing international human rights treaties, covenants, and conventions" (UNGA, 2016, IB). More and more, the right to the city is viewed as the framework in which human rights in the city are specified and developed (Reuter, 2019).

Other Rights and Freedoms in the City

Many other rights discussed in this collection, such as property rights and the right to housing, are encapsulated in the UDHR, the ICESCR, and other international conventions and treaties. Cities around the world, including Canada, are grappling with the issues of formal and informal property rights, affordable housing, and homelessness. While both property rights and the right to housing are key at the city level, they are not enshrined in the constitutions of many Western nation-states, including that of Canada. The Canadian state does not have the positive obligation to protect property rights or the right to adequate housing. Conversely, freedom of expression in public spaces is protected, although, as noted, it is not absolute. Canada imposes a reasonable limit on expression. In contrast, free speech is vigorously defended in the United States, and thus that country allows more latitude unless the expression falls into one of the categorical exceptions noted, such as incitement that carries an imminent danger of physical violence. Consequently, these rights and freedoms are bundled herein as other rights and freedoms in the city.

Outline of the Book

The book has nine chapters divided into three parts: "The Right to the City," "Rights in the City," and "Other Rights in the City." The parts consist of two to four chapters based on their thematic congeniality. In keeping with the purpose of this project, the chapters develop the three distinct themes, but, importantly, they also pull together, supporting, clarifying, and amplifying each other's particular focus. These intersections work to develop an understanding of how the complexity and interplay of rights—from individual human rights, to group versus collective rights (such as those of Indigenous Peoples), to specific rights (such as housing and property)—are shaping Canadian cities. Together the essays make a case that cities have become important hubs for rights-related activity and serve as key entities that shape, implement, and monitor policies dealing with social equity, justice, and inclusivity. Certainly, the book could be organized in other ways. For example, chapters could be grouped together based on the methods employed, on the nature of the issues pertaining to various disadvantaged groups, or on the scope of rights (international, national, or local). The chapter order exemplifies and illustrates the two conceptual frameworks of rights—the right to the city (RTTC) and rights in the city—and the other set of rights (such as housing and property) and freedoms (like that of expression) because they affect city dwellers in a significant way.

Part 1 attempts to explore Lefebvre's notional RTTC, as discussed before, through existing and notional rights. The section pursues its application in the issues that Canadian cities are currently facing, such as relationships between municipalities and First Nations and with cultural institutions, as a possible means through which the public can understand the importance of RTTC as a right and a legal mechanism. In the first chapter in Part 1, Alexandra Flynn, a legal scholar at the University of British Columbia, builds on the Ontario government's decision in 2018 to reduce the size of Toronto's city council. Using specific Canadian legislation, she focuses on Indigenous rights and the clash of rights between Indigenous and municipal claims. She argues in favour of enhanced local powers to support both the RTTC and the constitutional protections for First Nations. She also considers land interests at the urban scale within and adjacent to municipalities. The chapter concludes that the conceptualization of an RTTC for Canadian municipalities must always be prefaced with a clear understanding of the effects on First Nations and the obligations of local governments regarding Indigenous Peoples and communities.

Continuing this strand, Chapter 2 focuses on the RTTC as an emerging conceptual norm, oriented to rights that are not necessarily codified in law. The author, Jennifer Orange, a human rights scholar who recently joined the law faculty at Toronto Metropolitan University, acknowledges that no such right exists in domestic Canadian or international law. However, she argues that the RTTC could evolve into law. Her chapter describes how current human rights laws (such as the right to be free from discrimination) support but do not complete the RTTC concept. She shows how the RTTC is being taken up by cities' cultural institutions, such as museums, which can foster the public understanding of this right and the need for it to be entrenched in law. The chapter concludes by arguing that both codification and exhibitions about the RTTC support its norm development, moving it towards becoming a recognized human right. She recommends that policy-makers work with museums to gain access to knowledge of marginalized communities and to open up pathways for communication with city residents.

Together, the two chapters extend the terrain of the RTTC by making it more practical. They argue for the need to codify RTTC into law from the Indigenous lens, and they use a city's cultural institutions as a vehicle to promote the idea of RTTC and its importance as a legal right.

Part 2 focuses on human rights and their intersection with the city in various ways. The chapters examine rights issues in Canadian cities prior to the passage of the *Charter*; seek to understand group and collective rights, which are constitutionally protected and repeatedly upheld by the courts; explore how well Canadian municipalities follow their constitutional and quasi-constitutional obligations; and highlight the work of a non-governmental agency in helping a Canadian city to embrace human rights practices.

In Chapter 3, Sandeep Agrawal, the editor of this book and an urban planning and human rights scholar, documents the evolution of legislation of rights (human or civil) in Canada in the pre-*Charter* era, approaching this investigation through a municipal lens. Although Canadians celebrate the progress made on the human rights front in Canada, he makes it clear that this has not always been the case. He tells a sobering tale of how rights (in fact, the lack thereof) affected city dwellers before the adoption of the *Charter* in 1982. The chapter segments this historical look into two periods: from 1897 to the end of the Second World War in 1945, and from the post–Second World War years until 1982, when the Canadian *Charter* was adopted and the Constitution was repatriated from Britain. Agrawal's research uncovers several means by which discrimination manifested at the city level: race-based restrictive covenants; limited or no rights for women or minorities in municipal matters; infringements on freedoms of speech, religion, assembly, or political association; and additional municipal taxes and restrictive use of public facilities for people of colour. From a legal perspective, the problem resided in how the courts decided the cases; however, in reality few made their way to the courts. The courts interpreted the Constitution in the strictest sense, primarily on the grounds of the supremacy of Parliament and the principles of federalism, viewing municipal governments as having very little or no role in such matters.

Chapter 4 broadens the scope of human rights, shifting away from a focus on individual rights to the group and collective forms of human rights. Sandeep Agrawal and Eran Kaplinsky, members of the planning faculty and the law faculty, respectively, at the University of Alberta, examine how these rights play a role at the city level and thus affect urban issues. Through a spotlight on Canadian cities, these authors argue that several sections of the Canadian *Charter* and the Constitution guarantee group or collective rights to Canadians. The Canadian courts have upheld the two forms of rights on numerous occasions in urban matters. However, Agrawal and Kaplinsky also highlight that Canadian municipalities are still grappling with the application of group and collective rights. Particularly in Quebec municipalities, these struggles are further heightened by attempts to come to terms with the demands of religious or cultural groups, while satisfying French-Canadian Quebecois. As a collectivity, French-Canadian Quebecois are unwilling to relent at times. A further matter of concern that the authors explore is the lack of clarity by the judiciary or the provincial governments on how a municipality ought to deal with the collective rights of Indigenous Peoples, such as the Crown's duty to consult and the respect for treaty rights.

Sandeep Agrawal also wrote Chapter 5, which presents an empirical study examining whether Canadian municipal actions are consistent with the constitutional and quasi-constitutional requirements to comply with human rights. Using Alberta municipalities as case studies, he concludes that Canadian cities have made significant progress on the human rights front. Nonetheless, the chapter acknowledges that municipalities continue to face two sets of potential human rights challenges. One set comprises the perennial and outstanding issues of inclusion of user characteristics and minimum separation distances in the zoning bylaw, as well as inadequate provision of various forms of affordable and supportive housing, and limits on freedom of expression on municipal properties. These concerns arise out of court challenges premised on several sections of the *Charter*. The other set of challenges includes those created by recent changes to federal legislation, resulting in new issues like the location of safe injection sites, methadone clinics, and cannabis dispensaries.

Chapter 6, by Renée Vaugeois, reflects on the efforts of the John Humphrey Centre for Peace and Human Rights in making Edmonton, the capital of Alberta, a true human rights city—a place where all participate, are valued, and belong beyond its designation as a "human rights city." Using the "spatiality" of human rights, the author, a human rights advocate in Edmonton, describes the centre's contribution to human rights education, learning, and dialogue as a way to engage communities and the municipal government in applying rights at the local level. She reviews the principles and framework applied in the centre's work and recounts her experiences of translating human rights into practice. The chapter reflects upon the way in which the lessons from Edmonton can inform a path forward for other cities.

These four essays in Part 2 together narrate Canada's journey from discrimination in the past to strong defence of human rights in the present. They explore the thorny issue of the group rights of French Canadians and Indigenous Peoples, with suggestions on how human rights in local policy and practice might look. Following this, Part 3 extends the discussion of rights and cities by elaborating on different forms of rights and freedoms: for example, specific rights in the city, such as housing and property rights, which are not protected in Canada, and issues of and necessary limits to (in certain situations) freedom of expression in public spaces.

Michelle Oren and Rachelle Alterman, planning and legal scholars, contributed Chapter 7, which explores the right to housing in an international context. They analyze the constitutions of 189 UN member states against the UN criteria for the right to adequate housing that was included in the UN's ICESCR of 1966. Although this UN document does not oblige states to incorporate housing stipulations in their constitutions, this action is critical to the internalization of international legal norms. The authors' findings show that over half of the countries (including the United States and Canada) have not incorporated housing rights in their constitutions. However, a large and growing group of countries have done so. Oren and Alterman stress that housing rights in constitutional documents and the adequacy of housing services on the ground may not always match. The chapter identifies significant disparities across countries in addressing several of the UN criteria, but the authors find that housing tenure is the component most often referred to in the constitutions. In general, the language in the constitutions leaves the right to housing wide open to many interpretations.

Chapter 8 explores the extent of property rights in Canada, considering where property rights are not constitutionally protected. The author, Eran Kaplinsky, a legal expert in property and municipal law, identifies instances in which, in the absence of constitutional protection of property, the scope of government power over private property and the owner's entitlement to compensation become matters of statutory interpretation. Kaplinsky also uncovers an inconsistent approach to property rights across Canada, showing that it depends on whether private land is expropriated, restricted, or indirectly affected. This is further exacerbated by the courts' willingness to balance private and public interests and to apportion burdens and benefits. Decisions are animated by policy concerns, which vary greatly depending on the context. Further, planning legislation can be hindered by doctrinal ambiguity and inconsistency, which invites litigation and makes compensation contingent on arbitrary circumstances.

Rounding out the theme of other rights in the city, Chapter 9 presents a challenging dilemma of advocacy messaging in the city's public spaces and institutions. The authors, Ola Malik and Sasha Best, a former municipal solicitor and a Crown prosecutor respectively, explain that these are places we accept as providing citizens with a spontaneous, democratizing environment in which to meet one another, share, and disseminate opinions. Further, they are sites where people can express themselves and engage in lawful protest activity. Malik and Best lay out arguments about circumstances in which the government may appropriately limit freedom of expression, even freedom that is protected by the *Charter*. The chapter argues that "othering" speech, particularly when situated in a city's most public and visible places, raises serious public policy concerns that invite regulation. Othering speech consists of expressions that exclude certain groups by drawing on stigmatizing, discriminatory, demeaning, and stereotypical messaging.

Together, these three final chapters paint a murky picture of the right to adequate housing and the right to property in the absence of constitutional guarantees, while pointing to municipal challenges to keep public spaces inclusive and free of discrimination. Notably, the collection does not pretend to cover every issue and every form of human rights as they relate to the city. The ensemble of global human rights has evolved and expanded its focus from one of civil and political rights to one of economic, social, and cultural rights, with multiple treaties stipulating the rights of children, women, refugees, migrant workers, and, recently, people with disabilities (Oomen, 2016). Considerable gaps remain in addressing all of these rights; realistically, however, one volume cannot cover them all in a systematic way. Still, this multifaceted text contributes significantly to the current discourse on rights and the city by bringing forward the tensions between city residents' rights and a municipal regulatory framework for regulating spaces.

The discussion in this volume makes it clear that the Canadian state has come a long way in protecting its citizens' rights in the city. The judiciary has further clarified, applied, and even expanded the scope of rights in relation to various aspects of city life—with some exceptions, of course. These relate particularly to the provision of adequate housing and to municipal responsibilities towards the Indigenous Peoples of Canada. In response, municipalities have reviewed, revised, or even rescinded existing bylaws and practices; created new land use classes; or revised existing zoning or other municipal bylaws to accommodate new resulting land uses (Agrawal, 2020). The contributions, however, make it abundantly clear that Canadian municipalities still struggle to understand fully their legal and moral obligations *and* keep pace with the ever-evolving judicial interpretations of the *Charter*.

Of note, the collection elicits multiple perspectives on rights that apply to individuals and/or social groups—whether or not they are constitutionally guaranteed—and the limits to which they can be subjected. Our work here also demonstrates that rights issues in cities are complex, multifaceted, and dynamic in nature. Municipal efforts and engagement to rectify concerns remain a work in progress. This quest involves every stakeholder: state, regional, and local governments; academia; the private sector; and, above all, the civil society.

Certainly, codified rights are not a remedy for all urban problems. Law and legal processes and their interpretations are limited in the degree and extent to which they can deal with wide-ranging, deep, and entrenched economic and social issues. The chapters present the tensions that exist within Canadian municipalities when they deal with various rights and protect (or not) people who are marginalized, poor, or need housing. As Qadeer (2016) also contends, even if rights exist in law, their actual realization depends on the institutionalization of equality in economic, social, and cultural matters. The reality is that entrenched institutional and structural biases and power politics still prevent legal progress. Many of the ongoing issues are attributable to planning practitioners' and local politicians' poor awareness of human rights.

This anthology may leave the reader wondering whether the glass is half full or half empty. What is most evident, certainly, is that municipal planners and policy-makers have their work cut out for them. The increasing complexities of urban issues, coupled with both existing and new forms of rights emerging through new legal interpretations, are challenging planners in unprecedented ways. Clearly, cities are becoming the new frontiers of rights-based human development, social justice, and policy innovation. Many hope that "cities [will] deliver where nation states have failed" (Oomen, 2016, p. 2).

NOTES

1. The idea found its way into both the American *Declaration of Independence* of 1776 and France's *Declaration of the Rights of Man and the Citizen* of 1789.

2. According to Mitchell (2003, p. 23), the individual nature of human rights protects the interest of an individual at the expense of others' rights and hence suffers "indeterminacy," "reification," and "political disutility."
3. Kantian imperfect obligation requires the rational being to pursue a policy that admits exceptions, as opposed to perfect obligation that does not allow any exceptions.
4. For Sen, public reasoning involves an open public discussion, which encompasses respect for pluralism and tolerance for different points of view.

REFERENCES

Agrawal, S. (2014). Balancing municipal planning with human rights: A case study. *Canadian Journal of Urban Research, 23*(1), 1–20.

Agrawal, S. (2017). Human rights 101 for planners. *Plan Canada, 57* (2, Summer), 6–9.

Agrawal, S. (2020). Human rights and the city: A view from Canada. *Journal of American Planning Association.* doi:10.1080/01944363.2020.1775680

Alterman, R. (Ed.). (2010). *Takings International: A comparative perspective on land use regulations and compensation rights.* American Bar Association.

Davy, B. (2012). *Land policy: Planning and the spatial consequences of property.* Ashgate.

Donnelly, J. (2013). *Universal human rights in theory and practice.* Cornell University Press.

Fainstein, S. (2011). *Just city.* Cornell University Press.

Garvey, J.H. (1981). Freedom and choice in constitutional law. *Harvard Law Review, 94,* 1756–1794.

Goodale, M. (2009). *Human rights: An anthropological reader.* Wiley-Blackwell.

Harvey, D. (1973). *Social justice and the city.* University of Georgia Press.

Harvey, D. (2013). *Rebel cities: From the right to the city to the urban revolution.* Penguin Random House.

Holston, J. (2008). *Insurgent citizenship: Disjunctions of democracy and modernity in Brazil.* Princeton University Press.

Hopgood, S. (2013). *The endtimes of human rights.* Cornell University Press.

Howie, E. (2018). Protecting the human right to freedom of expression in international law. *International Journal of Speech-Language Pathology, 20*(1), 12–15. doi:10.1080/17549507.2018.1392612

Huchzermeyer, M. (2018). The legal meaning of Lefebvre's the right to the city: Addressing the gap between global campaign and scholarly debate. *GeoJournal, 83,* 631–644.

Lefebvre, H. (1968). *Le droit à la ville* [Right to the city]. Economica.

Lefebvre, H. (1992). *The production of space* (D. Nicholson-Smith, Trans.). Wiley-Blackwell.

Lefebvre, H. (1996). *Writings on cities* (E. Kofman & E. Lebas, Eds. and Trans.). Blackwell.

Mahmud, T. (2010). Surplus humanity and the margins of legality: Slums, slumdogs, and accumulation by dispossession. *Chapman Law Review, 14*(1), 1–73.

Marcuse, P. (2009). From critical urban theory to the right to the city. *City, 13*(2–3), 185–197.

Merry, S.E., Levitt, P., Serban Rosen, M., & Yoon, D.H. (2010). Law from below: Women's human rights and social movements in New York City. *Law and Society Review*, 44(1), 101–128.

Miraftab, F. (2012a). Planning and citizenship. In R. Weber & R. Crane (Eds.), *Oxford handbook of urban planning* (pp. 1180–1204). Oxford University Press.

Miraftab, F. (2012b). Right to the city and the quiet appropriations in the heartland. In M.P. Smith & M. McQuarrie (Eds.), *Remaking urban citizenship: Organizations, institutions, and the right to the city* (pp. 191–202). Transaction Publishers.

Mitchell, D. (2003). *The right to the city: Social justice and the fight for public space*. Guilford Press.

Needham B. (2006). *Planning, law and economics: The rules we make for using land*. Routledge.

Oomen, B. (2016) Introduction: The promise and challenges of human rights cities. In B. Oomen, M.F. Davis, & M. Grigolo (Eds.), *Global urban justice: The rise of human rights cities*. Cambridge University Press.

Public Health Ontario. (2020). *COVID-19 in Ontario: A focus on diversity*. https://www.publichealthontario.ca/-/media/documents/ncov/epi/2020/06/covid-19-epi-diversity.pdf?la=en

Purcell, M. (2002). Excavating Lefebvre: The right to the city and its urban politics of the inhabitant. *GeoJournal*, 58, 99–108.

Reuter, T.K. (2019). Human rights and the city: Including marginalized communities in urban development and smart cities. *Journal of Human Rights*, 18(4), 382–402.

Qadeer, M. (2016). *Multicultural cities: Toronto, New York and Los Angeles*. University of Toronto Press.

Qadeer, M., & Agrawal, S. (2011). The practice of multicultural planning in American and Canadian cities. *Canadian Journal of Urban Research*, 20(1), 131–155.

Sandel, M. (1998). *Liberalism and the limits of justice*. Cambridge University Press.

Sandercock, L. (2003). *Cosmopolis II*. Continuum.

Sen, A. (2004). Elements of a theory of human rights. *Philosophy and Public Affairs*, 32(4), 315–356.

Sen, A. (2005). Human rights and capabilities. *Journal of Human Development*, 6(2), 151–166.

Statistics Canada. (2020). *Impacts on immigrants and people designated as visible minorities*. https://www150.statcan.gc.ca/n1/pub/11-631-x/2020004/s6-eng.htm

UN General Assembly. (2016). *Policy paper 1: Right to the city and cities for all*. United Nations General Assembly Doc. A/CONF.226/PC.3/14. http://habitat3.org/wp-content/uploads/Policy-Paper-1-English.pdf

UN General Assembly. (2017). *71/256. New urban agenda: Resolution adopted by the General Assembly on December 23, 2016*. https://www.un.org/en/development/desa/population/migration/generalassembly/docs/globalcompact/A_RES_71_256.pdf

UN Human Rights Committee. (1996). *CCPR general comment no. 25: Article 25 (Participation in public affairs and the right to vote), The right to participate in public affairs, voting rights and the right of equal access to public service.* UN Doc. CCPR/C/21/Rev.1/Add.7, 12. http://www.refworld.org/docid/453883fc22.html

Webster, C., & Lai, L. (2003). *Property rights, planning and markets: Managing spontaneous cities.* Edward Elgar.

I
THE RIGHT TO THE CITY

1
WHOSE RIGHT TO WHAT CITY?
Indigenous Rights amidst Claims for Constitutionally Empowered Cities

ALEXANDRA FLYNN
—

Introduction

The right to the city (RTTC), articulated by scholars Henri Lefebvre (1996, 1970) and David Harvey (2003, 2008), is a reminder to pay attention to the unequal distribution of power at the local scale. This chapter focuses specifically on narratives of municipal power amidst Indigenous rights.[1] I first place this paper's arguments within the theoretical framework of RTTC, advancing that the meanings of the terms *right* and *city* must be conceptualized within the context of colonialism. Second, I explain what we mean when we talk about the empowerment of cities. I set out the constitutional role of Canadian municipalities, exploring the legal nudges made by the Supreme Court of Canada (SCC) to recognize the democratic importance of local governments through the development of principles such as subsidiarity and co-operative federalism within the constraints of Section 92(8) of the *Constitution Act, 1982*.[2] Third, I outline the effects of a more expansive understanding of municipal authority on First Nations. I draw on the early promise of reimagined Indigenous–municipal relationships, coupled with increasing local obligations to

First Nations, as indicative of legal duties owed by municipalities to Indigenous communities.

To illustrate the argument, I draw particular attention to the City of Toronto, Canada's largest municipality and the fifth largest government in the country, which is currently engaged in numerous political efforts to assume greater autonomy (see Charter City Toronto, 2019a). The chapter explains how a particular political moment unleashed a series of arguments by applicants, respondents, and interveners, and many advocacy efforts, aimed at protecting local democracy without considering the constitutional rights of or relationships with Indigenous Peoples and communities.[3] I conclude that an RTTC in the Canadian context—and in Toronto in this case—must be prefaced with a clear recognition of the constitutional rights of Indigenous Peoples and communities, and the resulting responsibilities of municipalities.

The Right to the City

The RTTC asserts that urban residents are essential participants in struggling against the international capitalism that affects the quality and fair distribution of city life (Purcell, 2002; Soja, 2010; World Urban Forum, 2004). Lefebvre's (1996) account drew on Marxist theory to conceptualize the RTTC as a right to urban life. There are two interrelated facets to RTTC literature. The first is a right to participate, and to be heard, in the city (Lefebvre, 1996). A second way of understanding RTTC is by recreating or changing the city, sometimes called a "right to difference" (Butler & Lefebvre, 2012). Harvey (2003) described this second facet as a collective human right that is "far more than the individual liberty to access urban resources: it is a right to change ourselves by changing the city" (p. 23). In this second conceptualization, "rebel cities" are urban centres with active resistance and revolutionary movements opposing capitalist urbanization; the Occupy Wall Street movement is an example of the struggle to reclaim a collective RTTC (Harvey, 2003, p. 71). In both of these conceptions of RTTC, theoretically and practically, cities are key spaces of struggle (Corntassel, 2012; Johnson, 2010; Regan, 2010).

The notion of an RTTC—as participation and difference—has gained considerable global traction in academic writing and in legislative change. For example, the UN enshrined the concept of the RTTC in its *New Urban Agenda*, which states::

> We share a vision of cities for all, referring to the equal use and enjoyment of cities and human settlements, seeking to promote inclusivity and ensure that all inhabitants, of present and future generations, without discrimination of any kind, can inhabit and produce just, safe, healthy, accessible, affordable, resilient, and sustainable cities and human settlements, to foster prosperity and quality of life for all. We note the efforts of some national and local governments to enshrine this vision, referred to as right to the city, in their legislations, political declarations and charters. (UN & Habitat III, 2016, p. 5 para 11; see also UN-Habitat, 2016)

It is unclear what this section and the RTTC specifically entail once prescribed in law (Njoh, 2017), including what exactly a legal RTTC looks like or how it challenges, complements, or replaces existing rights (Purcell, 2006). Two key questions, however, relate to the Truth and Reconciliation Commission (TRC) and Indigenous Peoples in relationship to this chapter. The first asks what we mean by *rights*. Law has been an important vehicle for advancing Indigenous rights, especially in relation to property and land (Borrows, 2002). Across the world, Indigenous Peoples have used law and resistance to claim power and land (Vanegas, 2012). Even so, there are limitations in the extent to which law can serve as a framework for advancing Indigenous self-determination, because courts to date have upheld Crown sovereignty, leaving Indigenous dispossession intact (Coulthard, 2007). Legal reform and resistance can be linear and overlapping, with each just one of the many tools that Indigenous Peoples may use to effect change (Blomley, 1994).

Jurisprudence can be meaningful in shaping political representation and land rights, including at the local scale (Peña, 2011). Courts have affirmed that urban Indigenous communities are self-organized, self-determining, and distinct communities (Belanger, 2013). Until these cases and other forms of resistance took place, municipalities had long rejected their role in Indigenous engagement, asserting that the relationship between Indigenous and Canadian governments was the responsibility of the federal government (Belanger & Dekruyf, 2017). These attitudes have softened more recently in some cities, although the focus has been on service delivery, not on true power for Indigenous Peoples. The challenge to framing Indigenous rights within an RTTC umbrella is conceptualizing urban cities as being capable of transforming and transcending existing political structures, rather than being understood within dominant notions of power (Stead, 2015). Indigenous urban populations are not expressly referenced in the *New Urban Agenda* or any other legal articulation of an RTTC, but international-scale legal rights have been advanced through the *United Nations Declaration on the Rights of Indigenous Peoples* (UNDRIP).[4]

A second question is what we mean by *a city* and to whom it means this (Tomiak, 2016). Under Canadian law, municipalities are defined as public entities that are provincially created with particular mandates and are delegated specific responsibilities. As Blomley (2004) notes, "the city is a site of particular ideological, material, and representational investments on the part of a settler society" (p. 127). Cities are manifestations of the settler state and are defined as "specific, yet unstable and varied, socio-spatial formations that are at once the products and vehicles of settler colonialism and its logic of displacing Indigenous bodies, peoples, ontologies, and rights" (Tomiak, 2016, p. 10). The local scale is relevant as a reminder that the settler state moves and creates categories and jurisdictions that require attention (Coulthard, 2014).

The city as we know it is rooted in Western notions of property law and governance (Nejad et al., 2019). Coulthard (2014) describes Indigenous spaces within cities as "urbs nullius"—urban spaces that do not have an "Indigenous sovereign presence," where gentrification has eliminated Indigenous Peoples from cities (p. 176). Indigenous boundaries do not map along municipal ones, and particular localities may hold political, spiritual, and economic meaning to Indigenous communities.

Indigenous planning scholars urge a commitment to political change inspired by Indigenous world views, knowledges, and methodologies (Prusack, Walker, & Innes, 2015), including what we mean by the boundaries and definitions of urban spaces. In considering the RTTC, the conceptualization of the city and who is defining it require careful attention.

A "Right" to Toronto?

The displacement of Indigenous communities in cities like Toronto is a fundamental and often omitted part of the lore of cities (Prusack et al., 2015). Systematic campaigns by colonial powers pushed Indigenous nations from urban centres, and their land and rights were eradicated (Coulthard, 2014).[5] Even so, Indigenous Peoples have long resided within colonial cities, never leaving. Toronto, for example, is built on the lands of many nations, including the Mississaugas, the Haudenosaunee, the Huron-Wendat, and the Seneca, and is home to many Indigenous Peoples from across Turtle Island. Toronto is subject to Treaty 13 and the Williams Treaties.[6] It is subject to the *Dish With One Spoon Wampum Belt Covenant*, a treaty agreement between the Haudenosaunee Confederacy, the Ojibwe, and allied nations to peaceably share and care for the resources around the Great Lakes. The Mississauga tribe of the New Credit received ten shillings for the 250,880 acres of what became the City of Toronto, yet many history books omit any mention of the treaty or the sale, which has become the basis of a land claim (Freeman, 2010). Instead, the city places its origin story at 1834, not the *Treaty of Toronto*, which was signed in 1787, briefly revoked in 1794, and reasserted in 1805 (Freeman, 2010). The forgotten narrative of the Indigenous origin of Toronto and other Canadian municipalities ignores the legal protections for Indigenous Peoples under Section 35 of the *Constitution Act, 1982*. Section 35(1) states that "Aboriginal and treaty rights of the aboriginal peoples of Canada are hereby recognized and affirmed."[7] Many First Nations have treaty and land interests such as reserves, urban reserves, and fee-simple title at the urban scale, both within and adjacent to municipalities, and about half of all Indigenous Peoples live within cities across Canada (Norris, Clatworthy, & Peters, 2013; Tomiak, 2011). There are treaty relationships and Indigenous claims within and adjacent to cities, but localities often claim uncertainty in regard to the obligations they owe to First Nations (Dorries, 2012). According to 2011 census data, 56% of Indigenous people now live in urban areas in Canada (Indigenous and Northern Affairs Canada, 2013).

Changes to municipal authority affect Indigenous–municipal legal relationships, given the constitutional protection of Aboriginal rights under Section 35 and the legal status of cities under Section 92(8) of the *Constitution Act, 1982* (Hoehn & Stevens, 2018). In August 2018, in the middle of Toronto's election, the Province of Ontario enacted Bill 5, legislation that drastically reduced the size of the city council.[8] The result defied the city's authority under the *City of Toronto Act, 2006*,[9] just months after the city council had changed the number of electoral districts following a years-long ward boundary review (City of Toronto, 2016). The City of Toronto successfully challenged the law at the lower-court level, with the decision overturned in a 3–2 split in favour of the Province at the Court of Appeal.[10] The decision was appealed to the SCC, where Bill 5 was upheld in a 5–4 decision.[11] Other Canadian provinces, perhaps buoyed by the Ontario example, have used their constitutional power to cancel plans for expanded local autonomy (Giovanneti & Tait, 2019).

Bill 5 has drawn attention to the precarious legal status of Canadian municipalities. In this legal drama, however, RTTC claims have been subverted as a right *of* the city to execute decision-making within the governance structures of the incorporated municipality, as structured by the state. As the next section of the chapter explains, many advocacy groups and politicians have called for greater protection of municipalities, using RTTC rhetoric to advance constitutional protection for municipalities while omitting reference to Indigenous rights (Charter City Toronto, 2019a). The section also explores municipal calls for empowerment in various forms, including through the courts.

Municipal Empowerment

Under Section 92(8) of the *Constitution Act*, municipal status and jurisdiction appears to be crystal clear: "Municipal institutions" are within the province's exclusive authority and have no protection against changes to the design and power imposed on them by provinces (Makuch, Craik, & Leisk, 2004). This constitutional brevity has led municipalities to be called "creatures of the province," with provincial governments empowered to set rules regarding what municipalities can and cannot do (Levi & Valverde, 2006, p. 416). Municipalities must act within their "defined jurisdictional sphere," with a failure to do so resulting in "the courts quashing the municipal action as *ultra vires*, or beyond its legal competence" (Makuch et al., 2004, p. 81). Cities have sought more power in three ways—the courts, new legislation, and constitutional protection—which are reviewed below.

The Courts

First, although cities are left out of the Constitution as a level of government (see Weistock, 2015), courts have become more deferential to municipal acts over the last 20 years.[12] For example, in the 2000 case *Rascal Trucking*, the court stated that "municipalities balance complex and divergent interests" in decision-making, thus warranting that "*intra vires* decisions of municipalities be reviewed upon a deferential standard."[13] That same year, the court decreed that "municipal governments are democratic institutions through which the people of a community embark upon and structure life together."[14] In *R v Guignard*, decided just two years later, the court affirmed that municipal powers "must be given a generous interpretation because their closeness to the members of the public who live or work on their territory make them more sensitive to the problems experienced by those individuals."[15]

Despite this seemingly progressive jurisprudence, judges have, to date, declared that they will not reread the Constitution to include municipalities as a protected order of government.[16] For example, in *East York v Ontario (Attorney General)*, several municipalities challenged the Province of Ontario's decision to create the Toronto megacity in 1998 without the consent of the amalgamated six municipalities.[17] The

Superior Court concluded that the unilateral action did not exceed the Province's constitutional authority to make laws relating to municipal institutions in the province.[18] Likewise, Justice LeBel cautioned in *Spraytech* in 2001 that courts must not "invent municipal authority where none exists."[19] This means that the courts have not read Section 92(8) or any other section of the *Constitution Act* as displacing provincial governments or protecting municipalities from provincial interference.

New Legislation
Over the last two decades, municipalities have acquired more autonomy through the strategy of provincial action. Across the country, provinces have given more expansive powers to large municipalities—following extensive lobbying efforts—including more options for raising revenue and greater oversight in matters such as infrastructure and housing.[20] For example, the *City of Toronto Act, 2006*, was meant to confer governmental status to Toronto via provincial legislation. Section 1 of the Act reads: "The City of Toronto exists for the purpose of providing good government with respect to matters within its jurisdiction, and the city council is a democratically elected government which is responsible and accountable."[21] As a government, the City of Toronto has the power to "determine what is in the public interest for the City" and to "respond to the needs of the City," as well as a host of other seemingly expansive powers.[22] In 2016, the Province of Quebec introduced legislation that gave greater autonomy to Quebec City and Montreal, the latter of which was given special official status as a metropolis (Fletcher, 2016). Among other new fiscal and regulatory powers, Montreal gained new authority in areas of housing, heritage preservation, and social policy relating to homelessness and immigration, which are currently administered by the Quebec government (CBC, 2018).

While provincial governments could arguably constrain their power by requiring a two-thirds vote or municipal agreement to make particular decisions, provinces remain the government in charge of decision-making when it comes to municipal authority. This is evidenced in Alberta, where the province introduced a charter for Calgary and Edmonton, its largest cities, in 2018, after a decade of negotiation (Dippel, 2018). Calgary's new city charter contained 44 new authorities, a new fiscal framework with cost-sharing and enhanced revenue tools, more requirements for community input, and a more mature government-to-government relationship between the city and the province.[23] After the election of a new provincial government in 2019, these powers were threatened (Giovanneti & Tait, 2019). Thus, even if a municipal act is called a charter it does not, on its own, have a special status that protects it from interference by provincial governments. It also means that provincial governments can impose and delegate responsibilities such as the procedural duty to consult Indigenous Peoples, as will be discussed later in this chapter.

Constitutional Protection

The notion of constitutionally recognized city charters is gaining traction, given the court's narrow reading of municipal authority and the power of provinces to enact legislation. This is becoming the third means by which cities are seeking more power. On June 7, 2018, the Ontario Conservative Party won a majority of seats in the provincial legislature, and Doug Ford, a previous Toronto councillor, became the premier. Bill 5, *The Better Local Government Act*, was enacted in law on August 14, 2018, amending the *City of Toronto Act, 2006*, by reducing the size of city council to 25.[24] Several candidates for city council, mainly women and historically marginalized people, and the City of Toronto challenged the decision (Flynn, 2018).[25] The action succeeded at lower court but was overturned in a 3–2 decision by the Ontario Court of Appeal, which was upheld in a 5–4 decision by the SCC in 2021.[26]

This approach operationalizes Section 43 of the *Constitution Act, 1982*, which reads:

> An amendment to the Constitution of Canada in relation to any provision that applies to one or more, but not all, provinces, including
>
> a)   any alteration to the boundaries between provinces, and
> b)   any amendment to any provision that relates to the use of the English or the French language within the province,

may be made by proclamation issued by the Governor General under the Great Seal of Canada only where so authorized by resolutions of the Senate and House of Commons and of the legislative assembly of each province to which the amendment applies.

Canada's formula for amending the *Constitution Act, 1982*, is very restrictive, requiring the consent of the federal government and the legislatures of seven provinces representing 50% of Canada's population.[27] However, a single-province amendment, used a handful of times, requires only the consent of a provincial legislature and the House of Commons (Newman, 2013). Several prominent political actors at the local, provincial, and federal levels have already expressed support for the idea of a constitutionally protected City of Toronto (Charter City Toronto, 2019a). This would constitutionally enshrine a charter in the Constitution and would require both federal and provincial governments' amendments going forward (Charter City Toronto, 2019a). While the initiative faces unprecedented political hurdles, if successful, it would remove the unilateral power of the province to determine the City of Toronto's authority and would elevate the city as a constitutionally protected government (Charter City Toronto, 2019b).

In summary, these three measures—courts, legislation, and constitutional protection—represent efforts to seek greater municipal power while avoiding engagement with the constitutional obligations to First Nations and Indigenous Peoples. They also avoid consideration of the obligations that these empowered cities would have in relation to Indigenous communities. This legal lapse ignores the constitutional protections of First Nations and Indigenous land interests at the urban scale, both within and adjacent to municipalities, as the next section explains (Freeman, 2010).

Indigenous Communities and Municipal Legal Obligations

Aboriginal and treaty rights of First Nations are recognized and affirmed under Section 35(1) of the *Constitution Act, 1982*, and have been given additional context through the courts.[28] Although the Canadian constitution recognizes and affirms Aboriginal rights, and courts have been helpful in asserting constitutional rights,[29] the barriers to meaningfully exercising Section 35 are urgent (Fraser & Viswanathan, 2013; McLeod et al., 2015). Although treaties signify nation-to-nation relationships between Indigenous nations and the state, Canadian history is replete with examples of what then Chief Justice Beverley McLachlin of the SCC eventually called Canada's "cultural genocide" towards Indigenous Peoples, through the creation of reserves and residential schools, as well as the erosion of hunting and other rights (Howard-Hassmann, 2015). Governments have demonstrated a long history of systematic erosion of Indigenous rights (Truth and Reconciliation Commission of Canada, 2015) and have often refused to engage in discussions with Indigenous communities over treaty violations and Indigenous claims, such that legal actions have been required to bring the federal government to the negotiating table.[30] More recently, all but a small handful of governments have adopted UNDRIP, which, among other things, advances Indigenous rights in respect of heritage property and provides for free, prior, and informed consent related to the development of Indigenous lands.[31] UNDRIP is widely seen by Indigenous activists, scholars, and lawyers as a best practice in considering Indigenous-settler relationships (Craft et al., 2018).

Indigenous rights continue to be undermined through the delegating of different functions to specific jurisdictions, with governments and their agencies each imposing and applying laws that muddy their individual obligations to First Nations (Borrows, 2017). As applied to municipalities, Ritchie (2013) cautions that the expectation of municipal negotiation with First Nations may further water down the nation-to-nation relationship that exists between the federal government and First Nations, thereby compromising treaty and other relationships. She is exploring a conundrum in Ontario concerning whether municipalities have a duty to consult and accommodate. This duty arises when the Crown has knowledge (real or constructive) of the existence of the

Aboriginal right or title and contemplates conduct that might adversely affect it.[32] The Crown is understood by the courts to comprise the federal and provincial governments,[33] and it holds a non-delegable legal duty to consult and accommodate, although it may delegate procedural aspects of consultation to third parties.[34] The judicially stated goal of the duty is to achieve "reconciliation,"[35] although the term has not been given a definable legal meaning,[36] nor does it address the colonialism that underpins the legal system (Valverde & Weaver, 2015).

The issues of jurisdictional muddling and what it means to move towards reconciliation become pronounced when one considers the relationships between Indigenous Peoples and communities, and municipal governments. There are no SCC cases extending the duty to municipalities. The lower-court decisions raise serious questions about the meaning and limitations of the duty to consult and accommodate. The leading appeal court decision, *Neskonlith Indian Band v Salmon Arm (City)*,[37] states that municipalities have no independent constitutional duty to consult First Nations whose treaty and other interests may be affected by municipal decision-making (Imai & Stacey, 2014). In this case, the Neskonlith were unsuccessful in using the duty to consult and accommodate to challenge a decision made by the City of Salmon Arm, which allowed a permit for development to be issued in a flood-plain area located right beside their reserve. Even though Salmon Arm took steps to consult and accommodate the Neskonlith, the court held that the municipality did not owe a duty, in part because municipalities lack capacity.[38] A handful of other lower-court decisions have made the same conclusion.[39] A 2017 SCC decision augments the likelihood that the duty to consult would be extended to municipalities. In *Clyde River*, the SCC held that the Crown may rely on regulatory bodies (in this case, the National Energy Board or NEB, a form of administrative decision-maker) to satisfy the duty to consult.[40] Justices Karakatsanis and Brown, in writing for a unanimous court, stated:

> In our view, while the Crown may rely on steps undertaken by a regulatory agency to fulfill its duty to consult in whole or in part and, where appropriate, accommodate, the Crown always holds ultimate

responsibility for ensuring consultation is adequate. Practically speaking, this does not mean that a minister of the Crown must give explicit consideration in every case to whether the duty to consult has been satisfied, or must directly participate in the process of consultation. Where the regulatory process being relied upon does not achieve adequate consultation or accommodation, the Crown must take further measures to meet its duty.[41]

The court stated that the Crown must supplement consultation processes where necessary to ensure that the duty to consult is adequate.[42] An administrative agency may also assess the adequacy of its consultation process, unless the authority to do so is explicitly removed in statute.[43] In such cases, the body is understood as representing the Crown in regard to consultation. While it acknowledges that the NEB is not "strictly speaking" the Crown or an agent of the Crown, the NEB is acting on behalf of the Crown when making a final decision on a project application such that "any distinction between its actions and Crown action quickly falls away," as "the NEB is the vehicle through which the Crown acts."[44]

The same legal logic as that espoused in *Clyde River* applies to municipalities. Courts have long concluded that municipalities, although they are administrative bodies under a strict reading of the Constitution, are democratic governments.[45] Case law is rife with examples of the Crown being used to denote executive power (Hogg, Monahan, & Wright, 2011).[46] By statute, most municipalities, and certainly the City of Toronto, are referred to as governments, with autonomy to govern their affairs within the bounds of their statutory authority, with little interference by provincial governments—for example, in areas such as revenue and planning. Hoehn and Stevens (2018) agree, arguing that the combination of the *Clyde River* holding and the evolution of municipal autonomy means that third parties can be effectively considered arms of the Crown and therefore hold a duty to consult and accommodate. Angela D'Elia Decembrini and Shin Imai (2019) likewise voice that First Nations and municipalities have a long-standing history of entering into agreements and emerging legislative requirements for municipalities to consult and accommodate. In Ontario and British Columbia, for example, municipalities are expected to consult, and provinces rely on municipalities to do so (Decembrini & Imai, 2019; Imai & Stacey, 2014).

Indigenous Peoples have long advocated and campaigned for much-needed services and programs for Indigenous citizens and the modification of local governance practices to ensure Indigenous interests are heard (see Royal Commission on Aboriginal Peoples, 1996). In cities across Canada, Indigenous-led organizations now have statutory mandates in areas such as child welfare and education (Belanger, 2013). Referencing such shifts, Ontario Regional Chief RoseAnne Archibald said to municipal leaders in 2018:

> Across Canada, municipal governments and neighbouring First Nations are developing stronger relationships…[These relationships, aimed at] long-term prosperity and peace [are built through] lasting friendships, relationships and partnerships on the principles of truth and reconciliation. Municipalities, although not original partners to the treaties, are considered from a First Nations perspective, to be current and valuable partners and certainly benefactors of the Treaty process. (Archibald, 2018)

The 1996 report of the Royal Commission on Aboriginal Peoples (RCAP) was the first government report that acknowledged the vast number of Indigenous Peoples and agencies in large cities and the corresponding lack of political agency (Royal Commission on Aboriginal Peoples, 1996).[47] The RCAP envisaged urban government reform to take better account of Aboriginal perspectives and interests through means such as ensuring Indigenous representation on decision-making bodies, establishing Aboriginal Affairs committees, and co-managing urban initiatives (RCAP, 1996). The RCAP proposed two models of urban Indigenous governance: the reform of urban government and public authorities, calling for greater local political participation, political representation, and co-management of urban programs and services; and a community of interest with greater Indigenous political autonomy, including a larger, city-wide politically representative body.

A report by the Toronto Aboriginal Research Project states that Indigenous communities in Toronto are moving towards both approaches.[48] Indigenous community agencies are participating formally in local government through their representation on the city's Indigenous Affairs Committee, which is developing an urban Indigenous framework. A city-based Indigenous Affairs Office is helping to guide the municipal government in its relationships with Indigenous Peoples, including urban Indigenous communities, neighbouring First Nations and Métis Nation of Ontario, and Indigenous organizations (see Toronto City Council 2017a, 2017b; Wallace, 2016). Toronto has also introduced a number of initiatives focused on relationship building (Toronto City Council, 2009). In 2010 the city affirmed recognition and respect for the unique status and cultural diversity among the Indigenous communities of Toronto, including recognition of their inherent rights under the Constitution (City of Toronto, 2010). In 2014, Toronto City Council endorsed the calls to action from the report of the TRC and requested the development by staff of concrete actions to implement fully the calls to action that explicitly recognize the role of municipal governments (Toronto City Council, 2017a; Wallace, 2016). These measures included cultural competency training for the Toronto civil service, a 10-year capital project to incorporate Indigenous place-making in Toronto parks, and the implementation of plaques to commemorate Indigenous places. In addition, the city council has adopted an ongoing ceremony at its meetings and approved a public campaign to educate residents about the Year of Truth and Reconciliation Proclamation (Toronto City Council, 2014).

The City of Toronto also adopted UNDRIP in 2013 (Wallace, 2016). UNDRIP, sanctioned by many Indigenous scholars as a best practice, goes beyond the duty to consult in its recognition of Indigenous rights, most importantly in relation to free, prior, and informed consent. Although the City of Toronto has not specifically set out how and when this type of consent applies to project approval, the adoption of UNDRIP remains an important step in signalling the city's desire to build respectful reciprocal relationships with Indigenous communities. The City of Toronto has specifically acknowledged the right to practise and revitalize cultural traditions and customs under Article 11 of UNDRIP.[49] Importantly, the City noted "staff's legal duty to consult," particularly in relation to environmental assessments and heritage (Wallace, 2016).

The City's conception of itself as having legal or constitutional obligations to Indigenous Peoples and communities has not materialized when considering its own empowerment. As expressed, an RTTC for Toronto means self-determination for the municipality, as constituted and geographically defined by the provincial government, to govern itself without interference by other governments. In this conceptualization, legal protection is intended for the city government itself and, through it, any stakeholder rights that it identifies. Despite the efforts of Indigenous Peoples, the City of Toronto has not realized RCAP's aims; in particular, it has not yet developed protocols with Indigenous Peoples as to how consultation or consent would look, nor has it clearly articulated its obligations.

The undercurrent of the City's argument for greater power is that the city is a democratic government that alone has the power to represent its residents. An RTTC focusing purely on engaging Indigenous communities and peoples as stakeholders undermines any belief that they have power over decision-making, as partners or otherwise (Fawcett, Walker, & Greene, 2015). Municipalities seeking protection or asserting their roles as democratic governments within the Canadian federal landscape must understand their constitutional and legal obligations to Indigenous Peoples and communities. Greater legal protection of local governments must be balanced alongside the protection of Section 35 constitutional rights for Indigenous Peoples and communities; this means not merely being heard but participating in shaping, challenging, and reimagining the city. How this looks will depend on the relationships between Indigenous Peoples and communities, and the municipal governments, including the agreements they make together.

Conclusion

This chapter has queried the way in which the dialogue surrounding greater municipal autonomy intersects with Indigenous rights, with a particular focus on Toronto. RTTC claims lay bare an omission of the political rights of Indigenous Peoples or the idea that any entity other than the city government should be empowered to make decisions (Prusack et al., 2015). They also sidestep obligations related to the duty to consult and accommodate, both legally and morally. Such a duty likely applies now, given *Clyde River*[50] and the evolution of the treatment of municipalities in jurisprudence. The notion of constitutional change that lacks a candid dialogue with Indigenous Peoples and First Nations is untenable.[51] Any municipal empowerment must first grapple with the constitutional rights of Indigenous Peoples and communities, including what changes to local power might mean for the duty to consult and accommodate, and for obligations under UNDRIP. Municipalities must also strengthen Indigenous governance, through funded liaison efforts, co-management of parks or other public spaces, and the development of protocols with Indigenous Peoples and communities. The conceptualization of an RTTC for Canadian municipalities must always be prefaced by a clear understanding of the effects on First Nations and the obligations of local governments in respect of Indigenous Peoples and communities. Otherwise, the right to the city is merely a right *of* the city.

NOTES

1. This paper uses the term *Indigenous Peoples* to mean First Nations, bands as defined by the *Indian Act*, Inuit, Métis, Aboriginal Peoples, and other Indigenous Peoples. *First Nations* refers to Indigenous governments. *Aboriginal* refers to terminology used in the *Constitution Act, 1982*. Where possible, I use the name of the Indigenous community. All errors are my own.
2. *Constitution Act, 1982*, being Schedule B to the *Canada Act 1982* (UK), 1982, c 11.
3. *Toronto (City) v Ontario (Attorney General)* (C65861) Court of Appeal, Orders and Filed Documents, http://www.ontariocourts.ca/coa/C65861/.
4. UN General Assembly, *United Nations Declaration on the Rights of Indigenous Peoples: Resolution*, adopted by the General Assembly, 2 October 2007, A/RES/61/295, https://www.refworld.org/docid/471355a82.html.

5. See, for example, House of Commons Debate, 9 April 1911, in which Prime Minister Laurier stated: "where a reserve is in the vicinity of a growing town, as is the case in several places, it becomes a source of nuisance and an impediment to progress" (quoted in Coulthard, 2014, p. 412).
6. One interpretation of Tkaronto is as a Mohawk word meaning "a gathering place," and its association with what is now Toronto has a circuitous history. However, this story is by no means a solid one, and the term may actually apply to a site further north near Lake Simcoe.
7. *Constitution Act, 1982*, being Schedule B to the *Canada Act 1982* (UK), 1982, c 11.
8. *The Better Local Government Act*, SO 2018, c 11 [Bill 5].
9. *City of Toronto Act, 2006*, SO 2006, c 11, Schedule A at s 1(1).
10. *Toronto (City) v Ontario (Attorney General)*, 2018 ONCA 761.
11. *Toronto (City) v Ontario (Attorney General)*, 2021 SCC 34.
12. *Morton v British Columbia (Agriculture and Lands)*, 2009 BCSC 136 (CanLII), [2009] 7 WWR 690; 92 BCLR (4th) 314; 42 CELR (3d) 79; [2009] BCJ No 193 (QL); 174 ACWS (3d) 103 at para 107.
13. *Nanaimo (City) v Rascal Trucking Ltd*, [2000] 1 SCR 342 [Rascal Trucking] at para 35.
14. *Pacific National Investments Ltd. v Victoria (City)*, [2000] 2 SCR 919.
15. *R v Guignard*, [2002] 1 SCR 472, 2002 SCC 14 (CanLII) at para 17.
16. *Canada Post Corporation v Hamilton (City)*, 2016 ONCA 767 (CanLII) at para 85.
17. *East York v Ontario (Attorney General)*, (1997), 34 OR (3d) 789 (Gen. Div.), aff'd (1997), 36 OR (3d) 733 (CA), leave to appeal to SCC refused, [1998] 1 SCR vii.
18. *Ibid.*, 797–798.
19. *114957 Canada Ltée (Spraytech, Societe d'arrosage) v Hudson (Town)*, [2001] 2 SCR 241 [Spraytech] at 366.
20. See, for example, *Municipal Government Act*, RSO 1990, Ch M-26; *Charter of Ville de Montréal*, RSO 2000, c 56, Schedule I, Ch C-11.4.
21. *City of Toronto Act, 2006*, SO 2006, c 11, Schedule A at s 1(1).
22. *Ibid.*, at ss 2(1) and (2).
23. Alberta Regulation 40/2018, *Municipal Government Act, City of Calgary Charter*, 2018 Regulation. http://www.Qp.Alberta.Ca/Documents/Regs/2018_040.pdf.
24. *Toronto (City) v Ontario (Attorney General)*, 2018 ONCA 761.
25. *Toronto (City) v Ontario (Attorney General)*, 2018 ONSC 5151.
26. *Toronto (City) v Ontario (Attorney General)*, 2021 SCC 34.
27. *Constitution Act, 1982*, being Schedule B to the *Canada Act 1982* (UK), 1982, c 11, at ss 38–45.
28. *Haida Nation v British Columbia (Minister of Forests)*, [2004] 3 SCR 511 [Haida].
29. *Ibid.*, referencing, for example *R v Badger*, 1996 CanLII 236 (SCC), [1996] 1 SCR 771, at para 41; *R v Marshall*, 1999 CanLII 665 (SCC), [1999] 3 SCR 456.
30. *Delgamuukw v British Columbia*, [1997] 3 SCR 1010 [Delgamuukw].

31. But see Bill 41-2019, *Declaration on the Rights of Indigenous Peoples Act* (BC).
32. *Halfway River First Nation v British Columbia (Ministry of Forests)*, 1997 CanLII 2719 (BC SC), [1997] 4 CNLR 45 (BCSC), at 71, per Justice Dorgan.
33. When beneficial ownership was transferred to Ontario, Ontario took the place of Canada as the level of government with the capacity to take up lands, subject to the rights guaranteed by treaty (*Keewatin v Ontario (Natural Resources)*, 2013 ONCA 158 (CanLII), http://canlii.ca/t/fwjp2).
34. *Haida Nation v British Columbia (Minister of Forests)*, [2004] 3 SCR 511 [*Haida*]. See also *Clyde River (Hamlet) v Petroleum Geoservices Inc.*, 2017 SCC 40 (CanLII) and *Chippewas of the Thames First Nation v Enbridge Pipelines Inc.*, 2017 SCC 41 (CanLII).
35. *Chippewas of the Thames First Nation v Enbridge Pipelines Inc.*, 2017 SCC 41, [2017] 1 SCR 1099.
36. *R v Van der Peet*, [1996] 2 SCR 507.
37. *Neskonlith Indian Band v Salmon Arm (City)*, 2014 47.1 UBC Law Review 293–312 [*Neskonlith*].
38. *Ibid.*
39. But see for example *Morgan v Sun Peaks Resort Corporation*, [2013] BCSC 1668; *Squamish Nation v British Columbia (Community, Sport and Cultural Development)*, 2014 BCSC 991; *Cardinal v Windmill Green Fund LPV*, 2016 ONSC 3456.
40. *Clyde River (Hamlet) v Petroleum Geoservices Inc.*, 2017 SCC 40 (CanLII) was decided at the same time as companion case *Chippewas of the Thames First Nation v Enbridge Pipelines Inc.*, 2017 SCC 41 (CanLII).
41. *Clyde River (Hamlet) v Petroleum Geoservices Inc.*, 2017 SCC 40 (CanLII), at para 22.
42. *Ibid.*
43. *Ibid.*
44. *Ibid.*, at para 29.
45. See, for example, *Rascal Trucking* and *Pacific National Investments*.
46. *Clyde River (Hamlet)*, at para 28.
47. RCAP defines "urban community of interest" as a collectivity that emerges in an urban setting, includes people of diverse Aboriginal origins, and "creates itself" through voluntary association.
48. With a sample of over 1,400 individuals, 14 topics studied, and 7 methodologies utilized, the Toronto Aboriginal Research Project (TARP) study provides an extensive picture of the current situation, successes, aspirations, and challenges facing Aboriginal people in the Greater Toronto Area (GTA). The TARP study is also unique in that it is a community-based research initiative that has been overseen, from start to finish, by the Toronto Aboriginal Support Services Council in collaboration with the TARP Research Steering Committee.
49. "Article 11 states that (1) Indigenous peoples have the right to practise and revitalize their cultural traditions and customs. This includes the right to maintain, protect

and develop the past, present and future manifestations of their cultures, such as archaeological and historical sites, artefacts, designs, ceremonies, technologies and visual and performing arts and literature; and (2) States shall provide redress through effective mechanisms, which may include restitution, developed in conjunction with indigenous peoples, with respect to their cultural, intellectual, religious and spiritual property taken without their free, prior and informed consent or in violation of their laws, traditions and customs" (Indigenous Rights Radio, https://rights.culturalsurvival.org/undrip-article-11-right-cultural-practices).

50. *Clyde River (Hamlet) v Petroleum Geoservices Inc.*, 2017 SCC 40 (CanLII).
51. See for example *Godbout v Longueuil (City)*, [1997] 3 SCR 844, where the SCC emphatically stated that provincial governments may not sidestep their constitutional obligations by devolving powers on municipal bodies.

REFERENCES

Archibald, R. (2018). *Speaking Points.* AMO Conference in Ottawa. http://www.chiefs-of-ontario.org/news_item/orc-roseanne-archibald-speaking-points-at-amo-conference-in-ottawa

Belanger, Y. (2013). Breaching reserve boundaries: Canada v. Misquadis and the legal creation of the urban Aboriginal community. In E. Peters & C. Andersen (Eds.), *Indigenous in the city: Contemporary identities and cultural innovation* (pp. 69–87). UBC Press.

Belanger, Y., & Dekruyf, K. (2017). Neither citizen nor nation: Urban Aboriginal (in)visibility and co-production in a small southern Alberta city. *Canadian Journal of Native Studies, 37*(1), 1–28.

Blomley, N. (2004). *Unsettling the city: Urban land and the politics of property.* Routledge.

Blomley, N.K. (1994). *Law, space and the geographies of power.* Guilford Press.

Borrows, J. (2002) *Recovering Canada: The resurgence of Indigenous law.* University of Toronto Press.

Borrows, J. (2017). Canada's colonial constitution. In J. Borrows & M. Coyle (Eds.), *The right relationship: Reimagining the implementation of historical treaties* (pp. 17–38). University of Toronto Press.

Butler, C., & Lefebvre, H. (2012). *Spatial politics, everyday life, and the right to the city.* Routledge.

CBC. (2018, December 8). *Quebec proposes greater autonomy, grants metropolis status for Montreal.* CBC. https://www.cbc.ca/news/canada/montreal/quebec-proposes-greater-autonomy-grants-metropolis-status-for-montreal-1.3888329

Charter City Toronto. (2019a). A proposal to empower and protect Toronto. https://www.chartercitytoronto.ca/uploads/1/2/3/5/123582995/charter_city_proposal.pdf

Charter City Toronto. (2019b, October 30). *In the Media.* https://www.chartercitytoronto.ca/in-the-media.html

City of Toronto. (2010, July). *Commitment to Aboriginal communities in Toronto: Building strong relationships, achieving equitable outcomes*. http://www.trc.ca/assets/pdf/CityofToronto.pdf

City of Toronto (2016). *Toronto ward boundary review* [City Clerk, Executive Committee Decision on Final Report]. http://app.toronto.ca/tmmis/viewAgendaItemHistory.do?item=2016.EX15.2

Corntassel, J. (2012). Re-envisioning resurgence: Indigenous pathways to decolonization and sustainable self-determination. *Decolonization: Indigeneity, Education & Society*, 1(1), 86–101.

Coulthard, G.S. (2007). Subjects of empire: Indigenous peoples and the "politics of recognition" in Canada. *Contemporary Political Theory*, 6(4), 437–460.

Coulthard, G. (2014). *Red skin, white masks: Rejecting the colonial politics of recognition*. University of Minnesota Press.

Craft, A., Gunn, B.L., Knockwood, C., Christie, G., Askew, H., Henderson,...Lightfoot, S. (2018). UNDRIP *implementation: More reflections on the braiding of international, domestic and Indigenous laws*. Centre for International Governance Innovation. https://www.cigionline.org/publications/undrip-implementation-more-reflections-braiding-international-domestic-and-indigenous

Decembrini, A.D., & Imai, S. (2019). Supreme Court of Canada cases strengthen argument for municipal obligation to discharge duty to consult: Time to put Neskonlith to rest. *Alberta Law Review*, 56(3). doi:10.29173/alr2530

Dippel, S. (2018, April 6). Calgary finally has its city charter. CBC *News*. https://www.cbc.ca/news/canada/calgary/city-council-charter-1.4609322

Dorries, H. (2012). *Rejecting the "false choice": Foregrounding Indigenous sovereignty in planning theory and practice* (Unpublished doctoral dissertation). University of Toronto, Toronto.

Fawcett, R.B., Walker, R., & Greene, J. (2015). Indigenizing city planning processes in Saskatoon, Canada. *Canadian Journal of Urban Research*, 24(2), 158–175.

Fletcher, R. (2016, December 6). Quebec signs new partnership with municipalities. *Global News*. https://globalnews.ca/news/3110591/quebec-signs-new-partnership-with-municipalities/

Flynn, A. (2018, July 30). The legal case against Ford's assault on local democracy. *Spacing Magazine*. http://spacing.ca/toronto/2018/07/30/the-legal-case-against-fords-assault-on-local-democracy/

Fraser C., & Viswanathan, L. (2013). The Crown duty to consult and Ontario municipal–First Nations relations: Lessons learned from the Red Hill Valley Parkway project. *Canadian Journal of Urban Research*, 22(1), 1–19.

Freeman, V.J. (2010). "Toronto has no history!" Indigeneity, settler colonialism and historical memory in Canada's largest city (Unpublished doctoral dissertation). University of Toronto, Toronto.

Giovanneti, J., & Tait, C. (2019, October 25). Mayors of Calgary, Edmonton criticize funding cuts to cities in Alberta budget. *Globe and Mail.* https://www.theglobeandmail.com/canada/alberta/article-alberta-premier-jason-kenneys-budget-cuts-hit-calgary-and-edmonton/

Harvey, D. (2003). The right to the city. *International Journal of Urban and Regional Research, 27*(4), 939–41. doi:10.1111/j.0309-1317.2003.00492.xLegislation

Harvey, D. (2008). The right to the city. *New Left Review, 53.* https://newleftreview.org/issues/II53/articles/david-harvey-the-right-to-the-city

Hoehn, F., & Stevens, M. (2018). Local governments and the Crown's duty to consult. *Alberta Law Review, 55*(4), 971–1008.

Hogg, P.W., Monahan, P.J., & Wright, W.K. (2011). *Liability of the Crown* (4th ed.). Caswell.

Howard-Hassmann, R. (2015, July 13). *Cultural genocide of Canada's Aboriginal people.* Centre for International Governance Innovation. https://www.cigionline.org/articles/cultural-genocide-canadas-aboriginal-people

Imai, S., & Stacey, A. (2014). Municipalities and the duty to consult Aboriginal peoples: A case comment on *Neskonlith Indian Band v. Salmon Arm (City). UBC Law Review, 47*(1), 293–312.

Indigenous and Northern Affairs Canada. (2013). *Urban Aboriginal peoples.* https://www.aadnc-aandc.gc.ca/eng/1100100014265/1369225120949

Johnson, K. (2010). Exhibiting decolonising discourse: Critical settler education and the city before the city. *Studies in the Education of Adults, 48*(2), 177–193.

Lefebvre, H. (1970). *The urban revolution* (Robert Bononno, Trans.). University of Minnesota Press.

Lefebvre, H. (1996). The right to the city. In E. Kofman & E. Lebas (Eds. and Trans.), *Writings on cities* (pp. 147–159). Blackwell.

Levi, R., & Valverde, M. (2006). Freedom of the city: Canadian cities and the quest for governmental status. *Osgoode Hall Law Journal, 44*(3), 409–459. http://digitalcommons.osgoode.yorku.ca/ohlj/vol44/iss3/1?utm_source=digitalcommons.osgoode.yorku.ca%2Fohlj%2Fvol44%2Fiss3%2F1&utm_medium=PDF&utm_campaign=PDFCoverPages

Makuch, S., Craik, N., & Leisk, S.B. (2004). *Canadian municipal and planning law.* Thomson Carswell.

McLeod, F., Viswanathan, L., Whitelaw, G.S., Macbeth, J., King, C., McCarthy, D.D., & Alexiuk, E. (2015). Finding common ground: A critical review of land use and resource management policies in Ontario, Canada and their intersection with First Nations. *International Indigenous Policy Journal, 6*(1), 1–23. doi:10.18584/iipj.2015.6.1.3

Nejad, S., Walker, R., Macdougall, B., Belanger, Y., Newhouse, D., & Wenjack, C., (2019). "This is an Indigenous city; why don't we see it?" Indigenous urbanism and spatial production in Winnipeg. *Canadian Geographer, 63*(34), 413–424.

Newman, D. (2013). The bilateral amending formula as a mechanism for the entrenchment of property rights. *Constitutional Forum, 21*(2). doi:10.21991/C9238N

Njoh, A.M. (2017). The right-to-the-city question and Indigenous urban populations in capital cities in Cameroon. *Journal of Asian and African Studies, 52*(2), 188–200.

Norris, M.J., Clatworthy, S., & Peters, E. (2013). The urbanization of Aboriginal populations in Canada: A half century in review. In E. Peters & C. Andersen (Eds.), *Indigenous in the city: Contemporary identities and cultural innovation*. UBC Press.

Peña, G. de la. (2011). Ethnographies of Indigenous exclusion in Western Mexico. *Indiana Journal of Global Legal Studies, 18*(1), 307–319.

Prusack, S.Y., Walker, R., & Innes, R. (2015). Toward Indigenous planning? First Nation community planning in Saskatchewan, Canada. *Journal of Planning Education and Research, 21*(3), 31–11.

Purcell, M. (2002). Excavating Lefebvre: The right to the city and its urban politics of the inhabitant. *GeoJournal, 58*, 99–108. doi:10.1023/B:GEJO.0000010829.62237.8f

Purcell, M. (2006). Urban democracy and the local trap. *Urban Studies, 43*(11), 1921–1941.

Regan, P. (2010). *Unsettling the settler within: Indian residential schools, truth telling, and reconciliation in Canada*. UBC Press.

Ritchie, K. (2013). Issues associated with the implementation of the duty to consult and accommodate aboriginal peoples: Threatening the goals of reconciliation and meaningful consultation. *UBC Law Review, 46*(2), 397–438.

Royal Commission on Aboriginal Peoples. (1996). *Volume 2: Restructuring the Relationship* [Report]. http://data2.archives.ca/e/e448/e011188230-02.pdf

Soja, E. (2010). *Seeking spatial justice*. University of Minnesota Press.

Stead, V. (2015). Homeland, territory, property: Contesting land, state, and nation in urban Timor-Leste. *Political Geography, 45*(March), 79–89. doi:10.1016/j.polgeo.2014.05.002

Tomiak, J. (2011). Indigeneity and the city: Representations, resistance, and the right to the city. In A. Bourke, T. Dafnos, & M. Kip (Eds.), *Lumpen-city: Discourses of marginality, marginalizing discourses* (pp. 163–192). Red Quill Books.

Tomiak, J. (2016). Unsettling Ottawa: Settler colonialism, Indigenous resistance, and the politics of scale. *Canadian Journal of Urban Research, 25*(1), 8–21.

Toronto City Council. (2009, August 5). Development of an urban Aboriginal strategy for Toronto. http://app.toronto.ca/tmmis/decisionBodyProfile.do?function=doPrepare&meetingId=2207#Meeting-2009.CC38

Toronto City Council. (2014, March 19). Aboriginal year of truth and reconciliation and establishment of Aboriginal Office. http://app.toronto.ca/tmmis/viewAgendaItemHistory.do?item=2014.EX39.10

Toronto City Council (2017a, May 24). Implementing Indigenous cultural competency training in the Toronto public service. http://app.toronto.ca/tmmis/viewAgendaItemHistory.do?item=2017.MM29.6

Toronto City Council. (2017b, November 3). Proposed Aboriginal office for the City of Toronto. http://app.toronto.ca/tmmis/viewAgendaItemHistory.do?item=2017.EX26.25

Toronto City Council. (2019, October 2). Legal challenge to Bill 5, the Better Local Government Act, CC 10.3. https://www.toronto.ca/legdocs/mmis/2019/cc/bgrd/backgroundfile-138203.pdf

Truth and Reconciliation Commission of Canada. (2015). *What we have learned: Principles of truth and reconciliation*. http://www.trc.ca/assets/pdf/Principles%20of%20Truth%20and%20Reconciliation.pdf

UN-Habitat. (2016, May 30). *Urban agenda for the EU: "Pact of Amsterdam" (Agreement at the informal meeting of EU ministers responsible for urban matters)*. https://ec.europa.eu/regional_policy/sources/policy/themes/urban-development/agenda/pact-of-amsterdam.pdf

UN & Habitat III (UN conference on Housing and Sustainable Urban Development). (2016, October). *New Urban Agenda*. http://habitat3.org/the-new-urban-agenda/

Valverde, M., & Weaver, A. (2015). "The Crown wears many hats": The blackboxing of sovereignty in Canadian Aboriginal law. In K. McGee (Ed.), *Latour and the passage of law* (pp. 93–121). Edinburgh University Press

Vanegas, F.S.B. (2012). Indigenous resistance and the law. *Latin American Perspectives, 39*(1), 61–77.

Wallace, P. (2016, April 1). *Fulfilling calls to action from Truth and Reconciliation Commission report (Report from Toronto city manager)*. https://www.toronto.ca/legdocs/mmis/2016/ex/bgrd/backgroundfile-91816.pdf

Weistock, D. (2015). Federalism and cities. In J.E. Sterling, & J.T. Levy (Eds.), *Federalism and subsidiarity* (pp. 259–287). New York University Press.

World Urban Forum. (2004). *World charter on right to the city*. https://www.hlrn.org.in/documents/World_Charter_on_the_Right_to_the_City.htm

LEGISLATION

Alberta Regulation 40/2018 Municipal Government Act, City of Calgary Charter, 2018 Regulation. http://www.qp.alberta.ca/Documents/Regs/2018_040.pdf

The Better Local Government Act, SO 2018, c 11 [Bill 5].

Bill 41-2019, *Declaration on the Rights of Indigenous Peoples Act* (BC).

City of Toronto Act, 2006, SO 2006, c 11, Schedule A.

Constitution Act, 1982, being Schedule B to the *Canada Act 1982* (UK), 1982, c 11 at ss 38–45. *City of Toronto Act, 2006*.

Municipal Government Act, RSO 1990, Ch M-26; Charter of Ville de Montréal, RSO 2000, c 56, Schedule I, Ch C-11.4.

UN General Assembly, *United Nations Declaration on the Rights of Indigenous Peoples*. Resolution adopted by the General Assembly, 2 October 2007, A/RES/61/295. https://www.refworld.org/docid/471355a82.html

JURISPRUDENCE

114957 Canada Ltée (Spraytech, Societe d'arrosage) v Hudson (Town), [2001] 2 SCR 241 [Spraytech].

Canada Post Corporation v Hamilton (City), 2016 ONCA 767 (CanLII).

Cardinal v Windmill Green Fund LPV, 2016 ONSC 3456.

Chippewas of the Thames First Nation v Enbridge Pipelines Inc., 2017 SCC 41 (CanLII).

City of Toronto et al v Ontario (Attorney General).

City of Toronto v Attorney General of Ontario, SCC 38921 2020 (leave granted).

Clyde River (Hamlet) v Petroleum Geoservices Inc., 2017 SCC 40 (CanLII).

Delgamuukw v British Columbia, [1997] 3 SCR 1010.

East York (Borough) v Attorney General (1997), 34 OR. (3d) 789 (Gen. Div.), aff'd (1997), 36 O. (3d) 733 (CA), leave to appeal to SCC refused, [1998] 1 SCR vii.

Godbout v Longueuil (City), [1997] 3 SCR 844.

Haida Nation v British Columbia (Minister of Forests), [2004] 3 SCR 511.

Halfway River First Nation v British Columbia (Ministry of Forests), 1997 CanLII 2719 (BC SC), [1997] 4 CNLR 45 (BCSC).

Keewatin v Ontario (Natural Resources), 2013 ONCA 158 (CanLII). http://canlii.ca/t/fwjp2

Morgan v Sun Peaks Resort Corporation, [2013] BCSC 1668.

Morton v British Columbia (Agriculture and Lands), 2009 BCSC 136 (CanLII), [2009] 7 WWR 690; 92 BCLR (4th) 314; 42 CELR (3d) 79; [2009] BCJ No 193 (QL); 174 ACWS (3d) 103.

Nanaimo (City) v Rascal Trucking Ltd, [2000] 1 SCR 342.

Neskonlith Indian Band v Salmon Arm (City), (2014) 47.1 UBC Law Review 293–312 [Neskonlith].

Pacific National Investments Ltd. v Victoria (City), [2000] 2 SCR 919.

R v Badger, 1996 CanLII 236 (SCC), [1996] 1 SCR 771.

R v Guignard, [2002] 1 SCR 472, 2002 SCC 14 (CanLII).

R v Marshall, 1999 CanLII 665 (SCC), [1999] 3 SCR 456.

R v Van der Peet, [1996] 2 SCR 507.

Squamish Nation v British Columbia (Community, Sport and Cultural Development), 2014 BCSC 991.

Toronto (City) v Ontario (Attorney General) (C65861). Court of Appeal, Orders and Filed Documents, http://www.ontariocourts.ca/coa/C65861/

Toronto (City) v Ontario (Attorney General), 2018 ONCA 761.

2
THE RIGHT TO THE CITY AS AN EMERGING NORM
Codification and Cultural Institutions

JENNIFER A. ORANGE
—

Introduction

The right to the city (RTTC), as Henri Lefebvre originally described it in 1968, provided a vision of how to transform urban space and elevate the power of urban residents so that they could control the processes affecting their daily lives (Lefebvre, 1968). The RTTC is about participation in city life. It is about experiencing all that the city has to offer. It encompasses the inclusion of people from diverse backgrounds, in the physical situation that the city creates, where people from different cultures, ethnicities, and ways of life interact. Lefebvre's RTTC is a reaction to the alienation of the poor and working-class urban residents from the opportunities that cities can provide: to live, learn, work, and play in a rich community of ideas and experiences.

Lefebvre purposely used "rights" language in his characterization. He knew that the RTTC was a novel concept, one that was not recognized as a legal right at the time, but one that could be characterized as a bundle of rights that largely related to already existing legal rights. Using this discourse, Lefebvre pushed urban residents, and those who administered government institutions, to think about the claims residents could make and the duties owed to them. His use of rights language continues to push us today to think about the process of achieving rights.

Although many might argue that the RTTC is merely an idea and not a legal right per se, the emergence of the RTTC in human rights movements, and even in different types of legislation, provides an example of how human rights evolve from concept to law. In this chapter I explore two ways in which the RTTC is evolving through the process of norm development. In the first instance, states, sub-state governments such as cities, and civil society organizations have worked together to develop standards that underpin the substance of the RTTC and through codification have begun to assert it as a legal right. In the second case, I describe two interventions by museums and show how they are bolstering the need for an RTTC. Both approaches support the growth of the RTTC as a human rights norm that can develop the characteristics of a legal right.

How Could the RTTC Develop into a New Legal Right?
An analysis of the legal status of the RTTC provides a fascinating view of how ideas can transform over time into law. Simply put, Canadian law is typically created by legislative enactment or through the evolution of the common law through judicial decisions. International law plays a role in the development of domestic law, but the relationship between the two arenas is complex. Canadian law, including judicial interpretation of the Canadian *Charter of Rights and Freedoms* (the *Charter*), is influenced by Canada's commitments to international treaties and declarations—among its other activities as a member of the international community of states (Brunnée & Toope, 2002a). The Supreme Court of Canada has held that international human rights treaties should be used as guidance in interpreting rights under the *Charter*.[1]

For laws to effectively develop, however, either domestically or internationally, they first must be acknowledged generally as norms by the people they affect.[2] How do ideas evolve into generally accepted norms? And how do they then become law?

When Lefebvre acknowledged that rights start as customs, he was aligning aspects of his theory with those of norm development. Constructivist accounts in international relations provide models for the way in which norms develop and become law internationally, but these methods can also apply to domestic law. Finnemore and Sikkink (1998) defined norms as "a standard of appropriate behaviour for actors with a given identity" (p. 891). They further explained that "norms do not appear out of thin air; they are actively built by agents (norm entrepreneurs) having strong notions about appropriate or desirable behavior in their community" (p. 896). One argument advanced by Brunnée and Toope (2002b) is that norms are developed through shared understandings and "a construction dependent on mutual generative activity" (p. 278). Interactions between different people and groups can cause shared understandings, or norms, to emerge as actors develop expectations of appropriate behaviour in specific contexts.

Although I provide only one brief description of norm development, my hope is that it provides a basic platform upon which to build a discussion of the different ways in which the RTTC is emerging in Canada and internationally as both a norm and a legal right. The RTTC norm is being built by domestic and international efforts to codify the norm into law and by the work of cultural institutions, such as museums, to expand the public's understanding of a need for more robust rights for urban residents.

The Codification of the RTTC

Currently, there is no established RTTC under international or Canadian law. Lefebvre (1996) recognized this when he referred to the RTTC as a "pseudo-right" (p. 158) and observed the way in which rights are enacted into law: "Rights appear and become customs or prescriptions, usually followed by enactments" (p. 157). The RTTC, however, can be conceived as a bundle of rights that consists largely of rights that already exist in international law, although they do not specifically target the needs of city dwellers. As Lefebvre (1996) described,

> [t]he right to the city is not simply the right to access education or work. Rather it is the right to belong everywhere, to inhabit cities through independent exploration, to influence institutions as well as attain a livelihood. It is also the right to encounter difference: not only different people, but different experiences—not only a limited "leisure" experience, but meaningful encounters across social classes in daily life. (pp. 173–174)

Later in this same work, Lefebvre elaborates that the RTTC includes the "right to work, to training and education, to health, housing, leisure, to life" (p. 179). From these descriptions we can identify basic rights to life, education, work, housing, and culture, and to being free from discrimination. Each of these rights is set out in the numerous treaties that Canada has signed and ratified, such as the *International Covenant on Economic, Social and Cultural Rights* (1966), the *International Covenant on Civil and Political Rights* (1966), the *International Convention on the Elimination of All Forms of Racial Discrimination* (1965), the *Convention on the Elimination of All Forms of Discrimination Against Women* (1979), the *Convention on the Rights of the Child* (1989), the *International Convention on the Protection of the Rights of All Migrant Workers and Members of Their Families* (1990), and the *Convention Relating to the Status of Refugees* (1951). Furthermore, Canada voted to support the adoption of the *Universal Declaration of Human Rights* (1948) and the *Vienna Declaration and Programme of Action* (1993).

So, in one sense, the RTTC exists within many recognized rights but perhaps not in a package that characterizes the particular experiences of urban residents. Part of this experience is that residents have little access to participation or representation. Lefebvre (1996), among others, has focused on the importance of supporting urban residents in their having a say in the way they live. The RTTC can be interpreted as a cry from urban residents for more robust democratic standards—that is, for the ability to participate meaningfully in the decisions that affect them.

Over the last 20 years, advocates have made considerable progress in putting the RTTC on policy and legislative agendas in cities, states, and international organizations. At the municipal level a number of cities have implemented legal measures to improve the lives of city residents, such as Dakar's *Civic and Citizens' Pact* (2003), Montreal's *Charter of Rights and Responsibilities* (2006), and in Australia the Victoria *Charter of Human Rights and Responsibilities* (2006) (UN-Habitat, 2010; Whitzman, 2013). Montreal's *Charter*, for example, sets out rights, responsibilities, and commitments under the themes of democratic life, economic and social life, cultural life, leisure and sport, environment and sustainable development, and security and municipal services (*Montréal Charter of Rights and Responsibilities*, 2005/2017).

At the state level, Brazil's *City Statute* (2001) and Ecuador's new *Constitution* (2010) recognize the RTTC (Shaw et al., 2013). In the 1990s the Council of European Municipalities and Regions explored the practical meanings of the rights of urban residents; in 2006 the council published the *European Charter for Equality of Women and Men in Local Life* (Council of European Municipalities and Regions, 2006; Khosla & Dhar, 2013).

International meetings of activists and other experts in urban affairs have made significant headway in pushing the RTTC to the front of agendas. The World Social Forum, one such international meeting, brings together civil society organizations, including non-governmental organizations, from around the world to discuss problems on a variety of themes, such as human rights and the environment (World Social Forum, 2016). Meetings of activists, workers, and professionals at the World Social Forums from 2002 to 2005 defined the RTTC in the *World Charter for the Right to the City*, stating the following:

> The Right to the City is defined as the equitable usufruct of cities within the principles of sustainability, democracy, equity, and social justice. It is the collective right of the inhabitants of cities, in particular of the vulnerable and marginalized groups, that confers upon them legitimacy of action and organization, based on their uses and customs, with the objective to achieve full exercise of the right to free self-determination and an adequate standard of living. The Right to the City is interdependent of all internationally recognized and integrally conceived human rights, and therefore includes all the civil, political, economic, social, cultural and environmental rights which are already

regulated in the international human rights treaties. (World Social Forum, 2005)

Thus, the World Social Forum conceives the RTTC as an integrated, collective right that is interconnected with all recognized international human rights conventions, echoing established human rights discourse, such as that found in the *Vienna Declaration and Programme of Action*.[3] The RTTC, however, notes something more than what is available in the earlier conventions (Khosla & Dhar, 2013). It is the confluence of encounters and peoples, which intersect in cities, that requires legal rights to take on new meanings. The RTTC community argues that it is not enough for urban residents to use current human rights discourse to make rights claims. Instead, the particular needs and alienation experienced by urban residents require new forms of rights. By recognizing these new rights, governments can create new solutions to complex problems.

Other international organizations have followed on from the work of the World Social Forum. United Cities and Local Governments (UCLG), a global network of cities and local, regional, and municipal governments founded in 2004, defined the mandates of local governments within a human rights framework (UCLG, 2020). Its November 2010 conference adopted the *Global Charter-Agenda for Human Rights to the City*,[4] inviting local governments to create action plans (Khosla & Dhar, 2013). More recently, in its November 2019 world summit meeting in Durban, the UCLG promoted its manifestos, several of which targeted human rights issues in cities, such as gender equality, and the right to housing. The *Manifesto on the Future of Culture* stated that "we invite cultural sectors, institutions and organisations to strengthen their own efforts to the response to our common challenges as one humanity, and be bolder and more explicit in addressing human rights, gender equality, inequalities and climate change" (UCLG Congress, 2019, p. 2). As we will see, some museums are taking up the call.

The work of civil society organizations and city governments has also activated the United Nations. In 2016 the UN Conference on Housing and Sustainable Urban Development (Habitat III) in Quito, Ecuador, developed the *New Urban Agenda*. At the General Assembly meeting in December of that year, all UN members adopted this agenda, committing to a new way to plan, build, and manage cities (Habitat III Secretariat, 2017). As a result, Habitat III developed a comprehensive policy paper that further illuminates that the RTTC can address the rapid urbanization, poverty reduction, social exclusion, and environmental risk faced in cities across the globe (Habitat III Secretariat, 2017). With a focus on freedom from discrimination, enhanced access to resources, and participation in political and social life, the report defines the RTTC in these terms:

> The right of all inhabitants present and future, to occupy, use and produce just, inclusive and sustainable cities, defined as a common good essential to the quality of life. The right to the city further implies responsibilities on governments and people to claim, defend, and promote this right. (Habitat III Secretariat, 2017, p. 26)

The breadth of international support for this initiative and the detailed work entailed in the 92-page policy paper demonstrate that the RTTC is indeed emerging as an international right. From its initial conception in 1968, Lefebvre recognized that norms take time to evolve into codes, and the RTTC provides an exciting opportunity to observe such a development. In the next section I discuss how the RTTC is being taken up in cultural institutions in a way that can foster the public's understanding of the right and the need for its solidification in law.

Exhibiting the RTTC

Despite the broad work of civil society organizations, local governments, and states through UN bodies, I dare say that most Canadians have not heard of the RTTC. Perhaps in response to the call for more education on the issues at the core of the RTTC, there are new partnerships developing between museums and local organizations to describe these struggles of urban residents in comprehensive exhibitions. While museums are criticized as places for urban elites, the sheer numbers of museum visitors, along with museum trends, dispute this. In the United States, more people visit museums every year than attend major league sporting events and theme parks combined (American Alliance of Museums, n.d.). The power of museums to reach the public is vast.

A core function of museums is to inspire visitors (Gerrard, Sykora, & Jackson, 2017), and there is increasing pressure on museums to support social justice, by both domestic and international museum organizations. In 2019 the world's largest museum association, the International Council of Museums (ICOM), proposed a new definition of museums, stating that museums work to "enhance understandings of the world, aiming to contribute to human dignity and social justice, global equality and planetary wellbeing" (ICOM, 2019, para 2 of the definition).[5] Museums around the world, such as the Lower East Side Tenement Museum in New York, the District Six Museum in Cape Town, South Africa, and Liberty Osaka in Japan, have partnered with local communities and visitors to create dialogue, and at times political action, that supports social justice.

The Canadian Museum for Human Rights (CMHR), which opened in 2014 as a national museum, has a gallery titled "Inspiring Change," which is "intended to spark a personal reflection on how each of us may contribute to positive social change" (CMHR, 2020). It is within this trend that the Smithsonian Anacostia Community Museum (Anacostia Museum) and the Toronto Ward Museum (TWM) work both to raise awareness of the unique challenges that urban communities face and to inspire people to work for social justice. Although direct correlations between museum work and the establishment of RTTC movements have not yet been established, the examples herein demonstrate how museums disseminate key concepts and may inspire visitors to take action within their communities.

The following section describes two exhibitions with different approaches to the struggles of city life: an exhibition by the Anacostia Museum in Washington, DC, titled *A Right to the City*; and an exhibition and programming by TWM titled *Block by Block*. Both interventions describe residents' struggles for inclusion and participation in all aspects of city life, but particularly in housing, transportation, equal access to work and education, and a healthy environment. Although many of the themes and modes used in the exhibitions are similar, key differences are evident. For the purposes of this chapter, one important distinction is that the Anacostia Museum foregrounds "rights" language, while the TWM does not.

Smithsonian Anacostia Community Museum

> The Right to the City is the right of all inhabitants, present and future, to use, occupy and produce just, inclusive and sustainable cities, defined as a common good essential to a full and decent life.[6]

Founded in 1967, the Anacostia Museum has developed from a museum aimed at bringing national culture to an urban neighbourhood, to a museum that provides a way for members of that community to voice their concerns (SACM, 2018b). The museum has hosted exhibitions on a broad range of subjects, such as the civil rights movement, the infestation of rats, and African American baseball players. From April 2018 to April 2020, the museum displayed a comprehensive exhibition called *A Right to the City*. The museum described the exhibition like this:

> [It] explores the history of neighborhood change and civic engagement in the nation's capital by looking at the dynamic histories of six Washington, D.C., neighborhoods: Adams Morgan, Anacostia, Brookland, Chinatown, Shaw and Southwest. The exhibition tells the story of these communities through the eyes of the Washingtonians who have helped shape these neighborhoods in extraordinary ways. They have used their collective community power to fight for quality public education, healthy and green urban spaces, equitable development and transportation, and a truly democratic approach to city planning. (SACM, 2018b)

Human agency is a key aspect of the stories shared in this exhibition, which does not merely show the challenges that different neighbourhoods experienced but also highlights the ways in which community members took leadership roles and fought for their rights. Just as Lefebvre noted the need for urban residents to have a voice in the creation of their community, this exhibition focuses on the ways in which residents are actively shaping their society and ensuring representation in decisions that affect their daily lives. Another special feature of the exhibition is the "telephone hotline" that allows people to call in and hear one of the 200 oral histories collected for the exhibition (SACM, 2018b). The telephone was on site when I visited the museum in 2018, and visitors could also record their own story to add to the collection.

The title of the exhibition puts rights at the forefront, but text within displays as well as in the exhibition guide makes it clear that there is no established RTTC yet:

Do people have a right to the city?

Do they have a right to equal, and not separate, education for their children, and a right to accessible transportation to jobs and schools? Do people have a right to remain in their homes and in their neighborhoods? Do they, along with their neighbors, have a right to decide how their neighborhoods develop and change?

A Right to the City. It is both an idea and an ideal. As long as cities have been a feature of human civilization, they have been the site of ongoing struggles for human rights—to create and maintain healthy community life, to have equal access to resources and opportunities, to exercise self-government. (SACM, 2018a)

The museum does not explicitly answer whether or not there is an established RTTC, but it sets out the concept as an ongoing battle.

The exhibition is divided into six parts, each focusing on a particular neighbourhood struggle. First, "Southwest DC: Urban Renewal, Urban Removal" describes the displacement of 23,000 residents, from the 1950s to the early 1970s, who were forced from their homes due to a policy of city redevelopment. It depicts the community organizations that helped re-establish the community elsewhere, including the Southwest Neighborhood Assembly, which became one of the first racially integrated neighbourhood associations in the city.

The second part is titled "Anacostia: Segregation, Desegregation, Resegregation." It describes the desegregation of schools in the Anacostia neighbourhood after the Supreme Court case *Bolling v Sharpe*,[7] which resulted in whites fleeing the district and the community being effectively segregated once again. This section portrays the work of two neighbourhood organizations, Rebels with a Cause and the Band of Angels, who advocated for new recreation centres and pools, improved roads, their own schools, and improved access for families in receipt of public assistance (SACM, 2018a).

Third is "Shaw: With the People, By the People, For the People," which focuses on the participation of the community in redevelopment. To avoid some of the experiences of the Southwest neighbourhood, Reverend Walter Fauntroy founded the Model Inner City Community Organization to ensure community participation in the planning process. Although the organization achieved many results, this part concludes with a recognition that despite achieving many of its housing goals, the neighbourhood was overwhelmed by gentrification, and between 1970 and 2010 Shaw's African American population dropped from 90% to 30% (SACM, 2018a).

The fourth part is titled "Brookland: Fight the Freeways" and reviews the community's fight in the late 1960s against the threat of new freeway construction. This section highlights the activism of an interracial coalition called the Emergency Committee on the Transportation Crisis. The committee saved homes and maintained the small town, "leafy" character of the area. This neighbourhood, however, faces ongoing challenges due to rising rents and new construction (SACM, 2018a).

Fifth is "Chinatown: Preserving Our Place," which describes the waves of discrimination experienced by Chinese immigrants. Like residents of the other neighbourhoods, they were forced to move several times, eventually settling in the area of H Street North West and Sixth

Street. This section highlights the community organizations that helped support Chinese settlers: the On Leong Merchants Association, the Chinese Consolidated Benevolent Association, the Chinese Youth Club, the On Leong and Hip Sing fraternal organizations, and the Lee and Moy family associations. Despite the roots of the Chinese community and their businesses in this area, city planners approved major developments in the neighbourhood between the 1960s and the 1990s, including the Washington Convention Centre and Capitol One Arena, the present home of the National Hockey League team the Washington Capitals. While features of Chinatown remain, there are only about 300 Chinese American residents remaining in the area and few Chinese-owned businesses (SACM, 2018a).

The final part of the exhibition is titled "Adams Morgan: The Power of Unity in Diversity." Unlike the experiences of residents in Anacostia, after the *Bolling v Sharpe* decision, the parents of children at the all-white elementary school and the all-black elementary school joined together to form the Adams-Morgan Better Neighborhood Conference to work towards integration. This section describes the benefits of collaboration: better tenant and immigrant rights, educational equity, youth development, and one of the first community-controlled schools in the nation. Although increased gentrification and property values also threaten economic and ethnic diversity in the area, the elementary school still prioritizes a multicultural, multilingual, and equity-centred education, while tenant protections guard some affordable housing (SACM, 2018a).

A Right to the City ends with Rev. Dr. Martin Luther King Jr.'s call to the Shaw community in 1967:

> Prepare to participate, and you will give to your city and our nation an instructive example of how we can deal with one of the most serious problems confronting us today. That's the message I want you to carry away from this meeting today. Prepare to participate! (SACM, 2018a, p. 23)

This concluding message accords with Lefebvre's writings on the RTTC. It is critical for urban residents to be willing and able to participate in the decisions that affect their lives. The Anacostia Museum smartly connects Lefebvre's theory to the call of the American icon, Rev. Dr. King Jr., to participate, which he made within one of the neighbourhoods at the centre of the exhibition. Museums have the capacity to connect universal concepts to local experiences, making them all the more meaningful for visitors and participants in museum programming.

The Toronto Ward Museum

I am not aware of any Canadian exhibition that addresses the RTTC explicitly. However, a multitude of exhibits and programs examine the various constituent issues that make up the concept.[8] One of the most comprehensive exhibits on this front is the *Block by Block* exhibition created by the TWM.

The TWM was founded to facilitate the "preservation and sharing of personal stories of migrants in Toronto's history" (TWM, 2015). The museum does not have one physical site but engages its audiences through its website, temporary displays, and interactive programming. According to its website, the museum "envisions a society that values immigrants as makers of Toronto's past and present, bringing together people of all backgrounds to shape a more just, equitable and sustainable future" (TWM, 2015). By focusing on participation, agency, and social justice, the museum supports the RTTC's goals, documenting how city residents have long taken an active role in shaping their lives in Toronto, identifying the barriers they face, and empowering them to do more.

It is important to note that the mission of the *Block by Block* exhibition does not correspond explicitly with the RTTC concept:

> The goal of *Block by Block* is to deepen relationships in and between communities through the exchange of personal stories, reflections and resources. We hope to contribute to better public understanding of migrant settlement experiences and the roles that neighbourhoods play in those experiences. We think those experiences have been

underrepresented in Toronto and that there is a lot to learn from them. We also hope to encourage public dialogue about future city-building. (TWM, 2019a)

As we will see, however, the process that the museum followed to record and exchange personal stories of migrant settlement experiences and different neighbourhoods resulted in a platform that elucidates the reasons why an RTTC is emerging and has the potential to support norm development.

A key mode of the museum's work, used robustly in *Block by Block*, is its partnerships with different organizations and communities. As I have written elsewhere, museums that work to advance human rights and social justice regularly create *communities of practice* to help enhance their knowledge and expertise in challenging subjects.[9] These communities of practice may include museum staff, non-profit organizations, governmental organizations, and members of local community groups that have first-hand knowledge of particular experiences (Orange, 2016). The TWM epitomizes an actor working in a community of practice.

The museum, together with eight institutional partners, ran its first iteration of the *Block by Block* exhibition in 2017 in three historically immigrant neighbourhoods in different Canadian cities: St. John's Ward in Toronto, Côte-des-Neiges in Montreal, and Strathcona in Vancouver. The exhibition billed itself as a "community-led conversation" that started with three big questions:

What makes a neighbourhood inclusive and livable for new immigrants and refugees? How have newcomers shaped Canadian neighbourhoods and staked a place in them for future generations? What are the pleasures and challenges of living in a neighbourhood where most residents are first or second-generation Canadian? (TWM, 2017)

The exhibition team engaged 520 participants to capture the stories of newcomers and racialized persons through photographs, transcribed narratives, and audio and video recordings, including 30 oral histories. The material was presented through three local exhibitions, a co-curated online exhibition, and three "Block Parties where the research team and local partners animated neighbourhood stories with creative programming" (TWM, 2019d).

The second iteration of *Block by Block* ran from 2019 to 2021. It focused on four neighbourhoods in Metropolitan Toronto: Parkdale, Regent Park, Agincourt, and Victoria Park. The online platform divides the stories into four themes: "Arriving and Settling," "Supporting Each Other," "Place and Identity," and "Resistance and Resilience." Under each theme are individual narratives told in text, audio, and video.

Under the theme of "Arriving and Settling," participant narratives explain the barriers to feeling like one belongs in a new place when one arrives with refugee status, the challenges in accessing community resources, and the difficulties in finding work in one's profession because one lacks "Canadian experience." The final narrative describes the ways in which Elsaida Douglas of Regent Park worked to overcome experiences of racial injustice and gun violence in her neighbourhood and advocated for change in community housing policy (TWM, 2019b).

The stories under the theme of "Supporting Each Other" focus on the ways in which newcomers to the city have identified needs and worked with organizations or advocated to combat isolation and exclusion. One narrative focuses on the experience of Suriya Ibrahim, who recognized that the revitalization of Regent Park required community input to ensure that local residents were not left out of the end benefits, such as access to the new pool. She identified the "open swim" time and the fee for swimming as barriers to access for people with low incomes. She also emphasized the need for priority spaces for local residents so that people from other parts of the city did not take up all the spots in this beautiful new facility (TWM, 2019e).

Under the theme of "Place and Identity," the narratives focus on how residents create a sense of belonging in their neighbourhood, while the media and people from outside the area perpetuate stereotypes of poverty and racism. Laurie Okimawinew's story shows how coming to Regent Park and participating in the programming offered at Council Fire Native Cultural Centre helped her learn about and celebrate her own Indigenous culture and history. This programming helped her understand the harms that the residential school system had caused her family, and gave her tools to overcome them.

Finally, under the theme of "Resistance and Resilience," the narratives focus on the struggles that people lived with before they moved to Canada, such as discrimination, poverty, a lack of housing, and a lack of security. Although Canada provides numerous opportunities to newcomers, this section shows many of the obstacles that remain for new immigrants. In addition to the challenges of finding housing and work, huge challenges emerge from gentrification and the rise in both residential and commercial rents. Garab Serdok's story emphasizes the role that immigrants played in creating the small businesses that give the Parkdale neighbourhood its vibrant character. Serdok owns a restaurant called The Tibet Kitchen. As Parkdale becomes a trendier hub, more big-box stores have moved in, driving up rents. Serdok stated: "The small businesses help build the neighbourhood up and we deserve to stay" (TWM, 2019c).

Although the *Block by Block* exhibition does not focus on rights, or the RTTC in particular, it does connect to many issues of human rights and to several of Lefebvre's preoccupations. A number of the narratives focus on exclusion due to different language backgrounds, ethnicity, race, income, or the lack of Canadian work experience. The stories highlight actions by individuals to create or prevent change in their neighbourhoods. This attention to the ways in which newcomers are participating in the social and political lives of their cities aligns perfectly with the goals of the RTTC.

Similar Struggles, Different Frames

Although framed differently, the exhibitions in Anacostia and Toronto have much in common. They are both concerned with the alienation that urban residents experience, and they connect that experience to race, ethnicity, poverty, and immigrant status. They address housing, transportation, access to community resources, and education. Both exhibitions add to our understanding of what it is like to live in a city neighbourhood—from the various struggles described to the rich relationships that diverse cities offer.

There are obvious ways in which the two exhibitions differ. Physically, the Anacostia Museum is part of the federally funded Smithsonian Institution and has its own beautiful building; *A Right to the City* took up the main exhibition space. The TWM is a much newer organization, which created *Block by Block* as an online exhibition with programming through "Block Parties." Despite the difference in resources, the substantive content of the two exhibitions is impressive.

In terms of the subject matter, *A Right to the City* concentrates on the activism of community groups, going back in time to describe the discrimination faced by the African Americans under slavery and by Chinese immigrants under the 1882 *Chinese Exclusion Act*. Much of the focus of the exhibition is on events that occurred between the 1950s and the 1970s. *Block by Block*, in contrast, mentions some community groups but emphasizes the contributions of individuals in a more recent time frame. Both museums examine the experience of people who are racialized or marginalized, but because of the different immigration histories of the two cities, the backgrounds of the residents differ. It should also be noted that the experience of Indigenous people is not included in the narrative of the Anacostia exhibition. Nonetheless, the experiences of discrimination and exclusion and the active support of community members in the face of adversity are common themes to both exhibitions.

A Right to the City, as its name implies, uses rights language and includes discussions of law suits and discriminatory laws through its displays, whereas *Block by Block* does not. The different approaches beg the question of whether it is helpful to invoke rights and legal language when trying to advance a certain norm through a cultural forum. Without using rights language, *Block by Block* is extremely effective in leading the viewer to think about the ways in which newcomers and racialized people are excluded from different city resources.

The message of both museum exhibits is neatly tied together by a famous Marxist geographer, David Harvey, in his 2008 work on the RTTC. He says:

The question of what kind of city we want cannot be divorced from that of what kind of social ties, relationship to nature, lifestyles, technologies and aesthetic values we desire. The right to the city is far more than the individual liberty to access urban resources: it is a right to change ourselves by changing the city. It is, moreover, a common rather than an individual right since this transformation inevitably depends upon the exercise of a collective power to reshape the processes of urbanization. The freedom to make and remake our cities and ourselves is, I want to argue, one of the most precious yet most neglected of our human rights. (para. 3)

Foregrounding rights may not be necessary to make the point that inclusion and representation are important, but, as Don Mitchell (2003) wrote in his book on the RTTC:

[r]ights establish an important *ideal* against which the behavior of the state, capital, and other powerful actors must be measured—and held accountable. They provide an institutional framework, no matter how incomplete, within which the goals of social struggle can not only be organized but also attained. (p. 25)

In this way, highlighting the legal aspects of the RTTC may cause museum visitors to think about how they can attain their rights and hold powerful actors accountable. There may be a place and a time for both avenues in supporting the development of the norms that underpin the RTTC.

While it is difficult to ascertain direct connections between museum projects and policy development, the TWM captures the attention of urban policy-makers through its broad partnerships and events. Supporting partners for *Block by Block* included the City of Toronto Newcomer Office and the City of Toronto Music Office, along with multiple community agencies. In addition, Toronto City Councillor Gord Perks promoted a Block Party on his website (Perks, 2019). In October 2018 the Anacostia Museum hosted a symposium in conjunction with the *Right to the City* exhibition, engaging community organizations, academics from disciplines ranging from law and public policy to cultural studies, and museum professionals (SACM, 2018d). My sense is that interactive programming has the greatest potential for museums to engage members of different communities in ways that can influence policy-makers, but more study is needed to assess the impact.

Conclusion

This chapter has explored two different, but concurrent, approaches to supporting the RTTC as it develops from being an idea, to a norm, to a legal right. The work of non-governmental organizations, alongside sub-state governments and states, has codified the substance of the RTTC in an effort to move it towards legal acceptance. But this shift from concept to law cannot progress without an acceptance of the idea as a societal norm. The work of museums to communicate both the RTTC as a legal right and the daily struggles and successes of urban residents has the power to elevate the RTTC by ensuring that communities share understandings of the needs and values underpinning the RTTC.

From a policy perspective, the two museum exhibits demonstrate the different ways in which urban residents are involved in policy development. They show the importance of working through neighbourhood organizations and the strength and ability of key individuals to make change. These museums are community partners, giving a voice to people whom we do not hear often enough in mainstream media or at podiums in city halls. Owing to their community connections, museums can be useful conduits for connecting to marginalized communities. For international actors such as the World Social Forum or Habitat III that are focused on the codification of the RTTC, working with cultural institutions can open up pathways for communication to and from local city residents. We do not regularly think of museums when we work to create legal reform, but we should.

NOTES

1. *Reference re Public Service Employee Relations Act* (Alberta), [1987] 1 SCR 313 at 349; *Suresh v Canada (Minister of Citizenship and Immigration)*, [2002] 1 SCR 3, 2002 SCC 1, at paras. 46, 59–75.
2. If laws are implemented without the affected population understanding the norms upon which they are based, the laws will not be followed without government enforcement efforts (Brunnée & Toope, 2002a).
3. Article 5 of the *Vienna Declaration* states: "All human rights are universal, indivisible and interdependent and interrelated."
4. See https://www.uclg-cisdp.org/en/right-to-the-city/world-charter-agenda#:~:text=The%20Global%20Charter%2DAgenda%20for,without%20discrimination%20of%20any%20kind.
5. At the time of publication ICOM's consultation process on a new definition of the museum was ongoing.
6. Global Platform for the Right to the City (https://www.right2city.org/), cited in SACM (2018c).
7. *Bolling v Sharpe*, 347 US 497 (1954).
8. For examples, see the Picture 2050 contest and exhibit at Toronto's City Hall that envisioned a caring and climate-friendly city (http://picture2050.ca/) and the MyToronto photography contest that highlights issues of homelessness and poverty (https://mytorontocalendar.com/about/).
9. Community of practice theory was first developed by Etienne Wenger and Jean Lave. It has been more fully described by Wenger, McDermott, and Snyder (2002) as "groups of people who share a concern, a set of problems, or a passion about a topic, and who deepen their knowledge and expertise in this area by interacting on an ongoing basis."

REFERENCES

American Alliance of Museums. (n.d.). *Museum facts*. http://ww2.aam-us.org/about-museums/museum-facts

Brunnée, J., & Toope, S.J. (2002a). Hesitant embrace: The application of international law by Canadian courts. *Canadian Yearbook of International Law, 40*, 3–60.

Brunnée, J., & Toope, S.J. (2002b). Persuasion and enforcement: Explaining compliance with international law. *Finnish Yearbook of International Law, 13*, 273.

Canadian Museum for Human Rights. (2020). *Galleries*. https://humanrights.ca/exhibition/galleries

Council of European Municipalities and Regions. (2006). *The European Charter for Equality of Women and Men in Local Life*. https://www.ccre.org/docs/charte_egalite_en.pdf

Finnemore, M., & Sikkink, K. (1998). International norm dynamics and political change. *International Organization, 52*, 887–917.

Gerrard, D., Sykora, M., & Jackson, T. (May 2017). Social media analytics in museums: Extracting expressions of inspiration. *Museum Management and Curatorship, 32*(3), 232–250. doi:10.1080/09647775.2017.1302815

Habitat III Secretariat. (2017). *The right to the city and cities for all*. United Nations.

Harvey, D. (2008). The right to the city. *New Left Review, 53*. https://newleftreview.org/issues/II53/articles/david-harvey-the-right-to-the-city

International Council of Museums. (2019, July). *ICOM announces the alternative museum definition that will be subject to a vote*. https://icom.museum/en/news/icom-announces-the-alternative-museum-definition-that-will-be-subject-to-a-vote/

Khosla, P., & Dhar, S. (2013). Safe access to basic infrastructure: More than pipes and taps. In C. Whitzman, C. Legacy, C. Andrew, F. Klodawsky, M. Shaw, & K. Viswanath (Eds.), *Building inclusive cities: Women's safety and the right to the city* (pp. 117–140). Routledge.

Lefebvre, H. (1968). *Le droit à la ville*. Anthopos.

Lefebvre, H. (1996). *Writings on cities* (E. Kofman & E. Lebas, Eds. and Trans.). Blackwell.

Mitchell, D. (2003). *The right to the city: Social justice and the fight for public space*. Guilford Press.

Montréal Charter of Rights and Responsibilities, By-law 05–056. (2005). Fourth ed. (2017), http://ville.montreal.qc.ca/pls/portal/docs/page/charte_mtl_fr/media/documents/charte_montrealaise_english.pdf

Orange, J.A. (2016). Translating law into practice: Museums and a human rights community of practice. *Human Rights Quarterly, 38*(3), 706–735.

Perks, G. (2019). *Block by Block Toronto Launch Events*. https://gordperks.ca/block-by-block-toronto-launch-events/

Shaw, M., Andrew, C., Whitzman, C., Klodawsky, F., Viswanath, K., & Legacy, C. (2013). Introduction: Challenges, opportunities and tools. In C. Whitzman, C. Legacy, C. Andrew, F. Klodawsky, M. Shaw, & K. Viswanath (Eds.), *Building inclusive cities: Women's safety and the right to the city* (pp. 1–16). Routledge.

Smithsonian Anacostia Community Museum. (2018a). *A right to the city* [Brochure].

Smithsonian Anacostia Community Museum. (2018b, April 18). *Anacostia Community Museum opens signature anniversary exhibition "A Right to the City."* Smithsonian Institution. https://www.si.edu/newsdesk/releases/anacostia-community-museum-opens-signature-anniversary-exhibition-right-city

Smithsonian Anacostia Community Museum. (2018c). *Digital exhibit: A right to the city*. Smithsonian Institution. https://storymaps.arcgis.com/collections/34d99cccb2c5454da7b4f08e482c1987?item=1

Smithsonian Anacostia Community Museum. (2018d, October). *Symposium: A right to the city*. Smithsonian Institution. http://anacostia.si.edu/Events?trumbaEmbed=view%3Devent%26eventid%3D129180891

The Toronto Ward Museum. (2015, March 4). *Vision and mission*. https://www.wardmuseum.ca/about-us/mission-vision/

The Toronto Ward Museum. (2017, July 15). *Block by Block* exhibition 2017. http://www.wardmuseum.ca/blockbyblock/archives/blockbyblock-2017/exhibition/

The Toronto Ward Museum. (2019a). *Block by Block* FAQ.

The Toronto Ward Museum. (2019b). *Block by Block* Dreamer's Way. http://www.wardmuseum.ca/blockbyblock/regentpark/dreamers-way/

The Toronto Ward Museum. (2019c, October 9). *Block by Block* Built by the community. http://www.wardmuseum.ca/blockbyblock/parkdale/built-by-community/

The Toronto Ward Museum. (2019d, October 11). *Block by Block* About https://www.wardmuseum.ca/blockbyblock/about/

The Toronto Ward Museum. (2019e, October 17). *Block by Block* Call your neighbour. https://www.wardmuseum.ca/blockbyblock/regentpark/call-your-neighbour /

UCLG Congress. (2019). *Manifesto: The future of culture*. UCLG World Summit of Local and Regional Leaders. https://www.uclg.org/sites/default/files/en_manifesto_culture.pdf

UN-Habitat. (2010). *State of the world's cities 2010/11: Bridging the urban divide*. UN Human Settlements Programme. https://unhabitat.org/sites/default/files/download-manager-files/State%20of%20the%20World%20Cities%2020102011%20-%20Cities%20for%20All%20Bridging%20the%20Urban%20Divide.pdf

United Cities and Local Governments. (2020). *Who we are*. https://www.uclg.org/en/organisation/about

UN General Assembly. (1989, November 20). *Convention on the Rights of the Child*. UNTS, vol. 1577, p. 3. https://www.ohchr.org/Documents/ProfessionalInterest/crc.pdf

UN General Assembly. (1951, July 28). *Convention Relating to the Status of Refugees*. UNTS, vol. 189, p. 137. https://www.ohchr.org/Documents/ProfessionalInterest/refugees.pdf

UN General Assembly. (1966, December 16). *International Covenant on Civil and Political Rights*. UNTS, vol. 999, p. 171. https://www.ohchr.org/Documents/ProfessionalInterest/ccpr.pdf

UN General Assembly. (1966, December 16). *International Covenant on Economic, Social and Cultural Rights*. UNTS, vol. 993, p. 3. https://www.ohchr.org/Documents/ProfessionalInterest/cescr.pdf

UN General Assembly. (1979, December 18). *Convention on the Elimination of All Forms of Discrimination Against Women*. UNTS, vol. 1249, p. 13. https://www.ohchr.org/Documents/ProfessionalInterest/cedaw.pdf

UN General Assembly. (1965, December 21). *International Convention on the Elimination of All Forms of Racial Discrimination*. UNTS, vol. 660, p. 195. https://www.ohchr.org/Documents/ProfessionalInterest/cerd.pdf

UN General Assembly, (1990, December 18). *International Convention on the Protection of the Rights of All Migrant Workers and Members of their Families*. A/RES/45/158. https://www.ohchr.org/Documents/ProfessionalInterest/cmw.pdf

UN General Assembly. (1948, December 10). *Universal Declaration of Human Rights*. 217 III. https://www.ohchr.org/EN/UDHR/Documents/UDHR_Translations/eng.pdf

UN General Assembly (1993, June 25). *Vienna Declaration and Programme of Action*. https://www.ohchr.org/Documents/ProfessionalInterest/vienna.pdf

Wenger, E., McDermott, R.A., & Snyder, W. (2002). *Cultivating communities of practice*. Harvard Business Press.

Whitzman, C. (2013). Women's safety and everyday mobility. In C. Whitzman et al. (Eds.), *Building inclusive cities: Women's safety and the right to the city* (pp. 35–52). Routledge.

World Social Forum. (2005). *World Charter for the Right to the City*. http://hic-gs.org/document.php?pid=2422

World Social Forum. (2016). *About the World Social Forum: World Social Forum 2016*. https://fsm2016.org/en/sinformer/a-propos-du-forum-social-mondial/

LEGISLATION

Canadian Charter of Rights and Freedoms, Part 1 of the *Constitution Act, 1982*, being Schedule B to the *Canada Act* 1982 (UK), 1982, c 11.

JURISPRUDENCE

Bolling v Sharpe, 347 US 497 (1954).

Canada (A.G.) v Ontario (A.G.), [1937] AC 326 (PC) (the "Labour Conventions" case).

Reference re Public Service Employee Relations Act (Alberta), [1987] 1 SCR 313 at 349.

Suresh v Canada (Minister of Citizenship and Immigration), [2002] 1 SCR 3, 2002 SCC 1, at paras. 46, 59–75.

II
RIGHTS IN THE CITY

3
HUMAN RIGHTS AND THE CITY IN THE PRE-CHARTER ERA

SANDEEP AGRAWAL
—

Introduction

Canadians have become used to a "normal" state of affairs, one in which their human rights and fundamental freedoms are codified and protected in both constitutional and quasi-constitutional formats. This has not always been the case, however. Human rights have only been guaranteed at the federal and provincial levels since the latter half of the twentieth century. The decades that followed the adoption of the United Nations' *Universal Declaration of Human Rights*[1] in 1948 were instrumental in catalyzing changes in human rights protection in both international and domestic arenas. It is these changes that led to constitutional and quasi-constitutional rights protections; thus, they did not appear out of thin air but were decades in the making.

This chapter focuses on the evolution of rights legislation in Canada, human and civil, alongside the societal changes that influenced the move towards the codification of human rights in the country.[2] The research is unique in that it was conducted through a specific municipal planning lens—which has, thus far, received very little attention (Agrawal, 2014,

2020). Specifically, this chapter looks at how the Constitution, legislation, and local bylaws paint a story about the rights of city inhabitants. It does not purport to provide a detailed and complete history of human rights and planning.

The research involved a systematic review of the existing literature, including academic and grey literature, as well as legislative and policy documents. Case law and legal jurisprudence were also key resources in the analysis. Legal search engines, such as CanLII, WestlawNext, and LexisNexis, were used to uncover historical cases from the time of Confederation in 1867 until the signing of the *Charter* in 1982.

Two search methodologies were used to collect cases. The first method identified keywords used to describe human rights cases over time. The keywords search was expanded as more cases were reviewed, and the researcher became familiar with the terminology used in a given era. For example, the search began with terms used to describe human rights in the *Charter*, like *discrimination, equality, sex, age, colour, ethnicity, race,* and *disability*.

Cases were reviewed chronologically so that linguistic trends could be identified, and, concomitantly, search terms to describe civil or human rights issues better could be added or removed as they emerged in the courts. The search terms grew to include terms like *alien, natural-born, non-resident, class, colour, immigrant, Chinaman,* and *Indian*, which were much more common in the early decades of Confederation.

The second method introduced new keywords emerging from national and provincial human rights legislation and international human rights treaties. These search terms came to include *freedom of religion, freedom of speech, freedom of association,* and *freedom of the press*. This method also involved searching cases that cited particular legislation enacted both domestically and internationally. The legislation included the *Bill of Rights*, the *British North America Act*, and the *United Nations Declaration of Human Rights*.

The two searches together yielded hundreds of mildly related cases. From this, approximately 50 cases were selected for further examination; not all were relevant to the focus of the study, and not all those that were relevant are cited here. The selections were made based on the legal context in which the key terms were used and their applicability to the evolution of rights—specifically, human rights, civil rights, freedoms, and the like—and municipal planning. Those selected for inclusion display a pattern of the way in which discrimination and legal rights were viewed in Canadian society and how the judiciary responded to the legal challenges emerging from municipal issues.

The searches elicited few cases related to Indigenous Peoples, even though they were the most discriminated people in Canada at the time. The study findings were related to issues concerning Indian status under the *Indian Act*,[3] and Aboriginal title. No cases were found that related to municipal issues. The following few factors may have contributed to this: (1) the assimilation provisions set out in the *Indian Act* confined Indigenous Peoples to reserves as they were often in fear of losing Indian status; (2) reserves were managed by band government, not municipal government, reporting to the federal government, which in turn followed oppressive assimilation policies; and (3) the *Indian Act* barred Indigenous Peoples from hiring lawyers or seeking legal advice (Wilson, 2018).[4]

The remainder of the chapter is divided into three parts: Part 1 considers 1867 to the end of the Second World War; Part 2 investigates 1946 to 1982; and Part 3 offers some concluding remarks about the pervasiveness of discrimination and racism in the pre-*Charter* era.

From 1867 to the Second World War

During the post-Confederation decades, minimal rights protections existed at the federal and provincial levels. The meagre legal protections that were in place rested within the *Constitution Act, 1867*, and the common law. Women, Indigenous Peoples, and people of Asian descent were legally disenfranchised in the post-Confederation era; thus, they were relegated to the status of being outside the operations or membership of the democracy (Greene, 2014). Only a fraction of the issues were confronted legally, as only a few individuals had the means or the access to justice and a fair trial.

Constitution Act, 1867 (British North America Act) and Common Law

The *British North America Act*,[5] now referred to as the *Constitution Act, 1867* (and henceforth the same in this chapter to avoid confusion),[6] established a parliamentary system of governance in Canada. Through the Constitution, Parliament was given the responsibility of protecting and preserving the rights of the people belonging to the newly formed Confederation. The Constitution was crafted based on the British system, which had no written constitution, but rather "articulated rights with reference to British liberties that were protected through customary law, historical precedents and the supremacy of Parliament" (Clément, 2016, p. 33).

Rights were considered to be rooted in the British tradition, including the British common law tradition, with Quebec following a civil code as the exception (Black-Branch, 2018). As such, no actual written bill of rights is found in the Act. Whatever existed was in the narrow form of rights scattered throughout the Act, which Hogg (2009) referred to as a "small bill of rights" (Part 3, 34.4a). These rights had mainly to do with the use of both English and French languages in the government institutions, the right to language and denominational schools, independence of the judiciary, and guarantees to hold periodic elections.

Basic rights principles established in British common law and carried over to Canada—such as trial by jury, the presumption of innocence, and habeas corpus[7]—helped to lay the foundational principles of the overall legal structure and informed both parliament and court decisions (Sharpe & Roach, 2017). However, no written code firmly established these rights. The few constitutional rights that were codified resulted mainly from duties owed by governments through political compromises, rather than from the idea that individuals possessed natural (or moral) liberties without government interference, as was the case with the *United States Bill of Rights* (Greene, 2014).

Supremacy of Parliament and Federalism: Protectors of Rights?

The *Constitution Act* of 1867 solidified the supremacy of parliament and federalism (Sharpe & Roach, 2017). Both of these concepts played a pivotal role in the transformation of rights and municipal planning.

Federalism divides powers between Canada's parliament and the provinces,[8] with municipalities falling under the jurisdiction of the provinces. This ties into the supremacy of parliament, where elected officials have almost unfettered power to create laws (Sharpe & Roach, 2017). The role of the courts is to interpret those laws and to ensure that they comply with the Constitution, or to determine whether legislative matters fall within federal or provincial jurisdiction (Black-Branch, 2018). Given that municipalities fall under provincial jurisdiction, municipal bylaws were challenged in the courts to confirm their validity.

The following cases illustrate the use of federalism to quash local bylaws, by finding them *ultra vires* to the province and the municipality. Despite illustrating positive outcomes on their face, these cases do not spell out rights victories given that the federal government continued to enforce racist policies, rooted in their legislative authority to do so. Nonetheless, these cases are important as they represent the first challenges made to rights-based policies at the municipal level, and they demonstrate that the courts tend to overuse federalism to handle these issues.

Three relevant cases show that complainants were able to challenge successfully the limits placed on Asian Canadians' economic freedoms by local bylaws under the provincial act: *Sing v Maguire*,[9] *R v Chong*,[10] and *R v Mee Wah*.[11] In the *Sing* case the appellant challenged the right of local authorities to be able to seize and sell property and possessions of the employer of the people of Chinese descent who could not pay a licence fee to work in Canada. Under British Columbia's *Chinese Taxation Act*, the employer, who employed a Chinese worker, was held liable if employees did not pay the tax. In the *Wah* case the appellant challenged his conviction of operating a laundry without a licence, which a municipal bylaw required from businesses operated by those of Chinese descent. The municipal bylaw was enacted under British Columbia's *Municipal Amendment Act*. The *Chong* case addressed a challenge to local taxation and licensing bylaws that targeted people of Chinese descent. The judge in the case reasoned as follows: "I am compelled to think that restriction and not revenue was the very object of the tax. But it is clear that the Provincial Legislature has under the BNA Act no power to impose or authorize a tax for the purpose of driving any industry out of the city or the Province."[12]

Interestingly, all three judgments held that the right to eliminate nationalities or individuals from the capacity to receive trade licences was *ultra vires* to the provincial powers given to the local legislature under Sections 91 and 92 of the *Constitution Act, 1867*.[13] These cases later informed the decision in *R v Corporation of Victoria*,[14] in which the City of Victoria Council ordered that no "Chinaman" be issued a pawnbroking licence.[15] The court explicitly held that a municipality may not prevent certain nationalities from receiving their trade licences. To give the municipality this power would exclude a large portion of people of Asian origin from "gaining a livelihood, or indeed existing in the Province—a very wide interference with 'trade and commerce,' which is totally removed from their control by the BNA Act."[16] The court cited legal principles from the French colony of Cayenne and Paris, implying that similar principles applied in Canada—that is, infringements of "personal liberty, and of the equality of all men before the law."[17]

Despite a favourable decision to the appellants, it did not affect the continued existence of several discriminatory federal and provincial government pieces of legislation, given the continued dominance of parliamentary supremacy and federalism. For instance, the federal *Chinese Immigration Act* (i.e., the "Head Tax") of 1885[18] and British Columbia's *Chinese Taxation Act* or *Chinese Regulations Act* of 1884[19] continued to exist despite this decision.

The above cases illustrate how no large-scale remedial measures followed bylaws that were struck down as invalid. Judges were often reluctant to challenge the status quo due to their strictly limited judicial role, or to deviate from the practice of strictly interpreting the Constitution. Notably, the cases cited confirm that the *Constitution Act* of 1867 did not function to protect fundamental freedoms from any level of government (Greene, 2014; Sharpe & Roach, 2017).

Rights for Whom?

Canada has had a checkered history on the rights front. This can be seen, for instance, through problematic federal government policies that discriminated against the people of Chinese descent (*Chinese Immigration Act* of 1885 and the *Chinese Immigration Act* of 1923[20]); the Japanese Canadians during the Second World War, under the *War Measures Act*; and the Indigenous Peoples, using the *Indian Act* (Black-Branch, 1997). Not all Canadians had equal rights after Confederation, and discrimination was an unaddressed part of Canadian life. Adams (2009) eloquently addressed this idea when he wrote:

> Canada's common law constitution may have been suffused with rights, but they were rights of a particular sort, and certainly not rights for all…[with the courts] routinely denying equal treatment to women, workers, Aboriginal peoples, and racialized minorities. (p. 12)

The three cases discussed below illustrate these issues at the municipal level.

In the case of *Christie v The York Corporation*,[21] a tavern in Montreal refused to serve a Black man. The court found that the business was able to discriminate based on the principle of freedom of commerce; in other words, this meant that merchants were free to deal as they may choose with any individual member of the public. In this case, the court found that no other written law applied to trump the principle of freedom of commerce. Furthermore, Section 33 of the *Quebec Licenses Act* (relied upon by the lower courts), which prohibited a restaurant from refusing food to travellers, did not apply either because the appellant was not a traveller who was asking for food. The court held that the respondent owner of the tavern was "strictly within its rights" when refusing to serve the appellant based on the colour of his skin. The prevailing attitude was that such instances of discrimination were considered a matter of private business in which the state should not intervene (Patrias & Frager, 2001). Furthermore, any anti-discrimination legislation was also considered an unwarranted restriction of the rights of merchants to operate their business.

In Edmonton, Alberta, a city ordinance prohibited Black people from using a public swimming pool at the same time as white people were using it. In 1924 the city's Black community challenged the issue before the Edmonton city council, seeking bathing privileges (Mathieu, 2010; Zbed, 2014). The council sided with the Black petitioners and rescinded the order on the grounds that all taxpayers should have access to publicly funded pools. However, a strong push-back from white citizens followed, pressing the council to reverse its decision. Although the issue of mixed bathing was never resolved, the Black community eventually decided not to press the matter further (Mathieu, 2010; Zbed, 2014). This incident illustrates the general public sentiment at the time but concomitantly shows a rare expression of a local council's progressive view on the matter.

As mentioned, women had limited rights. They were excluded from any form of political participation, and their legal position was considered inferior to that of men (Clément, 2008). The case of *Ellis v Renfrew (Town)*[22] challenged the ability of a woman to vote on a municipal bylaw even though she was included on the list of eligible voters. The court held that, despite being the owner of the property and despite being named in the voter's list, as a woman she could not be an eligible voter, just like "an infant, an alien, or other disqualified person."[23]

Summary

This segment of the chapter has narrated how deeply entrenched discrimination and racism were in the society from the latter part of the nineteenth century until the Second World War. Citizens' rights as we currently think of them were the exception rather than the rule, especially given the lack of human rights policy or legislation. The section demonstrates that historically courts resorted to the use of federalism to determine whether the issues emanating at the local level fell within the appropriate jurisdiction, as opposed to addressing the root cause of the issues. In the decades following the formation of Confederation, opportunities to legally challenge rights violations were limited. Even when challenges were brought forward, the outcomes were mixed. Some progress was made, but this pace of progress picked up in the decades following the Second World War, which the next part of this chapter covers.

Post–Second World War to 1982
To understand the progress of human rights in Canada, one must look to the influential post–Second World War period. The ratification of the *Universal Declaration of Human Rights* (UDHR) is especially significant, followed by the passing of provincial and federal human rights legislation during the 1960s and 1970s (Black-Branch, 1997; Clément, 2016; Patrias & Frager, 2001). In the absence of such legislation, the 1940s and 1950s continued to witness challenges to discriminatory practices at the local level, including racially motivated restrictive covenants, prohibitions on distributing printed material in the streets, and denial of housing based on an individual's personal views or political association.

The 1940s and 1950s
The following cases illustrate legal challenges of local bylaws where the courts continued to employ parliamentary supremacy and federalism in their decision-making through the 1950s.

In the well-cited *Saumur v Quebec (City)*[24] case, the appellant was arrested for flouting a Quebec City municipal bylaw that prohibited the distribution of literature in the street. The appellant challenged the bylaw on the grounds that it was outside municipal jurisdiction and that it amounted to religious and political censorship. The courts determined that the municipal bylaw was beyond the power of the province and hence the municipality of Quebec City. Writing for the majority, Justice Kellock stated: "The bylaw is *ultra vires* as it is not enacted in relation to streets but impinges upon freedom of religion and of the press which are not the subject of legislative jurisdiction under s. 92 of the BNA Act [Constitution Act, 1867]."[25] Federalism and the division of powers in the Constitution determined the outcome of this case.

Another example is the *Switzman v Elbling & Quebec (AG)* case,[26] in which Quebec's *Act to Protect the Province Against Communistic Propaganda*

("The Padlock Law")²⁷ was challenged. The Padlock Law was enacted in 1937 in Quebec with the aim of preventing the dissemination of communist propaganda. It allowed local authorities to close any buildings suspected of being used for any communist activity (Fournier, 2004). The case involved Elbling, who refused to rent her apartment to Switzman, given that he was associated with communism. Switzman challenged this decision. The Supreme Court of Canada (SCC) held that the law was unconstitutional and *ultra vires* under the *Constitution Act, 1867*. The Chief Justice presiding over the case wrote on behalf of the majority:

> In my view it is sufficient to declare that the Act is legislation in relation to the criminal law, over which, by virtue of head 27 of s. 91 of the *British North America Act [Constitution Act, 1867]*, the Parliament of Canada has exclusive legislative authority.[28]

The two cases discussed below relate to racially motivated restrictive covenants, which was a standard tool used at the time to keep minorities and people of colour out of certain parts of cities. A racial restrictive covenant is an agreement among the owners of adjoining properties, where they can legally bind themselves and their successors to the promise of not renting or selling their properties to members of certain races (Walker, 1997). Such covenants were legal and considered a matter of private property rights. They were commonly used as a way to promote racial and religious discrimination (Ziff & Jiang, 2012). For instance, the municipal government of Calgary, Alberta, since the 1920s was engaged in institutionalized segregation through restrictive covenants to keep people of colour from purchasing homes in certain parts of the city (Mathieu, 2010).

A prominent case that invokes a race-related covenant is that of *Drummond Wren (Re)*[29] in which the Ontario High Court found a racially restrictive covenant invalid because it prevented the sale of land to "Jews or persons of objectionable nationality."[30] The court held that "such a covenant is contrary to public policy, in that it tends to create or deepen divisions between religious and ethnic groups, and is in conflict with prevailing public opinion, as exemplified in *The Racial Discrimination Act, 1944*,[31] and other statutes and public documents."[32]

In the second important case, *Noble et al. v Alley*,[33] the SCC held that a restrictive covenant at a summer resort in Ontario was invalid for a different reason. The restrictive covenant in question bound the property owners in a summer resort to not sell, lease to, or let the property be occupied by persons of Jewish heritage or persons of colour. The property owner, Noble, had arranged to sell her cottage to Wolf, who was Jewish. Property owners in the vicinity invoked the covenant to invalidate the sale. The court held that the covenant was invalid due to the uncertainty in the language within it, which made it impossible to set limits on the race or blood of the purchaser of the land.[34] In 1950, while the aforementioned *Noble* case was still going through the court system, Ontario passed the *Conveyancing and Law of Property Amendment Act*,[35] which declared racially motivated restrictive covenants null and void. However, the Act only applied to covenants created on or after the Act received royal assent.

Universal Declaration of Human Rights

With the adoption of the United Nations' UDHR in 1948, the momentum towards codifying rights protection was gaining ground (Clément, 2016). The UDHR introduced a new language of rights. Prior to this, rights conversations in Canada had focused mostly on civil and political rights tied to citizenship. The UDHR brought forward a new language of "human rights," which meant universal rights for all, regardless of an individual's race, sex, language, religion, or other status (Tunnicliffe, 2019). When Canada signed on to the UDHR in 1948, this foreshadowed future policy changes and rights protection in the country. Regardless of the strength of the influence on domestic policy at the time, the UDHR was instrumental in setting the tone globally for human rights dialogue, especially in existing and emerging liberal democracies at the time.

Canada's First Provincial Bill of Rights

Independent of the UDHR, in 1947 the Province of Saskatchewan passed the first provincial bill of rights[36] in Canada that provided protection for free speech, religion, and employment based on race, ethnicity, or religion. In 1950 the Act was put to use in the case of *R v Naish*.[37] Contrary to a municipal bylaw, which prohibited the distribution of religious content, the appellant was charged for distributing handbills with content related to Jehovah's Witnesses. Judge Wakeling, presiding over the case, dismissed the charges and noted the following: "Religion is a material issue in this case and that sec. 2 of bylaw 2954, being inconsistent with sec. 3 of *The Saskatchewan Bill of Rights Act, 1947*, is superseded by the latter in so far as religious handbills are concerned."[38]

Patrias (2006) has suggested that, despite the human rights success in *Naish*, the legislation largely turned out to be weak in terms of its enforcement, public acknowledgment, and legal impact. She attributes its shortcomings to the prevailing anti-minority, cold war, and anti-communist sentiments, which made it difficult for the government to enforce it. Furthermore, the crafting and adoption of the bill was a state-initiated exercise rather than the product of widespread social movement; therefore, it lacked broader acceptance in society. She suggests that the actual strength of the bill was never tested fully in the court. Significantly, the Saskatchewan bill was too progressive for its time and did not have broad public support. Even though the bill could not make much impact legally, it was an important landmark in Canadian history and inspired future human rights legislation in Canada (Clément, 2016; Patrias, 2006).

Human Rights and the Federal Bill of Rights

The ratification of the UDHR and the enactment of the *Saskatchewan Bill of Rights* eventually inspired the federal government to adopt the *Canadian Bill of Rights*[39] in 1960 (Clément, Silver, & Trottier, 2012). Unfortunately, the *Bill of Rights* stood on weak grounds given that it was a statute that could at any time be amended by Parliament. Additionally, the bill's primacy could have been easily weakened by other acts of Parliament (Black-Branch, 1997). It was also ineffective in practice, as only five of a total 35 claims were successful in court (Morton, 1987). Nevertheless, the bill was an essential step in bringing awareness to the issue of human rights (Lui, 2012).

In another case, appellants unsuccessfully tried to protect their religious freedom by invoking the *Bill of Rights*. They were convicted of operating their business of a bowling alley on a Sunday in contravention of the *Lord's Day Act*.[40] In upholding the sanctity of the Christian religion, the Act prohibited businesses from being open on Sundays. The appellants argued that the *Lord's Day Act*[41] contravened their freedom of religion, as guaranteed under Section 4 of the *Bill of Rights*. The majority at the SCC held that there was nothing in the Act that directly "affected the liberty of religious thought and practice of any citizen of [the] country."[42] Specifically, requiring the appellants to observe a day of rest was simply a business inconvenience and not akin to an infringement of religious freedom. Refraining from carrying out business produced a "purely secular and financial" result, not an infringement on religious freedom.[43] The court emphasized that legislation for the preservation of Sunday was long established in Canada and had never historically been considered an interference to freedom of religion.

The 1960 and 1970s

The political and social changes of the 1960s and 1970s, in Canada and abroad, began to drive changes within Canadian society. Rights discussions that had focused on the protection of civil liberties—such as free speech, association, religion, press, assembly, and due process—were now evolving to include equality and protection against discrimination based on race, skin colour, sexual orientation, and more (Clément, 2016). Despite this progress, human rights violations continued to occur in Canadian cities, such as the forced relocation of Africville in Halifax, Nova Scotia, from 1964 to 1967, and the passing of *Bylaw 3926* in Montreal in 1969, which limited the right to protest or assembly.

Africville

In the Africville case the changing language of human rights and urban renewal was used to justify the forced relocation of a minority community. In the 1960s the municipality of Halifax relocated residents of the all-Black community of Africville. City reports determined that the land should be expropriated for industrial development (but it was never developed) and for the alleged benefit of relocating the residents to clear the "slum." (Mackenzie, 1991; Nelson, 2000). Despite community residents' paying taxes, the city had neglected the area, for instance by not providing any services like paved roads, sewage, and running water (Nelson, 2008). Eventually, the Africville residents were given no choice and were forced out with little compensation.

In *Leblanc v City of Halifax*,[44] a property owner in Africville appealed the amount of compensation awarded from the city for the expropriation of her property. Judge Advocate Coffin at the Nova Scotia Court of Appeal acknowledged the fact that the appellant was being forcibly ejected from her property, which would require her to incur expenses and the inconvenience of moving elsewhere. Coffin allowed the appellant increased compensation due to a miscalculation of the property value at trial. Despite this, with respect to human rights, the court found that the claim that Africville properties involved matters of "sociological concern" or a special value to the owner "were not a guide for the determination of compensation in the instant case."[45]

Montreal's Bylaw 3926

In Montreal in the late 1960s, numerous demonstrations occurred for multiple reasons: student activism, support for Quebec's independence, and protests against the Vietnam War (Greene, 1989). In 1969 the City of Montreal passed a bylaw that banned all public demonstrations for a 30-day period, essentially outlawing the freedom of assembly (Clément, 2016). The validity of the bylaw was challenged in court; however, it was held *intra vires* and upheld (Greene, 1989).[46] Two reasons account for this: the right to hold public meetings on a highway or in a park was not part of the BNA Act; and the *Canadian Bill of Rights*, which allowed freedom of assembly, did not apply to provincial and municipal legislation.

Provincial and Federal Human Rights Legislation

Human rights codes enacted at the provincial level initially protected against discrimination based on race and religion. As time went on, additional protected grounds were added, such as gender, age, disability, and sexual orientation. The federal government enacted its own *Human Rights Act* in 1977,[47] which was differentiated from the *Bill of Rights* of 1960 by conferring the right of equality or non-discrimination on federally regulated activities. It did this by enlisting the prohibited grounds of discriminaton,[48] as opposed to just extending rights and freedoms (such as religion, speech, or assembly) in the bill.

By the mid-1970s more provinces had enacted provincial human rights legislation. Notable among them were Alberta, British Columbia, and Quebec. For example, in 1974 the Province of British Columbia passed the *Human Rights Code*, which was lauded as one of the most progressive human rights laws in the world at the time (Clément, 2013). The code was unique in that it incorporated a "reasonable cause" section, which went beyond the specific grounds typically enshrined in human rights legislation. For instance, women were able to use the reasonable-cause section to set precedents in areas such as pregnancy and sexual harassment.

In 1971, Alberta passed its own bill of rights[49] and subsequently repealed the *Communal Property Act*, which had existed since 1947. The *Communal Property Act* targeted the province's Hutterites, a group that believes in communal living and pacifism. It required new Hutterite colonies to be a minimum of 40 miles from other colonies and required permission from the province to purchase new land. The act was unsuccessfully challenged as unconstitutional in *Walter v AG for Alberta*,[50] but was repealed soon after the *Alberta Bill of Rights* was passed; the Alberta government felt it to be inconsistent with the *Alberta Bill of Rights* (Spencer, 1973).

After its quiet revolution[51] and to redeem itself from actions taken during the October Crisis,[52] Quebec passed its *Charter of Human Rights and Freedoms*[53] in 1975 (Greene, 1989). Quebec made this legislation paramount above all other laws, and it set a new standard of discrimination protection (Clément, 2016). It offered access to justice by allowing two options for complainants: a complaint could be filed in court or with the

Human Rights Commission (Eliadis, 2014). In 1976, New Brunswick's *Human Rights Code* was the first statute in Canada to add "disability" as grounds for discrimination (Jacobs, 2018). These examples demonstrate that within this short amount of time Canada "had established the most sophisticated human rights legal regime in the world" (Clément, 2016, p. 105). As a result, Canadians had an avenue to bring forth complaints at a local level related to housing, transportation, and other issues.

Affecting Human Rights at the Municipal Level

Although not linked with rights directly, *R v Bell* (1979)[54] was a landmark case that spawned challenges to bylaws for their unreasonableness or discriminatory nature (Agrawal, 2013; Leisk, 2011). The case challenged the Borough of North York's bylaw in which dwelling units were defined for use by individuals (no more than two) or families (more than two people bound by blood, marriage, or adoption). The appellant was a tenant in a detached duplex unit and lived with two other persons unrelated to him. He was charged with violating the bylaw.

The SCC held that "adopting 'family' as defined as the only permitted use of a self-contained dwelling unit is oppressive and unreasonable."[55] Therefore, the bylaw was found to be *ultra vires* of the municipality under the provisions of Ontario's *Planning Act*.[56] The court determined that municipalities had the right to control the use of properties but not who used them. This decision had profound implications on municipal planning, leading to changes to provincial planning acts as well as municipal bylaws across the country. Subsequent to *Bell*, however, case law does not take such a strong position (Agrawal, 2013). Zoning definitions that refer to users or personal attributes have been upheld subsequently by the courts. One such example is *Smith et al. v Township of Tiny*,[57] which was decided after *Bell*. The judge in the *Smith* case disagreed with the *Bell* decision and argued:

> There is a distinction, of course, between the relationship of people using premises and whether they are using it as their main place of residence. But I do not think it is a distinction in principle. The restriction here may equally be prompted by consideration of schooling, sewer

and water or other requirements, all of which are the direct concern of the municipality. It is for the municipality to determine the use that will be made of the property. It seems to me also that it is for the municipality to consider how much use should be made of it.

Soon after came the *Faminow v North Vancouver (District)* case,[58] which closely followed reasonings in the *Smith* case.

Given that the *Bell* decision came from the SCC (whereas the decisions in *Smith* and *Faminow* came from lower courts—the Ontario Supreme Court and British Columbia Court of Appeal, respectively), it technically remains the leading case in the area of people zoning in municipal law.

Summary

Part 2 has examined the period from 1946 until 1982, providing a snapshot of urban issues such as restrictions on freedoms of expression, religion, assembly, and political association, and restrictive covenants typical in the 1940s and 1950s. The court practice of drawing on federalism continued at least into the 1950s. This section also describes legislative changes in the post–Second World War era until 1982, especially in the 1960s and 1970s, when the human rights movement gained momentum internationally and on the domestic front. Several subsections expound on some key legal cases in the 1940s and 1950s that dealt with restrictive covenants and issues of freedom of religion or political association. The 1960s and 1970s reflect the influence of the UDHR, provincial human rights legislation, and the federal *Canadian Bill of Rights*[59] and *Canadian Human Rights Act*[60] on municipal matters.

Conclusion

This chapter presents a broad inquiry into the changes that occurred on the rights front between 1867 and 1982, and the implications these changes have had on cities and planning at the local level. Discrimination was embedded in Canadian society, with racism, sexism, ableism, and xenophobic views often seen as the norm. These discriminatory ideas were reflected in government legislation and policies, as well as in court decisions (see chronology of government legislation below). Limited rights inscribed in the *Constitution Act* of 1867, narrow interpretations of the Constitution by the judiciary, and, of course, overtly discriminatory laws were key reasons for the prevailing situation.

At the municipal level, discrimination manifested mainly in the form of (a) race-based restrictive covenants; (b) limited or no rights for women or minorities in municipal matters; (c) infringements on freedoms of speech, religion, assembly, or political association; and (d) the imposition of additional municipal taxes and restrictive use of public facilities on people of colour. Some of these issues were challenged in court but with mixed results and little or no changes in federal or provincial legislation or practice on the ground.

From 1867 until the 1950s, judicial review of municipal bylaws was primarily based on the founding principles of the Canadian Confederation: namely, the supremacy of Parliament and federalism. These were weak arguments, however, when it came to defending the civil or human rights of all people, especially those rights relating to local issues such as housing, use of municipal facilities, municipal taxes, and freedom of religion. Court decisions strictly followed principles of federalism as set out in the Constitution, and municipalities played virtually no role in political or legislative affairs for approximately a century following Confederation. The judiciary saw its role as an arbiter of the division of powers when an issue arose. Generally, the courts were limited to deciding "whether the 'correct' level of government had acted," in accordance with the categories of legislative powers set out in Sections 91 and 92 of the *BNA Act*, and "not whether any level of government could act" (Monahan, Shaw, & Ryan, 2017, p. 15). Eventually provincial legislation and statutes outlawed most discriminatory practices. Thereafter, the emergence of the *Charter* was largely responsible for eliminating many long-standing discriminatory practices.[61]

The early federal and provincial rights statutes in the 1960s and 1970s, though not that strong, helped to guide future legislation. These legislative changes mirrored changing societal attitudes and helped pave the way to strong rights protection at all levels. The adoption of the *Charter* and repatriation of the Constitution in 1982, together with the enactment of the quasi-constitutional forms at the federal, provincial, and territorial levels, helped consolidate human rights for all Canadians.

The 1982 amendment to the Constitution shifted the supremacy of Parliament to the *Charter* (Richard, 2005), so that Parliament is no longer supreme in its law-making authority. Legislation had to abide by the *Charter* and the Constitution and can now be challenged in the courts. The judiciary can evaluate government legislation against the *Charter*, while interpreting the *Charter* and the repatriated Constitution in possibly new ways (Black-Branch, 1997). However, critics allege that the *Charter* grants too much power and discretion to the judiciary (Sharpe & Roach, 2017; Smithey, 2001).

This is not to say that Canada has now reached a perfect state. Legal challenges to human rights violations are on the rise. Issues surrounding lack of affordable housing, universal accessibility, Indigenous and other minority rights, and freedom of religion still confound municipalities (Agrawal, 2020). In addition, new issues, such as locations of safe injection sites, methadone clinics, and cannabis dispensaries, have also come to the fore (Agrawal, 2018). Having legal and legislative human rights protections is only one piece of a larger puzzle; the rest remains with changing the deeply held institutionalized and systemic biases in Canadian society. We have come a long way in terms of human rights, but there is still a long way to go.

Canada: Chronology of Legislation Cited (1867–1982)

Date	Legislation	Jurisdiction	Description
1867	British North American Act	National	The Canadian Constitution, repatriated in 1982
1885	Chinese Immigration Act (Head Tax)	Federal	Required a high fee by Chinese immmgrants entering Canada
1914	War Measures Act (Emergencies Act since 1988)	Federal	Suspension of civil liberties. Came into force three times: First and Second World Wars and October 1970
1916–40	Amendments to provincial Elections Acts in different years	Provincial	Women received right to vote in provincial elections
1918	An Act to Confer the Electoral Franchise upon Women	Federal	Women received right to vote in federal elections
1923	Chinese Immigration Act of 1923 (Chinese Exclusion Act)	Federal	Banned most immigrants from China
1944	Racial Discrimination Act	Ontario	Prohibited the display of discriminatory signs and advertisements
1945	Social Assistance Act	British Columbia	Prohibited discrimination in social assistance programs
1947	Bill of Rights	Saskatchewan	The first ever Bill of Rights in Canada
1948	United Nations' Universal Declaration of Human Rights	International	Sets out, for the first time, fundamental human rights to be universally protected
1950	Conveyancing and Law of Property Amendment Act	Ontario	Prohibited future racial restrictive covenants
1960	Canadian Bill of Rights	Federal	The first federal law to protect human rights and fundamental freedoms
1960	Canada Elections Act	Federal	Parts of the Act were repealed in order to extend voting rights to Indigenous Peoples, with status
1962	Human Rights Code	Ontario	Prohibited discrimination on multiple enumerated grounds
1972	Bill of Rights	Alberta	Prohibited discrimination on multiple enumerated grounds
1973	Human Rights Act	New Brunswick	In 1976, New Brunswick amended its original Act to include disability
1974	Human Rights Code	British Columbia	The Code included "reasonable cause" and therefore was not limited to specific grounds
1975	Quebec Charter of Human Rights and Freedoms	Quebec	Holds precedence over all other provincial legislation
1977	Human Rights Act	Federal	Federal statute that prohibited discrimination in all government institutions
1982	Charter of Rights and Freedoms	National	Supreme law of Canada. Protects basic rights and freedoms of all Canadians

NOTES

1. *Universal Declaration of Human Rights*, GA Res 217A (III), UNGAOR, 3rd Sess, Supp No 13, UN Doc A/810 (1948) 71 [UDHR].
2. "Civil rights" are legal rights granted by virtue of having citizenship in a particular nation or state. "Human rights" arise simply by being a human being. Considerable overlap exists between the two types of rights. The chapter uses these rights interchangeably.
3. *Indian Act*, RSC 1985, c 1–5.
4. Section 141 of the *Indian Act* of 1927.
5. *British North America Act*, 1867, ss 1867, c 3.
6. *Constitution Act*, 1867 (UK), 30 & 31 Vict, c 3, reprinted in RSC 1985, Appendix II, No 5.
7. This requires a person to appear before a judge after arrest to prevent unlawful detention.
8. *Constitution Act*, 1867 (UK), 30 & 31 Vict, c 3, reprinted in RSC 1985, Appendix II, No 5 ss 91 & 92.
9. *Sing v Maguire*, 1 BCR (Pt 1) 101, [1878] BCJ No 2 [*Sing*].
10. *R v Chong*, 1 BCR (Pt 2) 150, 1885 Carswell BC 2 [*Chong* cited to BCR].
11. *R v Mee Wah*, 3 BCR 403, 1886 Carswell BC 15 [*Wah*].
12. *R v Chong*, 1 BCR (Pt 2) 150, 1885 Carswell BC 2, at para 23.
13. *Constitution Act*, 1867 (UK), 30 & 31 Vict, c 3, reprinted in RSC 1985, Appendix II, No 5 ss 91 & 92.
14. *R v Victoria (City)*, 1 BCR (Pt 2) 331, 1888 CarswellBC 5 [*Victoria* cited to BCR].
15. *Ibid.*, at para 1.
16. *Ibid.*
17. *Ibid.*, at para 5.
18. *Chinese Immigration Act*, 1885, SC 1885, c 71 [Head Tax].
19. *An act to regulate the Chinese population of B.C.* 1884.
20. *Chinese Immigration Act*, 1885, SC 1885, c 71 [Head Tax]; *Chinese Immigration Act*, 1923, SC 1923, c 38 [Chinese Exclusion Act].
21. *Christie v The York Corporation*, [1940] SCR 139, [1940] DLR 81 [*Christie*].
22. *Ellis v Renfrew (Town)*, 18 OWR 703, 1911 CarswellOnt 163 [*Ellis* cited to CarswellOnt].
23. *Ellis v Renfrew (Town)*, at para 20.
24. *Saumur v Quebec (City)*, 2 SCR 299, [1953] 4 DLR 641 [*Saumur* cited to DLR].
25. *Ibid.*, at 681.
26. *Switzman v Elbling*, [1957] SCR 285, 7 DLR (2d) 337 [*Switzman* cited to DLR].
27. *Act to Protect the Province Against Communistic Propaganda*, RSQ 1941, c 52.
28. *Switzman v Elbling*, [1957] SCR 285, 7 DLR (2d) 337, at 341.
29. *Re Drummond Wren*, 4 DLR 674, [1945] OR 778 [*Wren* cited to DLR].
30. *Ibid.*, at 674.

31. *The Racial Discrimination Act* of 1944 was an act passed in Ontario that prohibited any publications or signs that expressed racial or religious discrimination.
32. *Ibid.*, at 678.
33. *Noble et al. v Alley*, [1951] SCR 64, [1951] 1 DLR 321 [*Noble* cited to DLR].
34. *Ibid.*
35. *Conveyancing and Law of Property Amendment Act*, RSO 1950, s 22.
36. *Saskatchewan Bill of Rights Act, 1947*, SS 1947, c 35.
37. *R v Naish*, [1950] 1 WWR 987, 1950 CarswellSask 28 [*Naish* cited to Carswell].
38. *Ibid.*, at para 26.
39. *Canadian Bill of Rights*, SC 1960, c 44, s 1(a) [Bill of Rights].
40. *Lord's Day Act*, RSC 1952, c 171.
41. The *Lord's Day Act* was struck down as unconstitutional in 1985. This was a mere three years following the enactment of the *Charter*.
42. *Robertson and Rosetanni v R*, [1963] 41 DLR (2d) 485, SCR 651 at 652.
43. *Ibid.*
44. *Leblanc v City of Halifax*, 4 LCR 134, 39 DLR (3d) 672 (NSCA) [*Leblanc* cited to DLR].
45. *Ibid.*, at para 68.
46. Greene (1989) cited *Canada (Attorney General) v Dupond*, [1978] 2 SCR 770, 84 DLR (3d) 420 on this point.
47. *Canadian Human Rights Act*, RSC 1985, c H-6.
48. Section 3(1) states the following: "For all purposes of this Act, the prohibited grounds of discrimination are race, national or ethnic origin, colour, religion, age, sex, sexual orientation, gender identity or expression, marital status, family status, genetic characteristics, disability and conviction for an offence for which a pardon has been granted or in respect of which a record suspension has been ordered."
49. *Alberta Bill of Rights*, SA 1972, c 1.
50. *Walter v Alberta (Attorney General)*, [1969] SCR 383, 3 DLR (3d) 1.
51. The Quiet Revolution was a period of intense socio-political and socio-cultural change in the 1960s in the province of Quebec, characterized by the secularization of the provincial government, the creation of a state-run welfare state, and realignment of politics from ultra-conservative to liberal.
52. The October Crisis occurred in Quebec in October 1970 when a Quebec nationalist group, in an effort to gain Quebec sovereignty, kidnapped a high-profile politician and a British diplomat; this led the then prime minister (Pierre Elliott Trudeau) to invoke the *War Measures Act* to give police sweeping powers of arrest and detention.
53. *Charter of Human Rights and Freedoms*, RSQ c C-12.
54. *R v Bell*, 2 SCR 212, 98 DLR (3d) 255 [*Bell* cited to SCR].
55. *Ibid.*, at 213.
56. *Planning Act*, RSO 1990, c P.13.
57. *Smith v Tiny (Township)*, 107 DLR (3d) 483, 1980 CarswellOnt 489.

58. *Faminow v North Vancouver (District)*, 61 DLR (4th) 747, 24 BCLR (2d) 49.
59. *Canadian Bill of Rights*, SC 1960, c 44, reprinted in RSC 1985, Appendix III [*Bill of Rights*].
60. *Canadian Human Rights* Act, RSC 1985, c H-6 [*CHRA*].
61. *Canadian Charter of Rights and Freedom*s, Part I of the *Constitution Act, 1982*, being Schedule B to the *Canada Act 1982* (UK), 1982, c 11, s 91(24) [*Charter*].

REFERENCES

Adams, E.M. (2009). *The idea of constitutional rights and the transformation of Canadian constitutional law, 1930–1960* (Doctoral dissertation). University of Toronto. https://tspace.library.utoronto.ca/handle/1807/19019

Agrawal, S. (2013, February). *Opinion on the provisions of group homes in the city-wide zoning bylaw of the City of Toronto*. City of Toronto. https://www.toronto.ca/legdocs/mmis/2013/pg/bgrd/backgroundfile-56473.pdf

Agrawal, S. (2014). Balancing municipal planning with human rights: A case study. *Canadian Journal of Urban Research, 23*(1), 1–20.

Agrawal, S. (2018). *Human rights and Alberta municipalities*. Report submitted to the Alberta Human Rights Commission. https://cms.eas.ualberta.ca/UrbanEnvOb/wp-content/uploads/sites/21/2018/05/Report-to-AHRC_Agrawal-1.pdf

Agrawal, S. (2020). Human rights and the city: A view from Canada. *Journal of the American Planning Association, 87*(1), 3–10. doi:10.1080/01944363.2020.1775680

Black-Branch, J.L. (1997). *Rights and realities*. Routledge.

Black-Branch, J.L. (2018). *Rights and realities: The judicial impact of the Canadian Charter of Rights and Freedoms on education, case law, and political jurisprudence* (2nd ed.). Routledge Revivals.

Clément, D. (2008). "I believe in human rights, not women's rights": Women and the human rights state, 1969–1984. *Radical History Review, 101*(Spring), 107–129.

Clément, D. (2016). *Human rights in Canada: A history*. Wilfrid Laurier University Press.

Clément, D. (2013). Alberta's rights revolution. *British Journal of Canadian Studies, 26*(1), 59–77. doi:10.3828/bjcs.2013.4

Clément, D., Silver, W., & Trottier, D. (2012). *The evolution of human rights in Canada*. Canadian Human Rights Commission.

Eliadis, P. (2014). *Speaking out on human rights: Debating Canada's human rights system*. McGill-Queen's University Press.

Fournier, M. (2004). *Communisme et anticommunisme au Québec (1920–1950)* [Communism and anti-communism in Quebec, 1920–1950]. J.M. Tremblay. doi:10.7202/303885ar

Greene, I. (1989). *The Charter of Rights*. J. Lorimer.

Greene, I. (2014). *The Charter of Rights and Freedoms: 30+ years of decisions that shape Canadian life*. J. Lorimer.

Hogg, P. (2009). *Constitutional law of Canada* (5th ed.). Carswell.

Jacobs, L. (2018). The universality of the human condition: Theorizing transportation inequality claims by persons with disabilities in Canada, 1976–2016. *Canadian Journal of Human Rights, 7*(1), 35–66.

Leisk, S. (2011). Zoning bylaws: Human rights and Charter considerations respecting the regulation of the use of land. In International Municipal Lawyers Association, *2011 Annual Conference, Chicago: Canadian Meeting.* https://imla.org/wp-content/uploads/2020/images/2011conf/papers9125as/Leisk-Zoning%20By-laws_%20Human%20Rights%20and%20Charter%20Considerations%20-%20Paper%20for%20IMLA%20Chicago-.pdf

Lui, A. (2012). *Why Canada cares: Human rights and foreign policy in theory and practice.* McGill-Queen's University Press.

Mackenzie, S. (1991). *Remember Africville* [Film]. National Film Board of Canada.

Mathieu, S.-J. (2010). *North of the color line: Migration and Black resistance in Canada, 1870–1955.* University of North Carolina Press.

Monahan, P., Shaw, B., & Ryan, P. (2017). *Constitutional law* (5th ed.). Irwin Law.

Morton, F.L. (1987). The political impact of the Canadian Charter of Rights and Freedoms. *Canadian Journal of Political Science, 20*(1), 31–55.

Nelson, J.J. (2000). The space of Africville: Creating, regulating, and remembering the urban "slum." *Canadian Journal of Law and Society, 15*(2), 163–185.

Nelson, J.J. (2008). *Razing Africville: A geography of racism.* University of Toronto Press.

Patrias, C. (2006). Socialists, Jews, and the 1947 Saskatchewan Bill of Right. *Canadian Historical Review, 87*(2), 265–292.

Patrias, C., & Frager, R.A. (2001). "This is our country, these are our rights": Minorities and the origins of Ontario's human rights campaign. *Canadian Historical Review, 82*(1), 1–35. doi:10.3138/CHR.82.1.1.

Richard, J.D. (2005). Federalism in Canada. *Duquesne Law Review, 44*(1), 5–34.

Sharpe, R.J., & Roach, K. (2017). *The Charter of Rights and Freedoms* (6th ed.). Irwin Law.

Smithey, S.I. (2001). Religious freedom and equality concerns under the Canadian Charter of Rights and Freedoms. *Canadian Journal of Political Science, 34*(1), 85–107.

Spencer, J. (1973). The alien landowner in Canada. *Canadian Bar Review, 51*(3), 393.

Tunnicliffe, J. (2019). *Resisting rights: Canada and the International Bill of Rights, 1947–76.* UBC Press.

Walker, J.W.St.G. (1997). *"Race," rights and the law in the Supreme Court of Canada: Historical case studies.* Osgoode Society for Canadian Legal History.

Wilson, K. (2018). Pulling together: A guide for Indigenization of post-secondary institutions. [Professional learning series—foundations guide]. BC campus. https://opentextbc.ca/indigenizationfoundations/

Zbed, C. (2014, August 28). Racism colours the opening of two new city swimming pools. *Edmonton Journal.* https://edmontonjournal.com/news/local-news/aug-28-1924-racism-colours-the-opening-of-two-new-city-swimming-pools

Ziff, B., & Jiang, K. (2012) Scorched earth: The use of restrictive covenants to stifle competition. *The Windsor Yearbook of Access to Justice*, 30(2), 79–101.

LEGISLATION

The Act Respecting Communistic Propaganda of the Province of Quebec, RSQ 1941, c 52.
An Act to Regulate the Chinese Population of B.C. 1884.
Alberta Bill of Rights, SA 1972, c 1.
British North America Act, 1867, SS 1867, c 3.
Canadian Bill of Rights, SC 1960, c 44, reprinted in RSC 1985, Appendix III.
Canadian Bill of Rights, SC 1960, c 44, s 1(a).
Canadian Charter of Rights and Freedoms, Part I of the *Constitution Act*, 1982, being Schedule B to the *Canada Act 1982* (UK), 1982, c 11, s 91(24).
Canadian Human Rights Act, RSC 1985, c H-6.
Charter of Human Rights and Freedoms, RSQ c C-12.
Chinese Immigration Act, 1885, SC 1885, c 71.
Chinese Immigration Act, 1923, SC 1923, c 38.
Constitution Act, 1867 (UK), 30 & 31 Vict, c 3, reprinted in RSC 1985, Appendix II, No 5.
Conveyancing and Law of Property Amendment Act, RSO 1950, s 22.
Indian Act, RSC 1985, c 1-5.
Lord's Day Act, RSC 1952, c 171.
Planning Act, RSO 1990, c P.13
Saskatchewan Bill of Rights Act, 1947, SS 1947, c. 35.
Statutes of Ontario, The Racial Discrimination Act, 1944, 1944, c.51.
Universal Declaration of Human Rights, GA Res 217A (III), UNGAOR, 3rd Sess, Supp No 13, UN Doc A/810 (1948) 71.

JURISPRUDENCE

Canada (Attorney General) v Dupond, [1978] 2 SCR 770, 84 DLR (3d) 420.
Christie v The York Corporation, [1940] SCR 139, [1940] DLR 81.
Ellis v Renfrew (Town), 18 OWR 703, 1911 CarswellOnt 163.
Faminow v North Vancouver (District), 61 DLR (4th) 747, 24 BCLR (2d) 49.
Leblanc v City of Halifax, 4 LCR 134, 39 DLR (3d) 672 (NSCA).
Noble et al. v Alley, [1951] SCR 64, [1951] 1 DLR 321.
Re Drummond Wren, 4 DLR 674, [1945] OR 778.
Robertson and Rosetanni v R, [1963] 41 DLR (2d) 485, SCR 651.
R v Bell, 2 SCR 212, 98 DLR (3d) 255.
R v Chong, 1 BCR (Pt 2) 150, 1885 Carswell BC 2.
R v Mah, 3 BCR 403, 1886 Carswell BC 15.
R v Naish, [1950] 1 WWR 987, 1950 CarswellSask 28.
R v Victoria (City), 1 BCR (Pt 2) 331, 1888 CarswellBC 5.

Saumur v Quebec (City), 2 SCR 299, [1953] 4 DLR 641.
Sing v Maguire, 1 BCR (Pt 1) 101, [1878] BCJ No 2.
Smith v Tiny (Township), 107 DLR (3d) 483, 1980 CarswellOnt 489.
Switzman v Elbling, [1957] SCR 285, 7 DLR (2d) 337.
Walter v Alberta (Attorney General), [1969] SCR 383, 3 DLR (3d) 1.

4
GROUP RIGHTS AND COLLECTIVE RIGHTS
What Are They and How Do They Affect Urban Issues?

SANDEEP AGRAWAL & ERAN S. KAPLINSKY
—

Introduction

Liberal ideology, espoused by Locke, Kant, Mills, Rawls, and others, considers an individual human being as the claimant of human rights. As a moral unit, the individual has been the building block of the United Nations' *Universal Declaration of Human Rights*[1] and the rights embedded in the constitutions of many liberal democracies around the world, such as Canada and the United States.

In the last few decades, and under the guise of "equality for all," the assimilationist tendencies of liberal states, with some exceptions like Canada, have resulted in an increase in state-sponsored, coercive integration of minority groups in the larger society (Kymlicka, 1995). The principle of majority rule followed in these states supports the hegemony of the majority culture, leading to dissensions with minorities (Freeman, 1995). All this has brought into question the idea of individual-based rights; as a result, the ideas of group and collective rights have proliferated (Jones, 1999; Kymlicka, 1995; Miller, 2002). The term *group or collective right* denotes that a right belongs to a group rather than to an individual human being. This, however, does not preclude a member of the group from simultaneously holding individual rights (such as rights to due process, fair trial, and voting).

Several scholars, such as Kymlicka (1995), Freeman (1995), and Green (1991), argue that group and collective rights are human rights, while other scholars disagree, such as Miller (2002) and Ramcharan (1993). Others either conflate group and collective rights or discuss them interchangeably (Jones, 1999; Kymlicka, 1995; Miller, 2002). Without wading into this debate, this chapter follows Kymlicka's rights framework based on culture and identity. This framework has been largely embraced by Canadian courts (Dick, 2009), as well as by many liberal scholars (Appiah, 1994; Taylor, 1994; and others) with a few exceptions, such as Levrau (2019) and Heim (2016).

For ease of understanding and to expound clearly on the difference between group rights and collective rights, the chapter treats them as two separate categories of rights:

- A *group right* emerges when the members of a group are discriminated against. If the right of the group is protected *only while the discrimination continues*, then it is termed a group right—which is less powerful than collective rights as it only requires exemptions or accommodations within existing laws and institutions.
- *Collective rights* are stronger than group rights and are permanent because they *continue beyond the end of discrimination* against the group (or "collectivity," as explained later).

A group can hold either of these two rights, but the long-term goals and interests of the group may determine the right for which they may be eligible within a political context.

This chapter seeks to explore the role that these forms of human rights play at the city level, thus affecting urban issues. Some literature exists on the way in which individual human rights affect municipal matters (Agrawal, 2014, 2017, 2020); however, no literature delves into urban issues from the lens of a group right or a collective right, and these issues are on the rise in Canadian cities (Agrawal, 2020). Focusing on Canadian cities, the chapter relies on existing legal and political discourses and a select set of case law. This material is augmented by interviews with three key human rights lawyers in Quebec.[2]

We begin by delving further into the meaning of group and collective rights and then identify the specific sections of the Canadian *Charter* and *Constitution Act, 1982* (henceforth Constitution) where these rights are codified. We then review multiple case examples to link urban issues—such as restrictions on group homes, religious practice, and commercial signs; advertising on public properties; and a dispute with an adjoining First Nations community—and the relevant sections of the *Charter* and the Constitution, illustrating their impacts at the municipal level. The chapter concludes that the courts have upheld the two forms of rights on numerous occasions in urban matters.

French-Canadian Quebecois, as a minority in Canada but a majority in Quebec, have benefited the most from the collective right conferred to them constitutionally. They have been struggling, however, to handle the demands (group or collective rights) of the Indigenous, ethnic, and religious minorities living among them, as demonstrated in multiple lawsuits particularly in the post-*Charter* era. The tension between individual and group rights and the collective rights of French-Canadian Quebecois has given rise to some discord in Quebec.

The collective right of Indigenous Peoples to self-determination is constitutionally affirmed, and the courts have upheld it multiple times. Ongoing negotiations are being litigated, in addition to the title claims that are underway. One such a case is *Tsilhqot'in Nation v British Columbia* (2014),[3] in which the Supreme Court of Canada (SCC) decided that provinces could not unilaterally claim a right to engage the use of land protected by Aboriginal title; they must engage in meaningful consultation with the title holder before they proceed. How self-determination may look is still being negotiated between various Indigenous groups and the federal government, with only a few cases resolved to date, such as the Nunavut and Tlicho land claims and self-government agreements. The role of municipalities, however, remains unclear in tackling the Crown's duty, constitutionally obligated, to consult with Indigenous Peoples when the Crown's actions may adversely affect Aboriginal or treaty rights.

Meaning of Group Rights and Collective Rights
Group rights and collective rights are grounded in the interest of those who jointly hold the rights (Jones, 1999). Groups can be formed based on certain factors that distinguish a true group from just a category of people (Miller, 2002). For example, a group may be separated based on members' physical features (ability, race) or shared beliefs (religion). According to Lerner (1992), groups can also emerge through complex combinations, such as their self-perception as a group or their perception as such by the surrounding community. Group designation often occurs because a group requires rights protection; it can be experiencing or have experienced oppression or discrimination or have been adversely affected by state action, inaction, or decision (Miller, 2002, p. 179).

Miller (2002) and Jones (1999) argue two conditions for the emergence of group rights or collective rights. First, the right enjoyed by a member should be extended to the other members of the group. Aligned with this, the members collectively value the continued existence of their group, so that granting them a group right will help preserve the group. Second, the joint interest provides sufficient justification for imposing duties on others, which rise above the interest of a single individual within the group. However, Kymlicka (1995) follows Glazer's (1978) and Walzer's (1982) ideas to distinguish between the two types of rights. These scholars both argue that the difference depends on whether the state sees a group continuing to remain a permanent and distinct society or whether the state sees the group ideally integrating into or being assimilated by the larger society.

Group Rights
Theoretically, the major limitation of group rights is that they only exist so long as the discrimination continues (Sanders, 1991, p. 369). For instance, if discrimination against disabled people were to end,

the group would simultaneously cease to have a rights cause. In the Canadian *Charter*, groups are enumerated (such as the disabled, religious, and racialized). Several legal cases reflect this, such as *Alberta v Hutterian Brethren* (2009),[4] *Law Society of British Columbia v Trinity Western* (2018),[5] *and Withler v Canada* (2011).[6] Nevertheless, the *Charter* also opens up the possibility of adding groups not listed in it, which counters Lerner's (1992) and Ramcharan's (1993) contention that the term *group* lacks precise legal meaning. Analogous grounds are additional prohibited grounds, similar to the enumerated grounds in that they determine a group to be "disadvantaged in the social, political, legal, penal and rehabilitative sense"[7] and requiring protection. The courts are tasked with the responsibility of adding analogous grounds where necessary, on a case-by-case basis. Thus far, Canadian courts have identified sexual orientation, marital status, and citizenship as analogous grounds of discrimination.

Following this framework, Kymlicka (1995) approves of the demands from ethnic groups, such as for exemptions from existing laws and regulations that have placed them at a disadvantage. He interprets that such rights are relatively weak (in comparison to the collective rights discussed in detail in the next section) and only require accommodations in the existing institutions consisting largely of the majority. Two Canadian examples of these group rights are (a) Sikh men who wear a turban and seek exemption from the motor vehicle law that requires riders to wear motorcycle helmets, and (b) Orthodox Jews who ask for allowance to erect an eruv—a thin strand of the wire during their Sabbath—in a public space. It is important to note that both group rights have been granted by the courts.[8]

Collective Rights

A collective right is another type of group right; it is held by the group, or "collectivity" (Sanders, 1991 p. 369), whose interests and goals transcend the ending of discrimination against its members. The members of this collectivity are linked not simply by external discrimination but by an internal, stronger cohesiveness achieved by common cultural, language, or religious identities. Examples of such collectivities are the Indigenous Peoples and French Canadians in Canada, or Native Americans and Puerto Ricans in the United States. Collective rights are based on the collectivity holding a right that looks beyond access to equality for their individual members and instead seeks distinct "group survival" (Sanders, 1991, p. 370). This type of right is claimed only when the right is born by the group *qua* the group (Chandra, 2017, p. 52).

Kymilcka (1995) refers to the collectivities holding collective rights as "national minorities," as opposed to ethnic minorities who hold the group rights discussed earlier. His justification for conferring collective rights on Indigenous Peoples and Quebecois flows from his reasoning that these two communities had institutionally complete societies prior to being incorporated into British North America (Kymlicka, 1995, 1998). He agrees with the liberal state's sheltering national minorities from majority decisions, which he describes as external protections. He also acknowledges that the minority group can limit some liberties of its individual members, as internal protections, in the name of group solidarity or cultural purity. This issue of internal and external protections is further discussed later in the chapter.

In the Canadian context, the Canadian *Charter* and Constitution recognize and affirm the collective rights of the Indigenous Peoples, based on their need to preserve their culture,[9] and French-Canadian Quebecois, based on the need to preserve their French language and culture.[10] These rights are inherent and more permanent than the rights provided to other groups. They guarantee a measure of autonomy, including a collectivity's ability to make decisions in several areas of social, economic, and political life without any interference from the state. For instance, the Province of Quebec has extensive jurisdiction over matters crucial to the survival of the French language and culture, such as education, language, culture, and immigration (Kymlicka, 1995). The Indigenous Peoples of Canada have the inherent right of self-government, which essentially means devolution of political power to the group over their historical territory, including governance, social and economic development, education, health, lands, and taxation powers.

Group and Collective Rights within the *Charter* and the Constitution

Several sections of the *Charter* (Sections 1, 2, 15, 23, and 25) and the Constitution (Section 35) guarantee group or collective rights to Canadians. Section 2 of the *Charter* includes freedoms for individuals as well as groups, such as the freedoms of religion, expression, assembly, and association. Similarly, Section 15 of the *Charter* guarantees equality rights for both individuals and groups. The court has made clear that "the concept of equality [under Section 15] does not necessarily mean identical treatment and that the formal 'like treatment' model of discrimination may in fact produce inequality [to the individual or the group]."[11]

Section 2 of the *Charter* has been interpreted by courts to protect the freedoms of religious minorities or vulnerable groups in combatting prevailing right imbalances in society. The court has clarified that the purpose of this section (2[d] in particular) is to allow "the achievement of individual potential through interpersonal relationships and collective action."[12] The right to collective bargaining, equal recognition of a religious minority, and the freedom of the press are just a few such issues upheld by the courts under Section 2.[13]

Several legal scholars and political scientists (Elkins, 1989; Monahan, 1987; Richez, 2010) argue that the limitation on *Charter* rights, as found in Section 1 of the *Charter*, allows collective goals aimed at the greater good of Canadians to prevail over individualistic ones in certain instances—noting that rights and freedoms are "subject only to such reasonable limits prescribed by law as can be demonstrably justified in a free and democratic society." In most of the liberal states, rights are not absolute and are subject to limits if the state finds it necessary to achieve an important (collective) objective.[14] Political scientist and *Charter* scholar Hiebert (1996) explains:

> An expansive interpretation of Section 1 would allow Parliament and the provincial legislatures to promote, where justified, values other than those specifically enumerated in the Charter. This would enrich the Charter by embracing collective values that, like individual rights, are relevant to Canadian conceptions of a just and democratic society

yet are not adequately captured by the Charter's highly individualist language. (p. 138)

For Richez (2010), Section 1 not only gives power to the legislatures but also gives a considerable amount of power to the courts to determine whether or not individual rights should take precedence over collective ones.

Constitutional provisions for collective right consist of status rights for Indigenous Peoples under Section 25 of the *Charter* and Section 35 of the Constitution, and French-language protection to French-Canadian Quebecois under Section 23 of the *Charter*. These provisions are discussed in the next few sections. Accordingly, rights for these collectivities were entrenched in Canada's constitutional documents, based on the historical pattern of Confederation, treaties, and jurisprudence (Mendes, 2007, p. 63). The collectivities are "rooted in the territory or woven into the history and fabric of the nation" (Bhabha, 2016, p. 269), thus separating their collective rights from those of other groups.

Indigenous Rights

Section 25 of the *Charter* and Section 35 of the Constitution recognize and affirm the existing Aboriginal and treaty rights of the Aboriginal peoples of Canada. However, colonial settlement and the reception of English law overlay the pre-existing Indigenous communities and their legal systems. Related to this, the SCC defined the meaning and scope of Aboriginal rights in a series of decisions. In his majority judgment in *Van der Peet*,[15] Chief Justice Lamer acknowledged upfront that he was picking up where *R v Sparrow* left off,[16] observing that the essence of Aboriginal rights was derived from Aboriginal peoples' prior occupation of land and their prior social organization and distinctive cultures.

Indigenous group membership has been contested in the courts, revealing the tension between individual rights and collective rights of the Indigenous Peoples. Notable court cases among these are the following:

- *Alberta (Aboriginal Affairs and Northern Development) v Cunningham*,[17] in which the SCC held that the provision of the *Metis Settlements Act*

of Alberta[18] was protected under Section 15(2) of the *Charter* as an ameliorative program, allowing the Métis to maintain their separate identity and to regulate membership in a Métis settlement.
- *Miller v Mohawk Council of Kahnawà:ke*,[19] in which the court ruled that a band law prohibiting mixed-race couples from living in Kahnawà:ke Reserve or Territory infringed Sections 7 and 15 of the Canadian *Charter*.
- *Thomas v Norris*,[20] where the court ruled that the rights of an individual, who was physically harmed while being forced to participate in an initiation ritual, superseded Indigenous collective rights. In other words, the initiation ritual was not protected under Section 35. Case law suggests that courts have tried to balance the collective rights of Indigenous Peoples against individual rights of their members.

French-Canadian Quebecois

The Quebecois's French-language rights are protected under Section 23 of the *Charter*. In the *Mahe v Alberta* decision,[21] Chief Justice Dickson said this (on behalf of all the presiding judges):

> The general purpose of s. 23 is clear: it is to preserve and promote the two official languages of Canada, and their respective cultures, by ensuring that each language flourishes, as far as possible, in provinces where it is not spoken by the majority of the population. The section aims at achieving this goal by granting minority language educational rights to minority language parents throughout Canada.[22]

> My reference to cultures is significant: it is based on the fact that any broad guarantee of language rights, especially in the context of education, cannot be separated from a concern for the culture associated with the language. Language is more than a mere means of communication, it is part and parcel of the identity and culture of the people speaking it. It is the means by which individuals understand themselves and the world around them.[23]

Section 33 of the *Charter* allows provincial governments to override Section 2, and Sections 7 to 15 of the *Charter*, for a period of up to five years. Quebec has exercised this power most often. Similarly, the Quebec *Charter of Human Rights and Freedoms*,[24] Section 52, allows the Quebec legislature to abrogate other sections of the Quebec *Charter* in the name of parliamentary supremacy, but more practically, "under the circumstances in which society and State imperatives outweigh individual needs" (Rousseau & Cote, 2017, p. 374). By invoking the notwithstanding clause under Section 33 of the Canadian *Charter* or Section 52 of the Quebec *Charter*, Quebec has prioritized collective interests (*droits collectifs*) of the Quebec people over the interests of individual Quebecois (Rousseau & Cote, 2017). Furthermore, Gosselin (1991) argues that this prioritization may be the only way for Quebec to maintain its "distinct society" status, especially given that it is not specifically named as such in the Constitution.

Quebec has invoked the notwithstanding clause of the Canadian *Charter* 61 times, in addition to 45 references to the notwithstanding clause of the Quebec *Charter*, compared to just three times in the rest of Canada over the same period (Rousseau & Cote, 2017). Quebec's use of Section 33 demonstrates a strong legislative practice to abrogate the Canadian and/or Quebec Charters in the collective interests of French-Canadian Quebecois. To some scholars, like Rousseau and Cote (2017) and Kahana (2006), this practice raises a theoretical possibility of potential individual human rights violations in Quebec.

Multiple prominent human rights lawyers in Quebec, interviewed for the research, argued that the origins of *droits collectifs* lie in the civil law tradition of Quebec (*jus commune*). Samson and Langevin (2015) agree, observing that "the influence of human rights on Quebec civil law appears inherent in its codification and its status as the jus commune. It is the very essence of a Civil Code to translate the dominant values of the society it governs into law" (p. 744). The interviewees also pointed to Quebec's *Charter*, especially Section 9.1, which introduced collective elements to the balancing of individual liberties. This section has been influential in how cases are decided in Quebec courts. The section reads:

"In exercising his fundamental freedoms and rights, a person shall maintain a proper regard for democratic values, State laicity, public order and the general well-being of the citizens of Québec."

The three lawyers further argue that the Quebec *Charter* has been applied more often and in the strictest way to issues such as language, ethnicity, and religion. More recently, Quebec's Bill 21 has gone further in asserting the collective right of the francophone Quebecois, by banning public officials from wearing religious symbols. The bill also amended the Quebec *Charter* by explicitly adding the state's laicity[25] to be of fundamental importance. Following Kymlicka's conception of rights, Bouchard and Taylor (2008) support the notion of *droits collectifs*, which could impose some restrictions among the members of the Quebecois people. They state that

> some people's rights and freedoms must occasionally be restricted to maintain the full panoply of rights that the State must offer all of its citizens. Individual rights may thus be restricted to allow the State to achieve important collective purposes such as contributing to the common good, ensuring public order, and so on. For example, this is true when the government decides to restrict certain rights to foster the survival and vitality of the French language in Québec. (p. 173)

Case Law

As discussed earlier, plenty of case law on the five *Charter* sections and Section 35 of the Constitution exists in the context of group and collective rights. However, the following examples have been carefully selected to ensure they demonstrate the nexus of group rights or collective rights and urban issues in Canadian municipalities such as Winnipeg, Edmonton, and Outremont.

Group Rights

Alcoholism Foundation of Manitoba v Winnipeg (City)
In *Alcoholism Foundation of Manitoba v Winnipeg (City)*,[26] the Manitoba Court of Appeal found that aspects of the City of Winnipeg's bylaw

regarding the group-home zoning restrictions violated Section 15(1) of the *Charter*. The bylaw provided that group homes for aged, disabled, convalescent, or rehabilitated prisoners could only be located in certain areas of the city and had to maintain a minimum separation distance of 300 metres from each other. Municipalities are expressly authorized to pass zoning bylaws that make distinctions between different properties and uses of land. However, the appellant, the Alcoholism Foundation of Manitoba, argued that Winnipeg's bylaw unlawfully singled out people living in group homes based on their personal characteristics of age, convalescence, treatment, or rehabilitation, contrary to Sections 2(d), 7, and 15(1) of the *Charter*. Judge Monnin, who presided over the case, found the bylaw violated Section 15(1) by creating a disadvantage to the inhabitants of group homes. He declared the bylaw inoperative and of no force and effect.

This decision came soon after the pivotal case of *Andrews v Law Society of British Columbia*,[27] in which the SCC established a three-part test to prove discrimination, also under Section 15(1). Judge Monnin referred in his ruling to the protection of the group rights of disadvantaged people in society, many of whom may not be listed in Section 15(1). He explained:

> A complainant must show unequal treatment plus discrimination. The discrimination is defined as a legal burden or a limitation based on personal characteristics such as being aged, a former prisoner, an about-to-be released prisoner, a physically or mentally handicapped person. This category is not exhaustive, and the class or category of disadvantaged persons could be extended to cover single parents, widows, widowers, veterans, AIDS sufferers, etc. In fact the disadvantaged category or class has no limit, at least not as yet.[28]

This case fits the definition of group rights espoused by Miller (2002) and Jones (1999), where the interests of the group under Section 15 of the *Charter* sufficiently justify imposing duties on others. In exchange for the group's Section 15 rights being upheld, the judge placed a duty on the city council to "adequately draft zoning and other bylaws, to avoid the pitfalls of describing a class or category [group] of individuals as it did."[29]

The ruling in *Alcoholism Foundation of Manitoba* had serious implications for zoning bylaws, which explicitly include characteristics of the people occupying the zone and/or include the minimum separation distance. Specifically, the decision called into question the group-home zoning bylaws across the country, which led many municipalities to revise or rescind their existing bylaws (Agrawal, 2013, 2014).

Rosenberg v Outremont (City)

Rosenberg v Outremont (City)[30] is an example of the court upholding religious accommodation for a religious minority group based on Section 2(a) of the *Charter* (freedom of religion). The case was brought forward by individuals (*Rosenberg* and others) on behalf of the Hasidic Jewish community, against the Borough of Outremont. The city removed an eruv, a symbolic wire that sets a boundary outside in public areas and allows Orthodox Jews to perform daily functions during their Sabbath day (Saturday).

The court held that Outremont's Hasidic community was within its constitutional right to construct an eruv, which is protected under the *Canadian Charter* as well as the Quebec *Charter*. The court reasoned that the city did not exercise its proper authority, because "the City has a constitutional duty to provide accommodation for religious practices that do not impose undue hardship on its residents."[31]

This case shows the Province of Quebec imposing its collective interest on minority group rights. Bouchard and Taylor (2008) agree with the view that the state can restrict certain individual or ethnic minority group rights, such as that of religious practice, to maintain a collective purpose. In this case, the Borough of Outremont claimed state neutrality or secularism as an assertion of collective values, noting: "But, if such rigid neutrality makes members of minority groups feel unwanted in their own society, then it might have an effect contrary to the one intended" (Howard-Hassman, 2018, p. 167). Some liberal theorists (Abu-Laban & Stasiulis 1992; Tomuschat 1983) posit that when a minority group chooses to limit the liberty of its own individual members or sub-religious or sub-cultural groups in the name of maintaining its cultural purity—or in this case "neutrality"—this may be antithetical to liberal values.

The *Rosenberg* decision and other court decisions favour ethnic minorities,[32] which result in a face-off between two minorities. Bouchard and Taylor (2008) attribute the prevailing anxiety and hostility in Quebec to the fact that "Quebecers of French-Canadian ancestry are still not at ease with their twofold status as a majority in Québec and a minority in Canada" (p. 18).

Collective Rights

Ford v Quebec (Attorney General)
The Quebecois's French-language rights are protected under Section 23 of the Canadian *Charter,* and converge with the importance of preserving French identity and culture in Quebec to form collective rights. The case of *Ford v Quebec (Attorney General)*[33] is useful to distinguish between group rights and collective language rights. The respondents (Ford and other business owners) challenged the validity of Sections 58 and 69 of the Quebec *Charter of the French Language,*[34] arguing that they infringed on their right to freedom of expression in Section 2(b) of the *Canadian Charter*. The sections mandated that "public signs and posters and commercial advertising shall be in the French language only and that only the French version of a firm name may be used."[35] The SCC held that both of these sections, which mandated the use of the French firm name and the French language in public signs and posters, did indeed infringe on this *Charter* right because the right to express oneself in one's language of choice falls under the ambit of the *Charter*'s Section 2(b).

Though the case is well known for clarifying the use and impact of the notwithstanding clause, Section 33, it also highlights an important dimension of collective rights in Quebec. Notably, the court drew an important distinction under the umbrella of language rights. On the one hand, citizens have a general *freedom* to express themselves in the language of their choice. On the other hand, there are actual language *rights*. These two dimensions can be compared to group rights versus collective rights: group rights being the general freedom to express oneself under Section 2(b) of the *Charter,* and collective rights being rooted in Section 23 of the *Charter.* According to Judge Dickson in *R v Big M Drug Mart Ltd.,*[36] cited in *Ford:*

> Freedom can primarily be characterized by the absence of coercion or constraint. If a person is compelled by the state or the will of another to a course of action or inaction which he would not otherwise have chosen, he is not acting of his own volition and he cannot be said to be truly free. One of the major purposes of the *Charter* is to protect, within reason, from compulsion or restraint.[37]

The collective dimension of language rights is different, however. These collective rights require more pre-emptive and affirmative action by the government, rooted in a "special historical, political and constitutional basis."[38] According to the court, these language rights

> grant entitlement to a specific benefit from the government or in relation to one's dealing with the government. Correspondingly, the government is obliged to provide certain services or benefits in both languages or at least permit use of either language by persons conducting certain affairs with the government.[39]

As such, this differentiation between group rights and collective rights is used by the court in *Ford*. Collective rights in Quebec, as seen through language rights, are entrenched through Section 23 of the Constitution; they therefore warrant additional protection through state action. The court further solidified this concept, acknowledging that ample evidence shows that the French language is threatened in Quebec. The court stated that a policy enacted to counter this threat—such as the provisions in the Quebec *Charter of the French Language*—are "serious and legitimate."[40]

Despite considering the importance of language preservation and collective rights in Quebec, the SCC held that the Section 2(b) infringements were *not* justified under Section 1 of the *Canadian Charter* and Section 9.1 of the Quebec *Charter*. The court noted that prohibiting the use of any language other than French on commercial signs was not "necessary to the defence and enhancement of the status of the French language in Québec or…proportionate to that legislative purpose."[41] Thus, the provisions enacted to protect French collective rights in Quebec were struck down as unconstitutional. In response, Quebec used the notwithstanding clause of the Canadian *Charter* to mandate French-language signs. This case demonstrates that the judiciary recognizes that some collective rights need protection in Canada, but balancing collective rights against group rights against individual rights is challenging. It can be difficult to determine what should take precedence.

With respect to municipal issues specifically, this case sparked outcry and protests in Montreal and other municipalities in Quebec, particularly by those who believed that the preservation of French culture and language justified any potential Section 2(b) infringement for individuals not falling within the collective-right purview (Endleman, 1995; Martel & Pâquet, 2012; Mathieu, n.d.). The *Ford* case has been cited repeatedly by municipalities across Canada on the issue of language, signage, and commercial expression; for example, in *R v Pinehouse Plaza Pharmacy Ltd*,[42] *R v Mader's Tobacco Store Ltd*,[43] and *Canadian Newspapers Co v Victoria (City)*.[44] *Ford* affected the drafting of sign bylaws in several municipalities as to whether the municipalities could impose language requirements on commercial signs.

Neskonlith Indian Band v Salmon Arm (City)

In *Neskonlith Indian Band v Salmon Arm (City)*,[45] also discussed in Chapter 1, the Neskonlith Indian Band brought a petition to quash a permit approved by the City of Salmon Arm. The permit allowed a company to construct a shopping centre on private land on the city's delta and floodplain areas. The disputed land adjoined the Neskonlith Reserve #3, which the band regarded as part of its traditional territory. The concern was that the siting of the proposed development posed certain threats to the environment and to the band's interests in the adjoining lands. The crux of this case was about whether the Neskonlith Indian Band had been adequately consulted prior to the issuing of the development permit.

The court found that the development permit was valid and that the municipality did not need to engage in any duty to consult. It confirmed that the honour of the Crown "is non-delegable and rests at all times with the province,"[46] also confirming what the *Haida Nation* case had established.[47] Furthermore, and most importantly, *Neskonlith* confirmed that the duty to consult does not extend to municipalities. No municipality has an "independent constitutional duty to consult."[48] The court makes clear that the duty to consult stems from Section 35 of the Constitution and is entrenched and unavoidable. Justice Newbury wrote:

> The purpose of the duty is to protect Aboriginal rights while furthering the goal of reconciliation. The Supreme Court of Canada has said that the honour of the Crown must be understood "generously" in this context (*Haida*, at para 17) and in the Band's submission, a "generous and purposive application of the honour of the Crown requires consultation whenever government authorizes activities which interfere with Aboriginal rights and title, whether that authorization comes directly from the Province or from local governments exercising delegated provincial authority."[49]

The rights held by Indigenous groups in Canada, pursuant to Section 35, are collective rights, meaning they exist irrespective of any explicit discrimination. Similarly, in the context of the duty to consult, the right to be consulted exists and is engaged *prior to* any infringement actually occurring. The Crown's duty to consult is engaged when the Crown makes a decision that has the potential to adversely affect lands and resources to which Indigenous Peoples lay claim; arguably, this is a low threshold.

As a result, the court acknowledged that the Neskonlith Indian Band was entitled to consultation by the provincial Crown. However, the development was a municipal project, and, given the municipality had no duty to consult, the permit was ultimately allowed. The court held that the band would have to pursue other remedies to halt the permit.[50] Justice Newbury, writing on behalf of the three justices presiding over the case, said:

> By virtue of *Haida*[51] and *Rio Tinto*[52] alone, then, it seems to me this appeal must fail as a matter of law. It is not for this court to create an exception to or modification of the very clear statements the Supreme

Court has made. And while it is true that First Nations may experience difficulty in seeking appropriate remedies in the courts in cases like this one, it is also true that as creatures of statute, municipalities do not in general have the authority to consult with and if indicated, accommodate First Nations as a specific group in making the day-to-day operational decisions that are the diet of local governments.[53]

Imai and Stacey (2014), legal scholars, have criticized this case, suggesting that the decision runs contrary to the duty to consult because it incorrectly treated the duty like *Charter* rights (by asking whether the duty applied to the entity, similar to whether the *Charter* applies to the actor under Section 32). However, this duty is separate from that of the *Charter*, being enshrined under Section 35 of the Constitution. They further suggest that it is counterproductive to allow a third party or non-Crown actor—such as a municipality, which is not bound by this duty—to act in a way that may interfere with the Indigenous rights in question, given that municipalities recognize the Crown owes a duty to consult. This would mean, practically, that any non-bound actor, such as a municipality, could act freely, despite the Indigenous band's knowing that it is entitled to a duty to consult.

Therefore, despite Indigenous communities being entitled to collective rights in Canada, the application of such rights is inconsistent and controversial. The Truth and Reconciliation Commission of Canada's *Calls to Action* (2015) calls on all levels of government—including municipal governments explicitly—to fully adopt and implement the *United Nations Declaration on the Rights of Indigenous Peoples* as the framework for reconciliation. Municipalities and other provincial agencies are still grappling with this responsibility, with tools and resources still in development.

American Freedom Defence Initiative v Edmonton (City)
In *American Freedom Defence Initiative v Edmonton (City)*,[54] also discussed at length in Chapter 9, the City of Edmonton removed an advertisement from its public transit buses because it made explicit references to the so-called honour killings of Muslim girls. The applicant, the American Freedom Defence Initiative (AFDI), applied for a declaration that the

city's removal violated its right to freedom of expression under Section 2(b) of the *Charter*.

The city argued that the advertisement was removed because the city prohibited offensive and discriminatory advertisements on public transportation. The question before the court was whether or not this policy infringed on argued right, and, if so, whether or not the infringement should be upheld as a "reasonable limit prescribed by law as can be demonstrably justified in a free and democratic society" in accordance with Section 1 of the *Charter*. The court applied the *Oakes* test,[55] in which the SCC laid down the criteria to establish a reasonable and justified limit on *Charter* rights. Judge Gill wrote:

> I reiterate that there can be absolutely no argument with the proposition that honour killings in any form, and on any justification, are criminal acts and are repugnant to the very foundations of Canadian society…However, the City in applying its policy is entitled to consider an advertisement as a whole, in this case, the term "Muslim" in reference to "honour killings," the "Islamization of America" logo as well as the background and history of…AFDI. In doing so, the City concluded that the advertisement is properly understood as an attempt by AFDI to mask its discriminatory anti-Muslim and/or anti-Islamic agenda in the form of an advertisement which purports to offer help to young women in danger.[56]

AFDI employs Section 1 in favour of the collective interest and moral values of Canadians. It makes it clear that even if the right to freedom of expression may be a zealously guarded *Charter* right, it is not limitless. Of note, the city initially approved the posting of the advertisement and posted it throughout its transportation network. It then pulled the advertisement in response to public complaints and outcry. Based on this case, the city's administrative approval process will need to be more vigilant by proactively vetting the advertising material to avoid protracted legal entanglements. Municipalities will have special challenges to determine what expression may not be appropriate for its communities and what might be offensive to "the moral standards of the community."[57] If public complaint is a criterion, how many public complaints will it take to decide that a message offends a community's moral standard (collective interest)?

Conclusion

This chapter set out to explore how group rights and collective rights play a role at the city level and thus affect urban issues. The foregoing discussion makes it abundantly clear that the Canadian state protects its citizens' group rights and collective rights alongside citizens' individual rights. The judiciary has further clarified, applied, and even expanded the scope of human rights in relation to various aspects of city life, although the expansion of the scope has added more judicial uncertainties.

The analysis of the five cases reveals that Canadian municipalities are still grappling with the application of these forms of rights and that some decisions remain contentious—among them, setting limits on expression on public properties, consultations with Indigenous communities, and considering the requiring of English signage on commercial establishments outside of Quebec. The struggles seem more pronounced among Quebec municipalities, where many are dealing with the matter of how to balance the rights of individual and/or sub-religious or sub-cultural groups with those of French-Canadian Quebecois as a collectivity. At the municipal level such issues have surfaced in the form of erections of Jewish eruvs in Outremont, the siting of ethnic places of worship—for example with *Lafontaine (Village)*[58] and *Centre Islamique Badr*[59]—and the construction of Sukkots in Montreal.[60] In all these cases the courts upheld individual rights or the group rights of the minority. However, they sparked intense controversy about these issues and lengthy legal trials, which ultimately led to large-scale public dissent in Quebec. Although not a municipal issue per se, several cases about who can or cannot become a member of Indigenous communities also surfaced. Notably, both the Quebec and the Indigenous cases exhibit the consequences of Kymlicka's (1995) argument of placing internal restrictions within these communities.

Unfortunately, how a municipality deals with Indigenous Peoples' collective rights, such as the Crown's duty to consult and the respect for treaty rights, remains unclear. As discussed earlier, the *Neskonlith* case[61] muddies this issue further by making a determination that municipalities, as non-Crown actors, do not have a role in the Crown's duty to consult. While municipal governments want to strengthen and develop mutually beneficial relations with the Indigenous governments in their vicinity, the judiciary and provincial governments have provided little or no guidance in this regard.

All in all, the response of Canadian cities to group rights and collective rights remains a work in progress. Recognition of these rights is not a remedy for all urban problems. Nevertheless, these rights are influencing urban issues in ways that are, at times, inconceivable to municipal planners, policy-makers, and elected officials. As a way forward, municipalities must train their planners and elected officials *and* educate their residents to help them understand the municipal government's constitutional obligations and the judicial interpretations, along with their implications for planning policies and practice.

NOTES

1. *Universal Declaration of Human Rights*, GA Res 217A (III), UNGAOR, 3rd Sess, Supp No 13, UN Doc A/810 (1948) 71 [UDHR].
2. We promised to protect the anonymity of our interviewees.
3. *Tsilhqot'in Nation v British Columbia*, 2014 SCC 44.
4. *Alberta v Hutterian Brethren of Wilson Colony*, 2009 SCC 37, [2009] 2 SCR 567.
5. *Law Society of British Columbia v Trinity Western University Hutterian*, 2018 SCC 32, [2018] 2 SCR 293.
6. *Withler v Canada (Attorney General)*, 2011 SCC 12, [2011] 1 SCR 396.
7. *Alcoholism Foundation of Manitoba v Winnipeg (City)*, 69 DLR (4th) 697, 1990 CanLII 8022 (MB CA), at 39 [*Alcoholism*].
8. *Dhillon v British Columbia (Ministry of Transportation & Highways)*, [1999] BCHRTD No 25, Carswell, BC 3191; *Rosenberg v Outremont (City)*, [2001] RJQ 1556, 2001 CanLII 25087.
9. Section 35 of the *Constitution Act, 1982*, Schedule B to the *Canada Act 1982* (UK), 1982, c 11.
10. *Canadian Charter of Rights and Freedoms*, s 23; Part 1 of the *Constitution Act, 1982*, being Schedule B to the *Canada Act 1982* (UK), 1982, c 11.

11. *R v Kapp*, 2008 SCC 41, at para 15; citing *Andrews v Law Society of British Columbia*, [1989] 1 SCR 143, at 165, 56 DLR (4th) [*Andrews*].
12. *Dunmore v Ontario (Attorney General)*, 2001 SCC 94, at para 17.
13. *Mounted Police Association of Ontario v Canada*, 2015 SCC 1; *Edmonton Journal v Alberta (Attorney General)*, [1989] 2 SCR; *Chamberlain v Surrey School District No. 36*, [2002] 4 SCR.
14. *Canada (Attorney General) v JTI-Macdonald Corp*, [2007] 2 SCR 610, para 36.
15. *R v Van der Peet*, [1996] 2 SCR 507, 137 DLR (4th) 289. [*Van der Peet* cited to SCR].
16. *R v Sparrow*, [1990] 1 SCR 1075.
17. *Alberta (Aboriginal Affairs and Northern Development) v Cunningham*, 2011 SCC 37.
18. *Metis Settlements Act*, RSA 2000, C M 14.
19. *Miller v Mohawk Council of Kahnawà:ke*, 2018 QCCS 1784.
20. *Thomas v Norris*, [1992] 2 CNLR 139, 1992 BCSC CarswellBC 740.
21. *Mahe v Alberta*, [1990] 1 SCR 342 1990, 68 DLR (4th) 69 [*Mahe* cited to SCR].
22. *Ibid.*, at para 31.
23. *Ibid.*, at para 32.
24. *Charter of Human Rights and Freedoms*, CQLR C C-12.
25. This is the separation of state and religions, the religious neutrality of the state, the equality of all citizens, and freedom of conscience and freedom of religion.
26. *Alcoholism Foundation of Manitoba v Winnipeg (City)*, 69 DLR (4th) 697, 1990 CanLII 8022 (MB CA), at 39.
27. *Andrews v Law Society of British Columbia*, [1989] 1 SCR 143, 56 DLR (4th).
28. *Alcoholism Foundation of Manitoba v Winnipeg (City)*, 69 DLR (4th) 697, 1990 CanLII 8022 (MB CA), at 39.
29. *Ibid.*
30. *Rosenberg v Outremont (City)*, [2001] RJQ 1556, 2001 CarswellQue 1312 [*Rosenberg*].
31. *Ibid.*, at para 46.
32. Other examples are *Multani v Commission scolaire Marguerite-Bourgeoys*, [2006] 1 SCR 256, and *Syndicat Northcrest v Amselem*, [2004] 2 SCR 551.
33. *Ford v Quebec (Attorney General)*, [1988] 2 SCR 712, 54 DLR (4th) 577 [*Ford* cited to SCR].
34. *Charter of the French Language*, CQLR C C-11.
35. *Ibid.*, at 721.
36. *R v Big M Drug Mart Ltd.*, [1985] 1 SCR 295 at 336, 18 DLR (4th) 321 [*Big M Drug Mart*].
37. *Ford v Quebec (Attorney General)*, [1988] 2 SCR 712, 54 DLR (4th) 577, at 751, citing *R v Big M Drug Mart Ltd.*, at 336.
38. *Ford v Quebec (Attorney General)*, [1988] 2 SCR 712, 54 DLR (4th) 577, at 751.
39. *Ibid.*
40. *Ibid.*, at 778.
41. *Ibid.*, at 779.
42. *R v Pinehouse Plaza Pharmacy Ltd*, [1988] SJ No 232, [1988] 3 WWR 705.
43. *R v Mader's Tobacco Store Ltd*, 2013 NSPC 29.

44. *Canadian Newspapers Co v Victoria (City)*, [1991] BCCAAA No 147, 1991 CarswellBC 2467.
45. *Neskonlith Indian Band v Salmon Arm (City)*, 2012 BCCA 379 [*Neskonlith*].
46. Ibid., at para 61.
47. *Haida Nation v British Columbia (Minister of Forests)*, [2004] 3 SCR 511 [*Haida Nation*].
48. *Neskonlith Indian Band v Salmon Arm (City)*, 2012 BCCA 379, at para 54.
49. Ibid., at para 61.
50. Ibid., at para 70.
51. *Haida Nation v British Columbia (Minister of Forests)*, [2004] 3 SCR 511.
52. *Rio Tinto Alcan Inc. v Carrier Sekani Tribal Council*, 2010 SCC 43 [*Rio Tinto*].
53. *Neskonlith Indian Band v Salmon Arm (City)*, 2012 BCCA 379, at para 70.
54. *American Freedom Defence Initiative v Edmonton (City)*, 2016 ABQB 555 [*AFDI*].
55. *R v Oakes*, [1986] 1 SCR 103, at paras 73–74, S26 DLR (4th) 200 (SCC) [*Oakes*].
56. *American Freedom Defence Initiative v Edmonton (City)*, 2016 ABQB 555, at paras 96–97.
57. Ibid., at para 71.
58. *Congrégation des témoins de Jéhovah de St-Jérôme-Lafontaine v Lafontaine (Village)*, 2004 SCC 48.
59. *Ville de Montréal v Centre islamique Badr*, 2017 QCCS 57.
60. *Syndicat Northcrest v Amselem*, [2004] 2 SCR 551.
61. *Neskonlith Indian Band v Salmon Arm (City)*, 2012 BCCA 379, note 41.

REFERENCES

Abu-Laban, Y., & Stasiulis, D. (1992). Ethnic pluralism under siege: Popular and partisan opposition to multiculturalism. *Canadian Public Policy*, 18(4), 365–386.

Agrawal, S. (2013). *Opinion on the provisions of group homes in the city-wide zoning bylaw of the City of Toronto*. Report submitted to the City of Toronto. https://www.toronto.ca/legdocs/mmis/2013/pg/bgrd/backgroundfile-56473.pdf

Agrawal, S. (2014). Balancing municipal planning with human rights: A case study. *Canadian Journal of Urban Research*, 23(1), 1–20.

Agrawal, S. (2017). Human rights 101 for planners. *Plan Canada*, (Summer), 6–9.

Agrawal, S. (2020). Human rights and the city: A view from Canada. *Journal of American Planning Association*. doi:10.1080/01944363.2020.1775680

Appiah, K.A. (1994). Identity, authenticity, survival: Multicultural societies and social reproduction. In A. Gutmann (Ed.), *Multiculturalism: Examining the politics of recognition* (pp. 149–164). (Expanded paperback edition). Princeton University Press.

Bhabha, F. (2016) Hanging in the balance: The rights of religious minorities. *Supreme Court of Canada Law Review*, 75(2), 265–284.

Bouchard, G., & Taylor, C. (2008). *Building the future, a time for reconciliation*. Report of the Consultation Commission of Accommodation Practices Related to Cultural Differences. Government of Quebec.

Chandra, R. (2017). Collective rights vs. individual rights. *International Journal of Multidisciplinary Research and Development*, 4(7), 51–55.

Dick, C. (2009). Culture and the courts revisited: Group-rights scholarship and the evolution of s.35(1). *Canadian Journal of Political Science*, 42(4), 957–979.

Elkins, D. (1989). Facing our destiny: Rights and Canadian distinctiveness. *Canadian Journal of Political Science*, 22(4), 699–716. doi:10.1017/S0008423900020217

Endleman, S. (1995). The politics of language: The impact of language legislation on French- and English-speaking citizens of Quebec. *International Journal of the Sociology of Language*, 116, 81–98. doi:10.1515/ijsl.1995.116.81

Freeman, M. (1995). Are there collective human rights? *Political Studies*, 43, 25–40.

Glazer, N. (1978). Individual rights against group rights. In E. Kemenka & A.E.-S. Tay (Eds.), *Human Rights* (pp. 87–103). London: Edward Arnold.

Gosselin, J. (1991). *La légitimité du contrôle judiciaire sous le régime de la Charte*. Éditions Yvon Blais.

Green, L. (1991). Two views of collective rights. *Journal of Law & Jurisprudence*, 4(2), 315–327.

Heim, D. (2016). "Old" natives and "new" immigrants: Beyond territory and history in Kymlicka's account of group rights. *Migration Letters*, 13(2), 214–227.

Hiebert, J. (1996). *Limiting rights: The dilemma of judicial review*. McGill-Queen's University Press.

Howard-Hassmann, Rhoda E. (2018). The "Quebec values" debate of 2013: Minority vs. collective rights. *Human Rights Quarterly*, 40(1), 144–167. Project MUSE, doi:10.1353/hrq.2018.0005

Imai, S., & Stacey, A. (2014). Municipalities and the duty to consult Aboriginal peoples: A case comment on *Neskonlith Indian Band v. Salmon Arm (City)*. UBC *Law Review*, 47(1), 293–312.

Jones, P. (1999). Human rights, group rights, and peoples' rights. *Human Rights Quarterly*, 21(1), 80–107.

Kahana, T. (2006). Legalism, anxiety and legislative constitutionalism. *Queen's Law Journal*, 31(2), 535–577.

Kymlicka, W. (1995). *Multicultural citizenship: A liberal theory of human rights*. Clarendon Press.

Kymlicka, W. (1998). Introduction: An emerging consensus? *Ethical Theory and Moral Practice*, 1, 143–157.

Lerner, N. (1992). *Group rights and discrimination in international law*. Martinus Nijhoff Publishers.

Levrau, F. (2019). Expanding the multicultural recognition scope? A critical analysis of Will Kymlicka's polyethnic rights. *The Pluralist*, 14(3), 78–107.

Martel, M., & Pâquet, M. (2012). *Speaking up: A history of language and politics in Canada and Québec*. Between the Lines.

Mathieu, N. (n.d.). Language conflict in Québec. McCord Museum. http://collections.musee-mccord.qc.ca/scripts/explore.php?Lang=1&elementid=103__true&tableid=11&contentl

ong#:~:text=Language%20conflict%20in%20Qu%C3%A9bec%20By%20Mathieu%20No%C3%ABl%2C%20under,in%20which%20French%20is%20the%20sole%20official%20language

Mendes, E. (2007). The Charter and its constitutional lineage: An evolving template of distributive justice for reconciling diversity, collective rights of national minorities and individual rights? *National Journal of Constitutional Law, 22*(1), 61–92.

Miller, D. (2002). Group rights, human rights and citizenship. *European Journal of Philosophy, 10*(2), 178–195.

Monahan, P. (1987). *Politics and the Constitution: The Charter, federalism, and the Supreme Court of Canada*. Carswell.

Ramcharan, B.G. (1993) Individual, collective and group rights: History, theory, practice and contemporary evolution. *International Journal on Minority and Group Rights, 1*(1), 27–44.

Richez, E. (2010, June). *The impact of Charter-based judicial review on social citizenship in Canada: The Case of Health Care Litigation*. [Conference presentation]. Canadian Political Science Association 82nd Annual Conference, Concordia University, Montreal.

Rousseau, G., & Côté, F. (2017). A distinctive Quebec theory and practice of the notwithstanding clause: When collective interests outweigh individual rights. *Revue generale de droit, 47*(2), 343–431. doi: 10.7202/1042928ar

Samson, M., & Langevin, L. (2015). Revisiting Quebec's jus commune in the era of the human rights Charters. *American Journal of Comparative Law, 63*(3), 719–746.

Sanders, D. (1991). Collective rights. *Human Rights Quarterly, 13*(3), 368–386. doi:10.2307/762620

Taylor, C. (1994). The politics of recognition. In A. Gutmann (Ed.), *Multiculturalism: Examining the politics of recognition* (pp. 25–74). (Expanded paperback edition). Princeton University Press.

Tomuschat, C. (1983). Protection of minorities under Article 27 of International Covenant on Civil and Political Rights. In R. Bernhardt et al. (Eds.), *Völkerrecht als Rechtsordnung Internationale Gerichtsbarkeit Menschenrechte* (pp. 950–979). Springer.

Truth and Reconciliation Commission of Canada. (2015). *Calls to action*. http://trc.ca/assets/pdf/Calls_to_Action_English2.pdf

Walzer, M. (1982). *Pluralism in political perspective: The politics of ethnicity*. Cambridge: Harvard University Press.

LEGISLATION

Canadian Charter of Rights and Freedoms, s 23, Part 1 of the *Constitution Act, 1982*, being Schedule B to the *Canada Act 1982* (UK), 1982, c 11.

Charter of Human Rights and Freedoms, CQLR c C-12.

Charter of the French Language, CQLR c C-11.

Constitution Act, 1982, Schedule B to the *Canada Act 1982* (UK), 1982, c 11.

Metis Settlements Act (Alberta), RSA 2000, c M 14.

Universal Declaration of Human Rights, GA Res 217A (III), UNGAOR, 3rd Sess, Supp No 13, UN Doc A/810 (1948) 71 [UDHR].

JURISPRUDENCE

Alberta (Aboriginal Affairs and Northern Development) v Cunningham, 2011 SCC 37.

Alberta v Hutterian Brethren of Wilson Colony, 2009 SCC 37, [2009] 2 SCR 567.

Alcoholism Foundation of Manitoba v Winnipeg (City), 69 DLR (4th) 697, 1990 CanLII 8022 (MB CA).

American Freedom Defence Initiative v Edmonton (City), 2016 ABQB 555.

Andrews v Law Society of British Columbia, [1989] 1 SCR 143, 56 DLR (4th).

Canada (Attorney General) v JTI-Macdonald Corp, [2007] 2 SCR 610.

Canadian Newspapers Co v Victoria (City), [1991] BCCAAA No 147, 1991 CarswellBC 2467.

Chamberlain v Surrey School District No. 36, [2002] 4 SCR.

Congrégation des témoins de Jéhovah de St-Jérôme-Lafontaine v Lafontaine (Village), 2004 SCC 48.

Dhillon v British Columbia (Ministry of Transportation & Highways), [1999] BCHRTD No 25, CarswellBC 3191.

Dunmore v Ontario (Attorney General), 2001 SCC 94.

Edmonton Journal v Alberta (Attorney General), [1989] 2 SCR.

Ford v Quebec (Attorney General), [1988] 2 SCR 712, 54 DLR (4th) 577.

Haida Nation v British Columbia (Minister of Forests), [2004] 3 SCR 511.

Law Society of British Columbia v Trinity Western University, 2018 SCC 32, [2018] 2 SCR 293.

Mahe v Alberta, [1990] 1 SCR 342 1990, 68 DLR (4th).

Miller v Mohawk Council of Kahnawà:ke, 2018 QCCS 1784.

Mounted Police Association of Ontario v Canada, 2015 SCC 1.

Multani v Commission scolaire Marguerite-Bourgeoys, [2006] 1 SCR 256.

Neskonlith Indian Band v Salmon Arm (City), 2012 BCCA 379.

Rio Tinto Alcan Inc. v Carrier Sekani Tribal Council, 2010 SCC 43.

Rosenberg v Outremont (City), [2001] RJQ 1556, 2001 CanLII 25087.

R v Big M Drug Mart Ltd., [1985] 1 SCR 295, 18 DLR (4th) 321.

R v Kapp, 2008 SCC 41.

R v Mader's Tobacco Store Ltd, 2013 NSPC 29.

R v Oakes, [1986] 1 SCR 103, 26 DLR (4th) 200 (SCC).

R v Pinehouse Plaza Pharmacy Ltd, [1988] SJ No 232, [1988] 3 WWR 705.

R v Sparrow, [1990] 1 SCR 1075.

R v Van der Peet, [1996] 2 SCR 507, 137 DLR (4th) 289.

Syndicat Northcrest v Amselem, [2004] 2 SCR 551.

Thomas v Norris, [1992] 2 CNLR 139, 1992 CarswellBC 740.

Tsilhqot'in Nation v British Columbia, 2014 SCC 44.

Ville de Montréal v Centre islamique Badr, 2017 QCCS 57.

Withler v Canada (Attorney General), 2011 SCC 12, [2011] 1 SCR 396.

5
HUMAN RIGHTS AND CANADIAN MUNICIPALITIES

SANDEEP AGRAWAL
—

Introduction

Applying human rights legislation to government action—including challenges to municipal action—is a growing concern. Government action that is consistent with human rights legislation is a constitutional requirement and, above all, a moral issue. Within such a context this chapter evaluates the soundness of plans and bylaws of Alberta municipalities in relation to the *Alberta Human Rights Act*[1] and the *Canadian Charter of Rights and Freedoms*.[2] It methodically analyzes a select set of municipal plans and municipal bylaws, such as zoning and community standards, as well as the narrative data from interviews with key informants in five major cities and five rural municipalities across Alberta.

The chapter begins with a background on the legislative context of human rights, including the *Alberta Human Rights Act*. It then describes how the study was conducted and details its findings. Much of the human rights issues at the municipal level concern affordable and social housing, such as secondary suites, permanent supportive housing, and group homes. Following this are new emerging issues associated with locating safe injection sites, methadone clinics, and marijuana retail and production places. The chapter concludes by sketching two broad sets of patterns observed across Alberta: (1) increasing challenges to municipal bylaws based on Sections 2, 7, and/or 15 of the *Charter* and court decisions in favour of protecting these rights; and (2) enactment of new federal legislation or amendments to existing federal regulations, resulting in new land uses that did not exist in the zoning bylaws.

Legislative Context of Human Rights

Human rights are the rights an individual has by virtue of being human; they represent one's dignity and are the equal, inalienable, and universal rights of all human beings. In Canada these rights are entrenched in the Constitution through the *Canadian Charter of Rights and Freedoms*. The *Charter* sets out the rights and freedoms of people *only* in relation to government activities, which distinguishes it from the quasi-constitutional legislation—the federal, provincial, and territorial human rights acts—that encompasses both private and public acts.

Constitutional guarantees are not, however, absolute. Section 1 of the *Charter* places "reasonable limits [on rights] prescribed by law as can be demonstrably justified in a free and democratic society." Section 32 of the *Charter* declares that it applies to the legislature and government of each province in all matters within the authority of the legislature of each province. Laws, including municipal government bylaws, that are inconsistent with the *Charter* or human rights legislation may be declared invalid and may lead to the payment of damages or other remedies. The Supreme Court of Canada decision *Godbout v Longueuil (City)*[3] established that municipalities are also subject to the *Charter*.

As the *Charter* does not apply to non-governmental activities, interactions *between individuals and organizations* (such as those between individuals and employers or landlords) are governed instead by human rights legislation, such as the *Alberta Human Rights Act*. However, regional human rights legislation and the *Charter* may overlap when an act of government occurs in an employment context or when services, facilities, or accommodations are provided by the federal, provincial, or municipal government. The following two subsections briefly describe the *Alberta*

Human Rights Act and the *Alberta Bill of Rights*, which seemingly guarantees property rights in Alberta.

Alberta Human Rights Act

The *Alberta Human Rights Act* has evolved over the years. The birth of the Act goes back to 1966 when the Alberta legislature passed it as a part of the nationwide effort to promote awareness of human rights. It was intended as a comprehensive system for dealing with discrimination, but it was understaffed, with only a single administrator. Fortunately, in 1972 the province strengthened the legislation by creating a human rights commission and by hiring staff to administer it. In 2000 the *Individual Rights Protection Act* of 1972 was renamed the *Alberta Human Rights Act* (henceforth, AHRA).

It is noteworthy that the Act was contested in the late 1990s for continuing to exclude sexual orientation as a ground of discrimination. The Supreme Court of Canada ruled in 1998 that the Act's omission of sexual orientation violated the *Charter*. The Act was eventually amended in 2009 to include protection against sexual orientation. Another amendment was added in 2015 to include gender identity and expression as further prohibited grounds of discrimination. The Act went through yet another amendment recently, following a court ruling in 2017, to add age as a prohibited ground of discrimination.

Alberta Bill of Rights

The *Alberta Bill of Rights*, enacted in 1972, is unique. The bill still exists alongside the AHRA, while carrying overlapping rights. Except for the federal government's *Canadian Bill of Rights* and the *Alberta Bill of Rights*, other provinces and territories, like Ontario and Quebec, have combined their bill and act provisions into one human rights act (or code).

The *Alberta Bill of Rights* contains only rights and freedoms extended or guaranteed by the Crown to individuals (and not corporations). It is a statute that imposes limits on the Alberta legislature only and can be overridden by the legislature as per the notwithstanding clause in Section 2 of the bill.[4] Usually, many of the rights and freedoms in a region's bill of rights[5] are guaranteed in the *Charter* and/or provincial and territorial acts. However, the *Alberta Bill of Rights* provides for the right to "enjoyment of property," which is not covered by the *Charter*, placing the bill at odds with the constitutional provision to Canadians. Also, the Alberta bill does not have a limitation clause similar to that of Section 1 of the Canadian *Charter*. So, in theory, it grants more rights than the *Charter* does.

The *Alberta Bill of Rights*' lack of status as ordinary non-entrenched legislation has resulted in a conservative approach to its interpretation (Bowal & Thul, 2013). The courts have generally avoided giving priority to the *Bill of Rights* so as to respect legislative supremacy (Greene, 2014);[6] in other words, the *Bill of Rights* is generally interpreted in such a way that it does do not take priority over other statutes.[7] The repeal of the *Communal Property Act* is the only significant example that relied on showing an alleged violation of the *Alberta Bill of Rights*, in that the Act was being used to restrict the growth of Hutterite communities. These interpretations[8] underscore Section 1a of the *Alberta Bill of Rights*, which allows the legislature to override the right of the individual to liberty, security of the person, and enjoyment of property by due process of law, as is the case with the *Canadian Bill of Rights* of 1960.

Municipal Planning and Human Rights Legislation

Many municipalities across Canada, irrespective of size or urban or rural status, face serious human rights challenges. Some of the areas where human rights have influenced land use regulations concern use restriction, limitations on numbers, parking standards, separation distances, and age restrictions. Many municipalities have responded to these issues with appropriate changes to their zoning bylaws. In several other jurisdictions, however, the issues remain very much alive. Toronto, Sarnia, Kitchener, and Smith Falls, for example, were all challenged, based on the definition of group homes and associated separation distances.[9] Delta, British Columbia, had a bylaw that allowed secondary suites only when occupied by family members—this was quashed by the Supreme Court of British Columbia.[10] Similarly, the Human Rights Tribunal found the mayor of Kelowna, BC, guilty of violating the *B.C. Human Rights Code* when he refused to proclaim gay pride week in the city.[11]

In Calgary, Edmonton, and Red Deer, issues of locating group homes and supportive housing have surfaced.[12] In Edmonton this author[13] argued against the pause on funding for supportive and affordable housing in certain inner-city neighbourhoods,[14] asserting that this was a violation of human rights. Calgary's issues have focused on the prohibition of secondary suites and livestock within the city limits. As well, the Calgary water safety bylaw was unsuccessfully challenged in the court as *ultra vires*[15] because it required the wearing of a personal flotation device in waterways, which was over and above the federal requirement.[16] As well, other real and alleged planning and human rights violations have come to light in Alberta cities.

Method

This study used a mixed-methods approach. It analyzed the literature collected on human rights and planning jurisprudence and the case law pertaining to Alberta municipalities. The legal analysis looked for potential human rights violations in municipal development plans and zoning bylaws. This was layered with semi-structured interviews with human rights advocates and city officials of five large cities (Edmonton, Calgary, Red Deer, Lethbridge, and Medicine Hat) and five municipal districts in Alberta (Red Deer County, Parkland County, Grande Prairie County, Lethbridge County, and Clearwater County). A few interviews were conducted in large cities outside of Alberta—Vancouver, Toronto, and Montreal—to contextualize and compare the findings with other parts of the country. These interviews were conducted in 2017 and 2018.

Findings

The study elicits possible concerns related to the *Charter* and human rights legislation violations in several areas. The bulk of the human rights issues that emerged in the study concern the provision of affordable and social housing, such as secondary suites, permanent supportive housing, and group homes. The next most common set of issues relates to locating safe injection sites, methadone clinics, and marijuana retail and production places. Freedom of expression issues in public spaces and on public properties, and issues concerning keeping livestock within the city limits, constitute the last group of concerns.

Housing
Secondary Suites
Restriction on developing secondary suites in certain parts of Calgary has been a perennial issue and has been repeatedly raised as a human rights issue by Calgarians, human rights advocates, and the Calgary mayor himself. The human rights aspect resides in how the ban on secondary suites restricts access to affordable housing. The new Calgary city council, however, took an extraordinary step in December 2017 (at the time the study was being conducted), making secondary suites a discretionary use across the city. Previously these units had been prohibited, especially in areas zoned for low density, single-detached housing residential districts, such as R-1, R-C1, and R-C1L, which constitute large sections of the city. This change from prohibited to discretionary use means that secondary suites can be handled by a normal development review process, without homeowners having to go to the city council for approval. Although still not straightforward, the revised process of discretionary use saves some time for applicants from a drawn-out and onerous approval process.

Supportive Housing
Supportive housing is a type of housing that provides permanent, affordable housing to at-risk populations under the supervision of on-site staff. Restrictive provisions in municipal bylaws affect the location and inhabitants of supportive and affordable housing, thereby turning the restrictions into a human rights issue. In several large and small municipalities across the country the most contentious issue concerns the placement of co-owned housing,[19] communal dwellings or cohousing,[20] rooming and lodging houses,[21] and transitional housing.[22] The issues related to group homes are explained later in the chapter. Some possible concerns in Alberta are related to the following aspects.

Direct Control Zones

Direct control (DC) zones are areas in which a municipality wishes to exercise control over the use and development of land or buildings. The uses in Calgary, such as emergency and temporary shelters, fall under the DC zones—which require the city council's approval. This practice adds time, costs, and potential barriers to services intended to most likely shelter *Charter*-protected groups, such as people with disabilities, persons of colour, or those with ethnic backgrounds. Thus, in Calgary, issues pertinent to DC land use zones are of interest to housing advocates.

No Specific Zones

One key problem that the Edmonton-based housing providers and advocates mentioned in the interviews is that very few sites in the city are zoned appropriately to allow for the building of permanent supportive housing across the city. Since most of Edmonton's neighbourhoods are zoned for single-detached housing, every multi-unit, high-density supportive-housing project requires a rezoning process, and a rezoning exercise for affordable housing is a hard and lengthy struggle. In Edmonton, getting a "buy-in" from the community regarding supportive-housing projects has also been a major challenge. At times the projects become embroiled in protracted legal battles with the community, resulting in further consternation and mistrust between the parties involved.

No Clear Land Use Definition

Another supportive-housing issue that the study informants identified is the absence of land use class definitions of supportive housing, especially in Edmonton's zoning bylaw. The supportive-housing use does not fit into any existing residential or other use definitions because of the unique nature of this housing and the combination of uses involved. As well, the building usually has independent units with a common kitchen and community spaces. As a result, several uses can be combined in a congregate-living setting. Some permanent supportive-housing programs also offer meals, peer-support programs, case management, and social activities, along with addiction, mental health, and health or medical services.

From the zoning perspective, because permanent supportive housing does not have its own classification, it straddles several already defined classes of use, including the following:

- apartment housing (because of the presence of multiple dwelling units);
- congregate living (because occupants share access to facilities like cooking, dining, laundry, or sanitary facilities);
- special residential facilities like group homes and lodging houses;
- extended medical treatment services, such as hospitals, sanitariums, isolation facilities, psychiatric hospitals, and detoxification centres.

For neighbourhood residents, all these uses—when linked together in supportive housing—raise red flags. Similarly, for the city's development authority these uses are exceptions to the rules prescribed in the city's zoning bylaw and thus warrant extra scrutiny.

The closest definition in Edmonton's zoning to supportive housing is "supportive community provision," which applies to apartment housing or group homes. This provision adds special criteria that the project must meet, such as indoor common space and amenities and outside landscaping, while incentivizing the development by allowing extra density and reduced parking. This use should also provide further additional benefits to developers to spur their interest.

In 2020, the city council created the new supportive housing use that encapsulates the temporary shelter services, seniors' housing and hospice care, group homes, and limited group home uses—allowing them as permitted use in many zones across the city. The rationale for the changes was to remove current barriers and align the zoning bylaw with a modern human rights–based approach to land use planning. Still, other forms of housing such as lodging houses have problems finding locations (City of Edmonton, 2020).

Calgary appears to have a slightly better approach to such situations. Its zoning includes definitions for multi-residential, apartment-style housing, and residential care that takes the form of on-site health and social support. It also allows up to 10 units, with one parking stall for three residents on the site in all residential zones. The residential care is, however, a discretionary use in the residential building; the city development officer is the individual with authority to approve this use, based on the compatibility, character, and other factors involved.

The advantage of having a zoning class of its own is that no barriers exist in constructing supportive housing. With such a unique zoning class, relevant projects would just need a development permit without going before council rezoning. In Calgary, while this permit may be appealed by the neighbours, the overall process is not as onerous as it is in Edmonton.

Lacking Strong Legal Ground

The housing advocates in Edmonton shared that it was difficult for them to challenge a rejection of a permanent supportive-housing project in the courts on human rights or *Charter* grounds. They argued that this was partly because either the project did not yet exist, or no units had been built at the time of an application being made to the court. Above all, no actual real-life clients existed who were being discriminated against.

Whether this argument holds any merit from a legal perspective remains an open question. A large body of case law exists on legal challenges to the municipal approval (or rejection) of development projects, based on a myriad of reasons: for instance, lack of due process, error in the application of relevant law, and/or jurisdictional overreach (*ultra vires*).

If we look at the issue raised by the housing advocates from the "standing" point of view,[23] two recent court decisions—*Abbotsford (City) v Shantz*[24] and *Downtown Eastside Sex Workers United Against Violence Society v Canada (Attorney General)*[25]—are important to cite. Both cases affirm a *liberal and purposive* approach to public interest standing. Public interest litigation allows a person or organization to bring a case, notwithstanding their lack of direct involvement in the matter or any infringement of their personal rights.

In *Abbotsford*[26] the British Columbia/Yukon Association of Drug War Survivors and the British Columbia Civil Liberties Association were granted the public interest standing to challenge the constitutionality of city bylaws that endangered lives of homeless people. In the *Downtown Eastside Sex Workers* case, the court granted an advocacy group, the Downtown Eastside Sex Workers United Against Violence Society,[27] the standing to challenge a broad range of laws against prostitution on the basis that they infringed several of their members' *Charter* rights. Noteworthy here is that these two judgments could help the housing advocates' standing to mount a legal challenge on behalf of their future clients.

Group Homes

Group homes are another form of supportive housing,[28] the location of which has raised issues across Canada. Alberta municipalities are no exception to this, with two specific issues documented in Red Deer and Edmonton. Red Deer has struggled over whether to allow a special form of group home in a residential area for people who have very severe mental health issues, so much so that the residents of the facility need to be physically restrained for their own safety, and the facility needs to be fitted with bullet-proof windows. This is an especially interesting example because the zoning actually allows these group homes to be situated right in the residential areas. The occupants of these group homes, however, might not be appropriate for living in such a residential setting.

The zoning in Red Deer is partially a product of its history of having Michener Centre in the city since 1923. Michener Centre is a government-run, residential facility for people with developmental disabilities. Furthermore, many social agencies look to locate these homes in Red Deer because of facilities and related supports that are already available in the city. Owing to this long institutional presence and other similar facilities, the City of Red Deer has had extensive experience in accommodating very complex special needs cases.

The Edmonton zoning has undergone its own set of changes in dealing with issues of group homes. In 1983 the city added the "limited group homes" zoning use class. In 2010, in response to a *Charter* challenge, the city removed user characteristics from this definition, as well as the minimum separation distance (MSD) of 150 metres. Nevertheless, in 2012, zoning was amended only to add new neighbourhood- and block-level thresholds to limit the number of group homes in a neighbourhood.

The current zoning allows group homes in almost all residential zones, as either permitted or discretionary use. The Edmonton zoning does not use an MSD between group homes to restrict the number of group homes, which is, or was, the case in many other municipalities across Canada. To avoid overconcentration, it limits their numbers in a neighbourhood by the following three criteria:

- A maximum of three facilities per 1,000 residents of a neighbourhood;
- Two facilities on a block in a residential zone;
- Twelve residents (discretionary use) and 30 residents (permitted use) in opposing block faces in a residential zone.

It is not clear whether this kind of restriction on the number of group homes in a neighbourhood contravenes human and *Charter* rights. Case law suggests that overconcentration of a use can be reason for a municipality to establish certain thresholds.[29]

Homelessness and Tent Cities

The tent-city phenomenon is not new to Canadian cities. By some accounts, the size of tent cities has increased over the years in places like Vancouver and Toronto. Edmonton and Calgary have long grappled with the emergence of such squatters, and have seen a rise in them, along with illegal camping in parks and river valleys and under city bridges. Housing advocates attribute this to rising homelessness coupled with a limited capacity of city-run emergency shelters, along with the limited supply of new supportive housing. In 2017, several tent-city residents were evicted from Calgary's Shaganappi Point Golf Course, just southwest of the downtown core, and from Edmonton's North Saskatchewan river valley. As recently as 2021, the raging pandemic and the limited capacity of the shelter system pushed more people to find shelter in encampments. Evictions from these encampments made their situation worse (Snowdon, 2021).

Such evictions may contravene *Charter* rights, just as what happened in *Abbotsford*[30] and *Victoria*.[31] In these tent-city cases the courts said that the homeless have a constitutionally protected right under Section 7 of the *Charter* to erect a temporary shelter and sleep overnight in parks. Neither of the two decisions, however, affirm that Section 7 grants the homeless with a constitutionally protected right to adequate food or shelter or any other necessities of life. Further, the cases do not impose any obligation on a municipality to provide individuals with adequate shelter.

These two decisions aligned with the Ontario Court of Appeal's decision in *Tanudjaja v Canada (Attorney General)*,[32] which upheld a Superior Court of Ontario's decision to strike an application brought under Section 7 of the *Charter*. This application sought to require the federal government and the Ontario government to provide "affordable, adequate, accessible housing."

Balancing the Rights of Charter-Protected and Other Groups

The issue here is how to balance the rights of an average Canadian with that of a *Charter*-protected group, such as Indigenous Peoples, in combatting a serious social problem such as homelessness. A study participant from a rural county raised this matter. How does a municipality prioritize one group's needs over another when providing accommodation and services? Alternatively, how does a municipality tackle a need that is more severe within the general population—in other words, one that is not specific to the *Charter*-protected group? One solution may lie in a collaboration of First Nations reserves and municipal governments so that together they can provide housing for both groups, rather than providing shelter exclusively for either group.

Definition of Uses

The analysis of zoning bylaws elicits three possible issues. Of note, at the time of the study, the City of Edmonton took the extraordinary step of comprehensively reviewing its zoning bylaws and making necessary adjustments to ensure consistency with the *Charter* and the AHRA.

Reference to User Characteristics

The study identified issues with the definitions of permanent supportive-housing facilities in the municipal zoning bylaws of Grande Prairie County, Calgary, Red Deer, and Lethbridge. These definitions explicitly identify *the users* of these facilities. However, by regulating users rather than *the use*, the bylaws could be declared as *ultra vires* (Agrawal, 2014). Some excerpts of the bylaws are below (the italicized text highlights potentially objectionable phrases):

> "Social Care Facility" means:
> a) places of care for persons who are *aged or infirm* or who require special care or a day care facility;
> b) a building or part of a building, other than a home maintained by a person to whom the children living in that home are *related by blood or marriage*, in which care, supervision or lodging is provided for four (4) or more children under the age of 18 years, but does not include a place of accommodation designated by the Minister of Family and Social Services as not constituting a child care institution; or
> c) a hostel or other establishment operated to provide accommodation and maintenance for *unemployed or indigent persons*. [Grande Prairie County]

> "Assisted Living Facility" means a building, or a portion of a building, operated for the purpose of providing live-in accommodation for six or more persons with chronic or declining conditions requiring professional care or supervision or ongoing medical care, nursing or homemaking services or for persons generally requiring specialized care. [Red Deer]

"Group Home" means development using a dwelling for a residential social care facility providing rehabilitative, and/or supportive care for 4 to 10 persons who, by *reason of their emotional, mental, social or physical condition*, require a supervised group living arrangement. [Lethbridge]

Restrictions on Who Can Occupy Which Type of Housing
Zoning here considers who can live in which type of housing. The following example is from Red Deer, which could potentially violate the *Charter* and the AHRA because of the nature of restrictions placed on the type of individuals who can occupy garden suites: "Garden Suites residence is restricted just to 'elderly parents' or 'cognitively impaired adult' of the registered owner."

Minimum Separation Distance
Zoning bylaws that take up the issue of minimum separation distance are concerned with prescribing MSDs to dissuade concentration of one type of use, especially when the use is permanent supportive housing. MSDs for certain controversial uses, such as adult mini-theatres and liquor stores, are common in the case studies. It might be challenging for municipalities to defend MSDs based on a planning rationale.

Keeping Livestock within the City Limits
The issue of keeping livestock within the city limits—such as bees, chicken, sheep, and other animals—has come up often in the last few years as a human rights issue. The rules surrounding backyard chickens vary across the country, with only a few major Canadian cities allowing them. Keeping chickens in the backyard is legal in cities such as Vancouver, Victoria, Kelowna, Surrey, and Montreal, but Toronto, Ottawa, Calgary, Halifax, Winnipeg, Regina, and Saskatoon prohibit the practice at the time of writing this chapter. As of 2015, a few Alberta cities, such as Grande Prairie, Airdrie, Peace River, and Fort Saskatchewan, allow the keeping of chickens within their municipal limits, although Edmonton and Calgary did not (McKechnie, 2015). Municipalities argue that keeping livestock in urban settings can present public health or cleanliness concerns.

A human and *Charter* rights case related to keeping livestock arose in Calgary a few years ago.[33] A city resident kept chickens in the backyard of his residential property in violation of the city's bylaw that prohibits this practice. He was fined by the city for illegal urban livestock operations, but he challenged the bylaw, arguing that it affected his right to make decisions about what he eats and what he grows or produces—in breach of his rights under Sections 2 and 7 of the *Charter* and human rights legislation. The city, however, argued that having a livestock (such as the chickens) within the urban area was considered a nuisance in terms of noise, odours, or accumulation of waste. The provincial court found the defendant guilty and ruled that the bylaw did not infringe upon the defendant's *Charter* rights. The issue of raising hens in backyards came to the city council for a vote in 2015, the second time in five years, but the council again rejected the idea.

Also in 2015, an urban farmer in Edmonton faced a fine of $500 per sheep (or $25,000 for 50 sheep) after a bylaw officer found him in contravention of the city's *Animal Licensing and Control Bylaw* that prohibits keeping any livestock—which is any large animal over 10 kilograms (in the case of Edmonton)—on residential property (Lazzarino, 2015). As of 2015, while keeping sheep is against city regulations, Edmonton allows residents to keep other creatures, including bees. A pilot project is currently underway to study the potential issues and concerns that are associated with keeping urban hens. As of May 2019, all backyard chicken coops are allowed in Edmonton. Limits are still in place for the number of pigeons or dogs one can keep at a property.

Freedom of Expression
Several *Charter* challenges have also taken up concerns with the use of public space by politically or religiously oriented signage or behaviour. Here are a few examples.[33]

Calgary
An Alberta provincial court decision upheld the city's traffic bylaw,[34] which prohibits joining or interfering with a parade or special roadway

event. Its violation is punishable by a maximum fine of $10,000 and costs, and up to 60 days imprisonment in default of payment. This bylaw was the basis for a street preacher to be charged with causing extreme noise and trespassing on the city's Stampede Parade. It was arguably the most highly visible challenge brought to a city bylaw, based on *Charter* Section 2(b), with an allegation that the *Charter* rights of freedom of religion and freedom of expression were infringed upon. The court decision stated that such a limitation is reasonable and demonstrably justified in a free and democratic society.

Edmonton

The Alberta Queen's Bench 2016 decision[35] required removal of an American Freedom Defence Initiative advertising sign that made explicit references to the honour killings of Muslim girls. Under *Charter* Section 1 the courts concluded that the city's policy imposed a reasonable limit that is justified in a free and democratic society.

Grande Prairie

An Alberta Queen's Bench decision[36] supported the city's refusal to allow a pro-life advertisement on the city buses.

Red Deer, Leduc, and Mountain View Counties and
Municipal District of Foothills

According to one of the study participants, Red Deer, Leduc, and Mountain View counties have teamed up to assert their authority to regulate and enforce their respective municipal bylaws on the type and number of signs on private properties along provincial highways, at the sections that pass within their municipal boundaries. In 2019, Foothills followed suit and prohibited signs attached to trailers or vehicles unless they are advertising the business for which the vehicle is being used.
The private landowners and signage companies claimed that the municipal prohibition of signs along the highway, which should be a provincial matter, violates their freedom of expression. While the provincial government has authority over land immediately adjacent to provincial roads,

it has deferred actions on signage to local governments. In the lawsuit against Foothills, the court ruled that although the vehicle signs are protected by Section 2(b) of the *Charter*, the local government's restriction on unattractive or distracting forms of advertising is a reasonable limit under Section 1 of the *Charter*.[37]

Effect of Changes in Federal Regulations

Recent changes to federal regulations related to safe injection sites, methadone clinics, and the consumption of marijuana have precipitated the need for the creation of new land uses at the municipal level. All of these federal regulatory changes emanated from legal decisions in which, under *Charter* Section 7, the courts found the benefits of safe injection sites,[38] methadone clinics, or marijuana use outweighed any potential detriment to the community or to society.

Safe Injection Sites

Municipal authorities must heed the Supreme Court decision when dealing with land use decisions related to safe injection sites.[39] If the public is not consulted or involved in siting such facilities, municipalities may run into tough opposition from their residents. For instance, a proposal by Edmonton City Council to place three of the four Health Canada–approved safe injection sites in the inner-city neighbourhoods came under fire from the residents of Chinatown in the area. In 2017 the residents applied to the federal court, seeking a judicial review of the federal health minister's decision to approve safe injection sites in Edmonton. They termed the city's decision "systemic ghettoization" of their neighbourhood, which they felt was already overrun by shelter beds and social agencies (Theobald, 2017). In 2019 the federal court allowed the requested locations of safe injection facilities, dismissing the argument that the residents were unfairly burdened by the facilities.[40]

Methadone Clinics

The location of methadone clinics is a persistent issue in many municipalities across Canada.[41] In Ontario the *Human Rights Code* covers a broad range and degree of disabilities, including addictions.[42] On this basis the Ontario Human Rights Commission advises several Ontario municipalities not to discriminate against people with addictions through restrictive zoning regulations for the methadone clinics; instead, the commission suggests including them as "medical clinics."

Relocating methadone clinics in the downtown areas of several Alberta municipalities, such as Lethbridge and Calgary, has become an issue as well. In Lethbridge, businesses in the area were opposed to the siting of such clinics because existing issues with the homeless, street drug users, panhandlers, and vandalism would be compounded by the clinics, which they argued would attract more opioid-addictive users. However, zoning in Lethbridge did allow such clinics as a right.

Marijuana for Medical Purposes
The new federal *Access to Cannabis for Medical Purposes Regulations* of 2016, which replaced the *Marijuana for Medical Purposes Regulations* (MMPR), responded to two court decisions that stated that the MMPR must allow reasonable access to marijuana[43] to protect the right to security as set out in Section 7 of the *Charter*.

Health Canada now requires applicants to meet existing municipal regulations pertaining to medical marijuana facilities. If no such regulations exist, Health Canada can still approve a facility without prior site approval from municipalities. Future marijuana grow operations could be seriously affected either by the absence of land use regulation or by overly rigid municipal restrictions—currently the case in many Ontario municipalities—which could lead to human rights challenges.

The Alberta Urban Municipalities Association (AUMA), now Alberta Municipalities, asked municipalities in its 2014 report to develop a specific land use class to regulate the siting and operation of medical marijuana production facilities (AUMA, 2014). This should be in place before the possibility of a production facility arises. They also suggested municipalities use their *Community Standards Bylaw*, which is intended to regulate the conduct of production facilities based on noise, odour, and unsightly appearance.

The Alberta Association of Municipal Districts and Counties (AAMDC), now Rural Municipalities of Alberta, issued a similar cautionary note to Alberta's rural communities, warning its membership to proactively address the siting of the facilities through land use bylaws (AAMDC, 2015). If a municipality does not have a land use bylaw in place that specifically addresses medical marijuana facilities prior to a development application being submitted, municipalities may miss their opportunity to have a say in the location of such facilities. AAMDC drew attention to potential negative externalities that the marijuana grow-ops carry with them, just like any other industrial operation. For example, if municipalities prefer that these facilities be situated in industrial-zoned areas rather than in agricultural areas, they must develop bylaws that establish this.

Marijuana for Recreational Purposes

A recent decision by the federal government to legalize marijuana for recreational purposes added further complications to municipal land use regulations because marijuana could be grown at home as of July 1, 2018. The federal decision, as well as corresponding provincial legislative changes to the sale, purchase, possession, and consumption of cannabis, affects municipalities in several ways, including land use management, business licensing, bylaws, public health and education, law enforcement, and human resource policies.

Both the AUMA and the AAMDC call for sufficient fire and building codes to regulate the growing of marijuana, particularly in residential properties. This is to ensure that current and prospective property owners are protected from the adverse effects that home growing can create. The Federation of Canadian Municipalities further suggests that land use planning bylaws, such as MSDs, need to be put in place to limit the proximity of cannabis dispensaries to schools and playgrounds (Federation of Canadian Municipalities, 2017). They can also define and classify cannabis retail and lounge facilities distinctly from other zoning categories like general retail, where alcohol sales are permitted.

Community Standards Bylaws

Community Standards bylaws in Alberta municipalities have a long and contentious history. They attempt to regulate individuals' behaviour and activities in public spaces, based on local standards of social and moral values, and issues related to the maintenance of private properties. They can regulate noise, graffiti, panhandling, littering, and loitering; they also place limits on public assembly. Critics argue that sections of the bylaws, such as those that put limits on peaceful assembly, go against the *Charter*, which allows "freedom of peaceful assembly" as a fundamental freedom assured to Canadians.

These bylaws came to greater public attention when a southern Alberta municipality, the Town of Taber, enacted a *Community Standards Bylaw* in 2015 that implemented a curfew period during which minors were not allowed in public places unaccompanied by an adult (CBC News, 2015). The bylaw puts strict restrictions on acceptable behaviour in public places, such as prohibitions on spitting, assembly, and panhandling.

Of note, it is not just Taber that developed this bylaw. A few other Alberta municipalities had similar bylaws in their books, long before Taber enacted its own. We located sections in municipalities such as the City of Red Deer, Strathcona County, and the Town of Ponoka,[44] which could lead to potential human rights violations. As an example, the following is an excerpt from *Community Standards Bylaw 3383/2007* of the City of Red Deer:

> No person shall be a member of an assembly of three or more persons in any public place or any place to which the public is allowed access where a peace officer has reasonable grounds to believe the assembly will disturb the peace of the neighbourhood, and any such person shall disperse as requested by a peace officer.

Of note is that the enforcement of these bylaws is not widespread, which begs the question of whether these bylaws are even effective or relevant today.

Conclusion

The study set out to evaluate whether the policies and bylaws of Alberta municipalities are consistent with the *Charter* and the AHRA. The findings show that municipal regulations are mostly congruent with the *Charter* and the AHRA. Two factors, in particular, are responsible for the way in which human rights have affected planning at the municipal level:

- increasing challenges to municipal bylaws and decisions based on Sections 2, 7, and/or 15 of the *Charter* and court decisions in favour of protecting these rights; and
- new federal legislation or amendments to existing federal regulations, which resulted from the court rulings that protected Canadians' right to life and security as guaranteed in the *Charter*.

These two factors have prompted municipalities to review, revise, or even rescind existing bylaws, create new land use classes, or revise existing zoning bylaws to accommodate new resulting land uses.

The new federal legislation influenced land use planning at the municipal level in an unprecedented way. At the same time, it gave rise to a new set of human rights issues, such as locating safe injection sites and cannabis dispensaries in the municipal fold. These issues are becoming part of the perennial and outstanding issues of secondary suites, user characteristics, minimum separation distances, and livestock kept within the city limits. All of this makes human rights, now more than ever before, a critical issue at the municipal level.

Nevertheless, over the years, both the province and municipalities have made significant progress on the human rights front. For instance, in the last decade or so the province revised the AHRA to include age (in relation to the provision of goods, services, accommodation, or facilities), sexual orientation, and gender identity, as well as expression, as grounds of discrimination.

Concomitantly, municipalities in Alberta have amended their bylaws to bring them in line with the AHRA and the *Charter*. Interestingly, many significant changes, especially in the provision of affordable and supportive housing, occurred while the study was in progress. For instance, Calgary removed the prohibition on secondary suites in residential areas. Edmonton introduced changes to the group-home use class, created a new use class for supportive housing, and approved the keeping of backyard chickens. Most potential human rights and *Charter* issues in other Alberta municipalities still involve the prohibition or exclusion of definitions of various forms of supportive housing, restrictions on their locations, and the problematic inclusion of user characteristics in the zoning class definitions.

The lack of legal aid services makes it difficult for Albertans to pursue a case on human rights grounds. This essentially amounts to the denial of justice to those who have encountered discrimination. The province is also missing any civil society organizations such as the Pivot Legal Society in British Columbia, which would help marginalized people challenge legislation, policies, or practices that undermine human rights.

The Alberta government's Property Rights Advocate Office documents concerns about individuals' property rights that are affected by various factors, including municipal planning and zoning decisions, and communicates these concerns to the provincial government. It, however, does not provide direct assistance for property rights disputes. The Property Rights Advocate Office could be a place to raise issues that result from the intersection of human rights and municipal planning and zoning. However, because of the lack of direct assistance and the potentially lengthy delays in government action, this office may not be the most effective means to provide immediate remedies.

A service in Alberta, similar to the Ontario Human Rights Legal Support Centre, may be most effective. Ontario's legal centre is a Government of Ontario–funded agency that provides direct legal services to individuals who have experienced discrimination. Such a legal centre could provide advice on human rights inquiries, assist individuals with human rights applications, and even represent applicants at mediations and hearings at the Alberta Human Rights Commission.[45]

NOTES

1. *Alberta Human Rights Act*, RSA 2000, c A-25.5.
2. *Canadian Charter of Rights and Freedoms*, Part I of the *Constitution Act, 1982*, being Schedule B to the *Canada Act 1982* (UK), 1982, c 11.
3. *Godbout v Longueuil (City)*, [1997] 3 SCR 844, 152 DLR (4th) 577 [*Godbout*].
4. Section 2 of the bill says this: "Every law of Alberta shall, unless it is expressly declared by an Act of the Legislature that it operates notwithstanding the Alberta Bill of Rights, be so construed and applied as not to abrogate, abridge or infringe or to authorize the abrogation, abridgment or infringement of any of the rights or freedoms herein recognized and declared."
5. Including the *Canadian Bill of Rights*, 1960, the *Saskatchewan Bill of Rights*, 1947, and the *Alberta Bill of Rights*, 1972.
6. Legislative supremacy provides judges with a guide for ranking legal rules. If a judge encounters a conflict between a statute and a cabinet order, or between a statute and the common law, the statute takes precedence in both cases because legislatures, which create statutes, are superior to cabinets and the judiciary. If there is a conflict between two statutes, the more recent one takes precedence because a current legislature is legally supreme at any given time.
7. *R v Big M. Drug Mart Ltd. et al.*, [1985] 1 SCR 295.
8. *R v Such*, [1992] AWLD 706, 132 AR 323; *Churgin v Calgary (City)*, [1988] 41 Alta. LR (3d) 112, 33 MPLR (2d) 247; and *Trelenberg v Alberta (Minister of Environment)*, [1995] AWLD 815, 31 Alta. LR (3d) 353.
9. The author's report to the City of Toronto was instrumental in obtaining recognition of the group that was inhabiting the group home and in having separation distances between them removed from the bylaw. It also helped in introducing human rights in Ontario's Public Policy Statement. See Agrawal (2013).
10. See *Tenants' Rights Action Coalition v Delta*, 1997 [1997] BCJ No. 2070, 151 DLR (4th) 729.
11. *Okanagan Rainbow Coalition v Kelowna (City)*, 2000 BCHRT 21, 37 CHRR D/122.
12. Supportive housing is a combination of housing and social services meant for those who may have health issues, including addiction or alcoholism, mental health concerns, HIV/AIDS, or diverse disabilities.
13. The author made a deputation to the Edmonton city council on April 12, 2016.
14. Although housing itself is not included as a human right, it has a place within the human rights discussion, especially given that it often applies to groups who are protected under the *Charter* or human rights legislation and who have trouble accessing affordable and safe housing.
15. This is a legal term for going beyond one's legal power or authority.
16. *Alberta v Latouche*, 2010 ABPC 166, [2010] 10 WWR 282.
17. *Calgary (City) v Hughes*, 2012 ABPC 250, [2012] AWLD 4346.

18. *R v Pawlowski*, 2011 ABQB 93, [2011] 6 WWR 83 [*Pawlowski ABQB*]; *R v Pawlowski*, 2014 ABCA 135, [2014] 7 WWR 241 [*Pawlowski ABCA*].
19. Co-ownership is ownership of the same housing, jointly and at the same time, by several persons, each of whom has privately bought a share in the right of ownership.
20. Cohousing is a collection of private homes with shared common facilities, such as a kitchen.
21. A rooming or lodging house is a private house in which rooms are rented to persons unrelated to each other, for living or staying temporarily, who share kitchen and bathroom facilities.
22. Transitional housing refers to temporary accommodations for displaced individuals and families, which also provide some supportive services.
23. *Standing* is the legal term for one's ability to bring a case in court against the conduct of another person.
24. *Abbotsford (City) v Shantz*, 2014 BCSC 2385, [2015] BCWLD 1393 [*Abbotsford*].
25. *Downtown Eastside Sex Workers United Against Violence Society v Canada (Attorney General)*, 2012 SCC 45, [2012] 2 SCR 524 [*Downtown Eastside Sex Workers*].
26. *Abbotsford (City) v Shantz*, 2014 BCSC 2385, [2015] BCWLD 1393.
27. *Downtown Eastside Sex Workers United Against Violence Society v Canada (Attorney General)*, 2012 SCC 45, [2012] 2 SCR 524.
28. Group homes are residential facilities in which a small number of unrelated people in need of care, support, or supervision live together. They include correctional group homes, juvenile group homes, residential care facilities, and group foster homes. The focus here is on residential care facilities.
29. See *Toronto (City) Zoning By-law No. 138-2003* 2004 OMBD No. 280 (*Deveau*); *Advocacy Centre for Tenants Ontario v Kitchener (City)* (2010) OMBD Case No. PL050611.
30. *Abbotsford (City) v Shantz*, 2014 BCSC 2385, [2015] BCWLD 1393.
31. *Victoria (City) v Adams* 2008 BCSC 1363, [2008] BCWLD 7764 [*Victoria BCSC*]; *Victoria (City) v Adams*, 2009 BCCA 563, [2009] BCJ No 2451 [*Victoria BCCA*].
32. *Tanudjaja v Canada (Attorney General)*, 2014 ONCA 852, 123 OR (3d) 161 [*Tanudjaja*].
33. *Calgary (City) v Hughes*, 2012 ABPC 250, [2012] AWLD 4346.
34. *R v Pawlowski*, 2014 ABPC 126, [2014] AWLD 3054.
35. *American Freedom Defence Initiative v Edmonton (City)*, 2016 ABQB 555, [2016] AWLD 4633.
36. *Canadian Centre for Bio-Ethics v Grande Prairie (City)*, 2016 ABQB 734, [2017] 4 WWR 182.
37. *Top v Municipal District of Foothills No. 31*, 2020 ABQB 521.
38. Safe or supervised injection sites are legally sanctioned, medically supervised facilities designed to reduce overdose mortality and communicable diseases through the sharing of needles. These sites provide a hygienic and stress-free environment in which individuals can consume illicit recreational drugs intravenously.
39. *Canada (Attorney General) v PHS Community Services Society*, [2011] SCC 44, [2011] 3 SCR 134.

40. *Chinatown Area Business Association v the Attorney General of Canada and Access to Medically Supervised Injection Services Edmonton*, 2019, FC 236.
41. A methadone clinic is a place where a person who is addicted to opioid-based drugs, such as heroin or prescription painkillers, can receive prescription-based methadone as a method of treatment.
42. See also *Entrop v Imperial Oil Limited*, 2000 CanLII 16800 (Ont. C.A.).
43. *R v Smith*, 2015 SCC 34, [2015] 2 SCR 602; *Allard v Canada*, 2016 FC 236, 263 ACWS (3d) 358.
44. Strathcona County and the Town of Ponoka are outside the scope of the study.
45. This chapter has been updated since it was first written in 2018 to account for some of the recent bylaw changes.

REFERENCES

Agrawal, S. (2013). *Opinion on the provisions of group homes in the city-wide zoning bylaw of the City of Toronto*. Report submitted to the City of Toronto. https://www.toronto.ca/legdocs/mmis/2013/pg/bgrd/backgroundfile-56473.pdf

Agrawal, S. (2014). Balancing municipal planning with human rights: A case study. *Canadian Journal of Urban Research, 23*(1), 1–20.

Alberta Association of Municipal Districts and Counties. (2015). *Marijuana Grow Op and Medical Marijuana Facilities report released*. http://www.aamdc.com/attachments/article/882/07%2029%2015%20Marijuana%20Grow%20Op%20and%20Medical%20Marijuana%20Facilities%20Report%20Released.pdf

Alberta Urban Municipalities Association. (2014). *Municipal Regulation of Federally Licensed Medical Marijuana Production Facilities*. https://www.auma.ca/sites/default/files/Advocacy/Document_library/municipal_tools_for_marijuana_regulation_oct_14.pdf

Bowal, P., & Thul, D. (2013, January 1). Bill of Rights in Canada. *LawNow*. http://www.lawnow.org/bills-of-rights-in-canada/

CBC News. (2015). Taber bylaw bans public swearing, spitting and yelling in Alberta town. https://www.cbc.ca/news/canada/calgary/taber-bylaw-bans-public-swearing-spitting-and-yelling-in-alberta-town-1.2988992

City of Edmonton. (2020). *Text amendments to Zoning Bylaw 12800 to Enable Supportive Housing Developments*.

Federation of Canadian Municipalities. (2017). *Cannabis legalization prime*. https://fcm.ca/Documents/issues/Cannabis_Legislation_Primer_EN.pdf

Greene, I. (2014.) *The Charter of Rights and Freedoms* (2nd ed). Lorimer.

Lazzarino, D. (2015, August 6). Edmonton bylaw officers tell local sheep farmer to get rid of his 50 sheep or face a $500 per animal fine. *Edmonton Sun*. https://edmontonsun.com/2015/08/05/edmonton-bylaw-officers-tell-local-sheep-farmer-to-get-rid-of-his-50-sheep-or-face-a-500-per-animal-fine/wcm/a31e9217-24ff-4481-91e9-44fe29dd27fe

McKechnie, B. (2015, June 16). What you need to know about backyard chickens. *Global News.* https://globalnews.ca/news/2054762/what-you-need-to-know-about-backyard-chickens/

Snowdon, W. (2021). Edmontonians living rough brace for winter as city shelters struggle to meet pandemic demand. *CBC News.* https://www.cbc.ca/news/canada/edmonton/edmonton-homeless-camps-winter-pandemic-strategy-1.6247159

Theobald, C. (2017, June 18). Inner-city communities protest concentration of supervised injection sites. *Edmonton Journal.* https://edmontonjournal.com/news/local-news/inner-city-communities-protest-concentration-of-supervised-injection-sites-in-their-neighbourhoods

LEGISLATION

Alberta Bill of Rights, SA 1972, c 1.

Alberta Human Rights Act, RSA 2000, c A-25.5.

Canadian Bill of Rights, 1960 SC 1960, c 44, s 1(a).

Canadian Charter of Rights and Freedoms, Part I of the *Constitution Act, 1982,* being Schedule B to the *Canada Act 1982* (UK), 1982, c 11.

Saskatchewan Bill of Rights Act, 1947, SS 1947, c. 35.

JURISPRUDENCE

Abbotsford (City) v Shantz, 2014 BCSC 2385, [2015] BCWLD 1393.

Advocacy Centre for Tenants Ontario v Kitchener (City), (2010) OMBD Case No. PL050611.

Alberta v Latouche, 2010 ABPC 166, [2010] 10 WWR 282.

Allard v Canada, 2016 FC 236, 263 ACWS (3d) 358.

American Freedom Defence Initiative v Edmonton (City), 2016 ABQB 555, [2016] AWLD 4633.

Calgary (City) v Hughes, 2012 ABPC 250, [2012] AWLD 4346.

Canada (Attorney General) v PHS Community Services Society, [2011] SCC 44, [2011] 3 SCR 134.

Canadian Centre for Bio-Ethics v Grande Prairie (City), 2016 ABQB 734, [2017] 4 WWR 182.

Chinatown Area Business Association v the Attorney General of Canada and Access to Medically Supervised Injection Services Edmonton, 2019, FC 236.

Churgin v Calgary (City), [1988] 41 Alta. LR (3d) 112, 33 MPLR (2d) 247.

Downtown Eastside Sex Workers United Against Violence Society v Canada (Attorney General), 2012 SCC 45, [2012] 2 SCR 524.

Entrop v Imperial Oil Limited, 2000 CanLII 16800 (Ont. CA).

Godbout v Longueuil (City), [1997] 3 SCR 844, 152 DLR (4th) 577.

Okanagan Rainbow Coalition v Kelowna (City), 2000 BCHRT 21, 37 CHRR D/122.

R v Big M. Drug Mart Ltd. et al., [1985] 1 SCR 295.

R v Pawlowski, 2011 ABQB 93, [2011] 6 WWR 83.

R v Pawlowski, 2014 ABCA 135, [2014] 7 WWR 241.

R v Pawlowski, 2014 ABPC 126, [2014] AWLD 3054.

R v Smith, 2015 SCC 34, [2015] 2 SCR 602.

R v Such, [1992] AWLD 706, 132 AR 323.

Tanudjaja v Canada (Attorney General), 2014 ONCA 852, 123 OR (3d) 161.

Tenants' Rights Action Coalition v Delta, 1997 [1997] BCJ No. 2070, 151 DLR (4th) 729.

Top v Municipal District of Foothills No. 31, 2020 ABQB 521.

Trelenberg v Alberta (Minister of Environment), [1995] AWLD 815, 31 Alta. LR (3d) 353.

Toronto (City) Zoning By-law No. 138-2003 (Re) [2004] OMBD No. 280.

Victoria (City) v Adams, 2008 BCSC 1363 [2008] BCWLD 7764.

Victoria (City) v Adams, 2009 BCCA 563 [2009] BCJ No 2451.

6
BECOMING A HUMAN RIGHTS CITY
Lessons from Edmonton

RENÉE VAUGEOIS
—

Introduction

In March 2005, I had the opportunity become the sole part-time staff member of the John Humphrey Centre for Peace and Human Rights (hereafter the John Humphrey Centre), a fledgling organization working to promulgate the values enshrined within the United Nations' *Universal Declaration on Human Rights* (UDHR). The organization emerged more than 30 years ago in Montreal as a satellite of the Human Rights Education Foundation established by the late John Peters Humphrey, the principal drafter of the UDHR. In 1998, Edmonton hosted the world's largest conference to reflect on the progress of the *Declaration* after 50 years, with attendance of over 700 delegates from 34 countries. Honoured guests who came to Alberta to discuss the state of human rights included (to name just a few) the great Archbishop Desmond Tutu, Mary Robinson, Cindy Gilday, and Antonio Lamer. Through the event it became clear that human rights education was critical to building world peace. Attendees from Edmonton committed to advancing human rights in that city, which led to the establishment of the John Humphrey Centre for Peace and Human Rights.

Since 2005 the core work of the John Humphrey Centre has focused on building from the centre out—that is, building a human rights community. Since its inception the centre's work has grown to cover the province of Alberta, to stretch throughout the prairies, and now to reach across Canada. It made a commitment to build Edmonton as a true "human rights city," a place where everyone participates, belongs, and is included. In doing so, the centre joined an emerging movement of other cities across the world that included Rosario in Argentina and Graz in Austria, and has been inspired by Shulamith Koenig and the People's Movement for Human Rights Education.[1] At the John Humphrey Centre we made a commitment to inspire learning on human rights, for human rights are the most real in those spaces closest to home. In Eleanor Roosevelt's words:

> Where, after all, do universal human rights begin? In small places, close to home—so close and so small that they cannot be seen on any map of the world. Yet they are the world of the individual person: The neighborhood he [sic] lives in; the school or college he attends; the factory, farm or office where he works. Such are the places where every man, woman, and child seeks equal justice, equal opportunity, equal dignity without discrimination. Unless these rights have meaning there, they have little meaning anywhere. Without concerted citizen action to uphold them close to home, we shall look in vain for progress in the larger world.[2]

The following is a reflection on the work of the John Humphrey Centre over the past 15 years to build human rights "spaces" at home in Edmonton, Alberta. In this time the centre has worked across many communities and sectors, which has resulted in the growth of a framework of theory and practice that informs its work. What has become clear in this journey is that human rights are the one thing that binds us and gives us a collective framework for demanding accountability and seeking to meet the needs of those most marginalized in our communities. Human rights are the only tool that we, as citizens, have to make claims to responsible authorities and to shine a light on the issues that often go unseen in communities.

In this chapter I use the term *space* to refer to a space that is not only absolute, which could be Euclidean or cognitive, but also relational, including emotional, spiritual, and intellectual, as argued by Lefebvre (1992; see Elden, 2009, and Kitchen, 2009, for ontogenetic discussion of space). For the intent of this chapter I will use the term *space* to denote the ideational, relational, and physical components necessary for building a culture of human rights. Many may associate human rights with the individual and with the legal aspect, but they are also relational as they are about us living together in space and time. Human rights are affected by the geographical space of an area, such as here where I write from the Treaty Six Territory in the colonial state of Canada upon the land of Turtle Island.³ We have to understand that the geographical space we occupy is also influenced by the history of that space. The present-day manifestations of colonization and genocide in Canada are alive in our social relations and in the physical or virtual spaces in which we may gather.

Human rights are also about this relational aspect. They are collective, but they also exist within a context. So, the spaces I speak of in this chapter encompass a complex narrative of history that influences the spaces we are in—the emotional, the physical, the spiritual, the intellectual. I am conscious of this as I sit here in ᐊᒥᐢᑿᒌᐚᐢᑲᐦᐃᑲᐣ (amiskwacîwâskahikan), the land stolen from the Papaschase and Shoal First Nations, as well as other Indigenous Peoples. To me, human rights are about a reconciliation of this past, through truth and the building of a human rights culture, or relations, at the community level. At the same time, it is a framework for state responsibility and accountability at the international level.

Four Pillars of Responsibility

When we apply the lens of the UDHR, it requires that we look at all people in our community, not just select specific groups, such as seniors, children, women, and those living with a disability. It demands that we shape our vision with an eye to seeing those who are most marginalized in our community and bringing their stories and experiences to light, while also applying an anti-oppression lens. When we do this, we expose deeper stories. We can build sustainable and appropriate solutions that reach those who most need them; this will ultimately strengthen human rights across the spectrum. This grounding is critical because it takes us into a perspective of universalism and inclusion. It locates us in a place of intersectionality. The trick is to reach those people who are most vulnerable, with their often overlooked reality, by assisting in bringing their voices and experiences to the forefront.

In detailing the *Convention on the Rights of the Child* in 1989, the United Nations articulates what is known as the three *P*s—participation, provision, and protection—which are tied to the broader concepts of dignity, security, and freedom, respectively. These three pillars provide a framework to understand children's rights, but at the John Humphrey Centre we link this framework to all human rights. We add one additional pillar, however, which we believe is necessary to fill out this framework— remedy, linked to the concept of justice. We use this four-pillared framework in our human rights education and programming.

Pillar One: Participation and the Right to Dignity
All humans, no matter their age or ability, have the right to participate in the decisions that affect them and their community. Without the participation of the individual who is affected by a decision, solutions will not be sustainable or relevant. Whether this is a child in a classroom or a senior in an old-age home, the voice and perspective of the person are critical in the defining of solutions to help that person live a life of dignity. The participation pillar calls on us to be human centred and responsive to the voice, needs, and perspectives of those affected by issues. State parties have a responsibility to ensure that people have the right to participate. This may include democratic voting measures, as well as the right to information, sovereignty, and decision-making over one's body in the health system. It may mean supporting student government, as it is about creating spaces for people to organize, engage, and

contribute so that they may explore relevant and appropriate solutions and collaborations to the issues they face.

Participation is a fundamental element of building long-term solutions to challenging issues in the community. Notably, the collective wisdom and contributions of those at the margins can also provide reasonable and tangible solutions. For a city to be a human rights city, it must make a committed effort to ensure that barriers to the participation of these and diverse voices are removed. I have seen at first hand the growth, transformation, and innovation that come from community members who are affected by issues and sitting alongside the decision- and policy-makers. Participation can include a review and revision of key processes, such as the city's procedures for joining a committee (which may present as burdensome and intimidating to some people) or how the city facilitates its public meetings. It may also mean going out into the community rather than expecting the community to come to the city, and putting safety and inclusion at the centre of their procedures—to value the voices of those who are affected. It is the voices of these individuals that must be heard, and they need spaces marked by dignity and respect.

Pillar Two: Provision and the Right to Security
The notion of the right to life and security of the person is at the centre of the second pillar of human rights. Provision requires that the state and related responsible authorities ensure that the necessities for survival and development are in place to support community members, with the maximum available resources. This includes elements such as health care, education, and housing.

The World Health Organization articulates that the right to health should be applied and assessed through four lenses: availability, accessibility, acceptability, and quality in health care (UN General Assembly, 2000, 2015). This orientation is useful when one looks at all areas of the right to provision, which is about the right to possess, receive or have access to certain resources, skills and services. *Availability* calls for sufficient health-care service. *Accessibility* ensures that people are free from discrimination when accessing health, but, further, that they have physical accessibility, economic accessibility or affordability, and access to information. *Acceptability* calls for a people-centred approach to health care that acknowledges the gender, language, or cultural sensitivities that participate in the rights of individuals. Finally, *quality* calls for health care that is safe, effective, timely, equitable, efficient, and integrated.

These same four principles can be applied to other forms of the right to provision, such as housing or education, as they set important standards for which provincial or federal bodies should aim related to these rights. While much of the right to provision is outside the purview of municipal governments in Canada, municipalities can certainly advocate to other levels of government to ensure these principles inform their pursuit.

Pillar Three: Protection and the Right to Freedom
Protection, as the third pillar, is concerned with our rights not to be violated by others, whether by state-related parties, businesses, organizations, or individuals. Meaningful protection means that mechanisms are in place to ensure that all people are protected from abuse, exploitation, or violation. In Canada we have the *Canadian Criminal Code* as a basis for protection rights for all citizens. We also have the *Canadian Charter of Rights and Freedoms*, which provides a fundamental basis for human rights law by establishing the value of human rights in this country. It provides the principles to which the state aspires and can be held accountable.

At the municipal level, one domain in which protection comes into play is law and bylaw enforcement. As the City of Edmonton funds our civic law enforcement, it has a responsibility to see that it equitably protects the rights of all people in the community. Notably, bylaws are mechanisms through which every day realities create or affect spaces of inclusion or exclusion. As an example, Edmonton has historically had bylaws that directly discriminated against certain groups, like the banning of Black community members from public pools and parks in 1924 (Zdeb, 2014).

Today exclusion can take many forms in bylaws, such as bans in public spaces or overwhelming bureaucracy and licensing for small businesses.

This red tape places increased burdens on those who may have different abilities, lack proficiency in English, are newcomers to the country, or are part of a group that is traditionally marginalized. In these times, when we are considering the role of law enforcement in systemic racism or violence, local bylaw enforcement is a fundamental component of systemic oppression; however, oversight of bylaw enforcement through peace officers is often overlooked.

Pillar Four: Remedy and the Right to Justice
Without a space to seek a remedy when rights have been violated, or a space to claim rights, in actuality we do not have rights. Thus, the concept and practice of remedy is a central and critical pillar when one addresses human rights. It requires all levels of government to provide accessible mechanisms for all people to bring forward concerns and violations as a pathway to learning and growth. Thus, this is a critical pillar for us at the John Humphrey Centre, given that access to justice for marginalized and/or excluded communities constitutes a major gap in Canada.[4] The United Nations Development Programme defines *access to justice* as "the ability of people to seek and obtain a remedy through formal or informal institutions of justice for grievances" (UN Development Programme, 2013, p. 5). Access to legal support that is universal, affordable, accessible, acceptable, and of good quality is not readily available to all. For example, for Indigenous Peoples in Canada, until 1961 when compulsory enfranchisement was removed from the *Indian Act*, it was illegal to raise funds for legal struggles and to fight for their lands or rights.

The inaccessibility to our remedy systems is a colonial legacy, as they were built on distrust, isolation, and fear, which are still alive today. All too many people in our community continue to become criminalized for even engaging in public spaces. I think of a friend of mine who can never seem to step on a university campus without being harassed and bullied by security. Numerous men and women with similar experiences may no longer be able to sustain their patience in the heat of this bullying and harassment, but when they finally lose their cool and defend themselves or their family, they end up criminalized. Having a criminal record changes everything. It makes one then unable to access income support and finds it markedly harder to be hired or to find a place to live.

These four pillars of responsibility for human rights provide an important foundation for the balancing of our collective well-being. We need to ensure that we find balance and create space to address all four of the pillars in the community.

Taking Action for Human Rights
Part of our work is to ensure that action on human rights is distributed evenly through a range of areas (Hunter, 2015), because many ways exist in which to engage and affect human rights. Each of the action areas discussed next plays an important role in the advancement and defence of human rights in our communities. Witnesses and those who document help to shift dynamics and give us the information and stories needed to effect systemic change. Educators enable radical learning and sharing of truths. Advocates help community members to access the supports they need. Organizers and facilitators provide space for collective connection and growth. All of these actors and actions provide fundamental intersections, and we must cultivate these connections in our communities.

Documenting and Witnessing
Enabling change related to human rights crucially depends on documenting issues and concerns in order to inform and influence policy and programming. In so doing, we create more efficient and relevant systems that are responsive to community needs and demands. This action area is therefore oriented to supporting individuals or groups who are striving to claim their rights. Documenting human rights at a community level is an important aspect of witnessing, which helps to build the case for systemic change. Witnesses walk alongside people and participate in shifting the power balance in processes that are often dominated by those with power.

The mere act of having someone witness a meeting with a doctor or a social worker, or participate in a remedy process, helps to balance the power in space. It is common for those seeking access to their rights to be fearful of sites they must enter or to lack confidence in their ability to engage constructively. Having a witness, then, not only provides a sense of comfort but also is a measure of accountability and objectivity. It is everyone's right to be able to have witnesses to support them in translating and meeting their needs. People's stories can be emotional, however, and those on the receiving end are sometimes defensive or find it hard to be empathic. Nevertheless, sharing experiences and working to build foundations of trust in order to hear and adapt remains an important goal. In particular, we must listen to the most marginalized. Creating a dynamic human rights system in a civil society demands that citizens' voices be *heard*, that we have *spaces* in which to be heard, and that documentation be *a part of this process*. This documentation, we believe, has to be independent of government influence or oversight.

Educating

The John Humphrey Centre was founded on the idea that human rights education is fundamental to embedding in society a culture of peace and human rights. Several important thinkers have spoken of this need. For example, Kofi Annan, former secretary general of the United Nations, has said, "Human rights education is much more than a lesson in schools or a theme for a day; it is a process to equip people with the tools they need to live lives of security and dignity" (United Nations, 2004). The educational philosopher Paulo Freire (n.d.) makes a related pedagogical point: "As long as the oppressed remain unaware of the causes of their own condition, they fatalistically accept their own exploitation." Martin Luther King (1963) has also touched on this relationship between those with power and those without, stating that "freedom is never voluntarily given by the oppressor; it must be demanded by the oppressed."

Education requires that we not only learn and teach what human rights are but also provide knowledge and the means to learn and understand the systems that contribute to oppression, along with providing spaces that allow remedy or access to human rights. Education requires a commitment to shine a light on hidden issues and speak truth to power.

Our work in education, the focal point of what we do at the centre, relies on popular education pedagogy to create a learning space that is grounded in people's experiences; we then translate these experiences into human rights language. Through the collective wisdom of many, including those who courageously share their lived experience, we can find meaningful strategies to advance human rights, without blinders. Our aim is to facilitate transformative shifts.

The early work of the John Humphrey Centre focused heavily on human rights education for the younger generation because we believed in the importance of planting these seeds in the hearts and minds of the child—and we continue this work today, through strength-based activities both in and out of schools, where children can express themselves while learning about human rights. We also now engage in public education through partnership with the Catherine Donnelly Foundation through the building of Righting Relations.[5] This pan-Canadian network of adult educators and community organizers works for a more just Canada based on intersectionality and a decolonial philosophy, an orientation that aligns well with the mission of the John Humphrey Centre.

Advocating

The third critical human rights action area is advocacy. Advocates recognize the importance of individual advocacy but also see systems as providing resources, even if they are broken and unfair. Advocates help people navigate those systems and use their own knowledge of them to help people fulfill their needs; they bend the systems to extract as much justice or resources from it as they can. Advocates are critical players in our effort to advance human rights, working at the front line to ensure that voices are heard and people's needs are met.

The tension of advocacy work lies in the dichotomy between efforts to meet an individual's needs and efforts to push for systemic change. The focus on meeting individual needs can be all consuming. Although that focus is critical, the emphasis can subtly shift towards charity, rather than the achievement of dignity and self-determination. Advocacy invokes the need to reflect, to find the balance in advocating for individual rights and in attending to a larger collective approach that works towards fairer systems. Advocacy is also linked to documentation: As advocates do the important work on the front lines, their efforts must be documented and captured as part of the drive to achieve systemic change. Their role may also entail acting as a translator of their clients' experiences, presenting them to those who can intervene on behalf of the clients in a manner that is most likely to elicit the desired response or outcome.

Organizing and Facilitating

Strong organization and facilitation are critical skills and zones of action in the fight for human rights. Organizers often work behind the scenes, pulling everyone together, while effective facilitators create a context that ensures equitable contribution, based on an anti-oppressive stance. This orientation provides the foundation for safe and inclusive spaces.

When they are tackling issues, the instinct of organizers and facilitators is typically to bring together those who are hurting, to identify the root causes of their concerns, and to build strategies for change. They often organize people who are at the margins of dominant systems into groups, in order to apply pressure to change systemic rules. Organizers traditionally create pressure by building groups external to the current system. They create connections in the community and facilitate collective learning through dialogue and engagement.

Facilitation can and should go beyond just working with those who are affected by a human rights issue. Facilitating engagements that bring groups with different vantage points and responsibility to the tables can be highly beneficial. Pivotal work involves facilitating inclusive spaces for people with lived experience on the front lines and those who are in the public sector; both of these perspectives are valuable in finding solutions to inequities. We also need to facilitate learning and dialogue with the broader community on human rights issues, to help shift behaviour and misunderstandings. Such community discourse is intrinsic to the work of finding decolonizing and sustainable long-term solutions, while helping to build relationships and trust.

To excavate the root causes of issues requires discussion grounded in multiple perspectives and diverse experiences. Careful and mindful facilitation is thus a crucial skill, one in which all levels of government need to invest to translate their community engagement into meaningful and strengthened community spaces and solutions. In our practice we use the talking circle as a process to facilitate equitable and shared space. While it is not the only tool for building a safe and relational space, it is a critical element in grounding a conversation and allowing people to step forward equitably and present their concerns.

Experiences in Edmonton: Lessons Learned and Best Practices
Foundations and Initial Challenges
The real journey towards Edmonton's becoming a human rights city began in 2004 even though the city had been designated as such a year earlier. The global movement has been unique in each city around the world that has taken on this vision. Graz, Austria, for example, was primarily led by the municipality itself and had resources from the start. This, however, did not necessarily translate into human rights taking hold in the community in a deep way. I have found that when government bodies lead initiatives to address rights-related issues, the initiatives often fall flat and implode. Many complex factors play a part here: among them, an aversion by the officials to do meaningful work, their fear of bringing people to the table who may have alternative perspectives and may slow processes down, or the community's distrust of participating in the work.

Certainly, the experience in Edmonton has not been without its challenges. As a non-governmental organization that is leading the work forward, the centre has encountered barriers. More importantly, we have also seen the slow but long-term growth of a human rights culture in our city.

At the beginning of the project a steering committee helped advance the work, which presented its own complexities and challenges because it largely comprised two types of people: those who wanted to see immediate shifts and changes to policy and practice in the city, and those who were coming from a more ephemeral, relational, and theoretical viewpoint with respect to building a human rights city. This latter group lacked the practicality that the former group was seeking. Both viewpoints are important, but they created frustration and conflict in the group. Nevertheless, great engagement and strategic action-planning were achieved to create a framework for change.

The second challenge we faced was spearheading a citizen-led initiative under the organizational umbrella. As the centre had its own governance structure through the board of directors, along with existing project work, such as our Rights in the Sun (with children), the presence of the project-steering committee began to create internal conflicts within the organization. As such, the organization had to negotiate priorities—the larger priorities of the organization and board of directors, and the priorities of the steering committee of the Human Rights City project. The process of accessing resources to support the work of the project, distinct from the larger work of the organization, conflicted. At this point, a couple of years into the work, the centre decided to fold the Human Rights City project into the centre's programming efforts. It became a priority *for the centre* rather than a separate project led by an independent group of people. In 2006 the board disbanded the steering committee; since then, the building of a human rights community has become one of four central strategic priorities for the organization. The steering committee's work was embedded into all our work, without creating a separate administrative burden. The funding reality for non-profit organizations is that sustaining long-term projects is difficult, so this strategy has allowed us to navigate around that challenge.

It was clear to us from the outset that building a human rights city required a commitment to creating spaces of discourse, dialogue, and learning on human rights. In so doing, we focused on the importance of building relationships in the community. Ultimately, human rights are connected to the notion of human relationships and our ability to live together in peace and harmony. Such relationships are a fundamental component of a rights-based framework, with the ensuing discourse supporting the growth of a mutual learning relationship. Further, human rights enter into the public space and become alive in the community. Human rights, of necessity, must be part of public discourse, or they do not exist or evolve. Harkening back to Roosevelt's comments cited earlier, this is a case of making human rights real and relevant at the local levels by inviting the community to discuss and reflect on them.

Youth Action Project
The John Humphrey Centre intentionally built two programs to support the growth of Edmonton as a human rights city. The first program, the Youth Action Project, targeted the younger generation, to equip them with knowledge of and skills in human rights. It allowed them to explore and learn about the ways in which human rights are alive in our community. Started in 2006, this project took a community-based learning approach: young people could engage in complex conversations with their peers, visit and learn from various agencies in our community and from people with lived experience, and create strategies to bring forward to our local government. This program has been a beautiful experience over the years for all involved, and we have seen young people grow into their careers with a human rights lens. Still today, I run into young people who were part of this program, and they speak about how every day in their work they use the lessons gained during that time. This gives me great pride.

In 2014 the mayor of Edmonton launched a task force to end poverty. We were concerned at the time about adequate representation on the task force of people who had lived experiences of poverty. Over the next three years the Youth Action Project helped to inform the city council's efforts to address poverty. Starting in 2015, this dialogue-to-action program worked with young people—those with lived experiences of poverty and those with experiences of privilege—through tough discussions related to poverty in Edmonton, which led to several calls to action. Members of this team also had personal experiences of being criminalized due to poverty, which deeply affected their lives in ways that others might not understand. Their participation in the task force contributed to advocacy efforts that shifted provincial legislation and decriminalized the accessing of public transportation.

Human Rights Facilitator Training Program

The second program we developed to strengthen human rights in the city was our Human Rights Facilitator Training Program, which also began in 2006. With this program we intended to create a learning space for members from diverse communities—representing various backgrounds, experiences, and abilities—to come together to find solidarity, to educate each other and others, and to build solid foundations for human rights facilitation in the community. Immediately, this program saw healthy outcomes, with people from different communities finding common connections and collaborating to expand education into their workplaces and broader communities. We have been honoured to deliver the training several times in other communities, including Winnipeg, Peace River, and Cold Lake.

The Future of These Programs

The programs are successful in large part because they are based on principles of popular education, which are participatory and emancipatory, allowing participants to take control of their own learning and to effect social change through relationship. These aspects move beyond the workshop and thus facilitate behavioural and attitudinal changes that promote human rights. As a methodology, popular education is thus intrinsically interconnected to the advancement of human rights. Each program also maintains a commitment to different perspectives and experiences, valorizes conversation and connection, and supports intercultural linkages across diverse community groups. The richness of the learning is based on the richness of experiences that participants bring to the collaborations.

Both the Youth Action Project and the Human Rights Facilitator Training Program remain relevant today because they are powerful models for other communities to use, to catalyze conversations and create connections and movement on human rights. However, funding constraints limit our capacity to operate these programs on an ongoing basis. Our dream is to have sustained funding so that we can continue to deepen and extend our culture of peace and human rights in the city, while also informing policy. Although many have recommended we conduct them on a cost-recovery basis or as a social enterprise, this is untenable: most people seeking our education come from low-income communities that lack access to resources for participating in continued education. Thus, we are committed to making these accessible, affordable, and available to all—whenever we offer them.

Implementation Challenges

An important insight that arises from the work of the John Humphrey Centre is the significance of coalescing around those at the grassroots level and working within community organizations over the long term. A great frustration has been the temporary nature of public-sector employees and elected officials. Finding bureaucrats in a position long enough to commit to and achieve long-term change is challenging at best. However, even then, they often face significant barriers in pushing forward meaningful community-based work. Or they may be risk averse and do not want to take a chance on moving towards effective change.

Further, we have been frustrated by having to start again at building relationships when someone leaves a key position they have held for a few years. This has happened with law enforcement personnel or teachers, for example, who usually remain in their positions for only two to three years. Just as we begin to gain traction and effect some change, they leave for a position elsewhere, mandating that we rebuild relationships from the ground level. This is comparable to the four-year cycle of elected officials. Overall, these truncated timelines present major obstacles to sustained change, within both the municipal and the provincial bureaucracies.

Over the course of my career I have witnessed a workplace culture of fear and toxicity in many public sector (provincial and municipal) and institutional spaces. This tone creates an infection, which I understand as a state of risk mitigation: people are afraid of repercussions in their work so they become stagnant and do not push for meaningful change. This has the effect of innovative ideas being quickly shot down and a culture of complacency developing. Along the same lines, progress sometimes stagnates because those who do decide to "show up" are concerned that other significant participants are absent. Trusting that those who are present and ready to do the work are the right people for that work will keep things moving.

Further, sometimes diversity "tokenism" may occur, and people from marginalized communities who show leadership become overburdened. However, the more we strengthen capacity and invite engagement from more people in our community, the better. This puts less demand on the ostensible leaders. In other words, we must find ways to encourage a greater diversity of the people who are involved, to create opportunities for new leaders to emerge. We need to enable dialogue and discussion on the tensions and realities in our world and community, making room for a wide variety of speakers. I want to invite courageous conversations that bridge political divisions and narratives, to facilitate analysis and to discover commonalities.

In communities affected by trauma—but which nevertheless need to be known and heard—the very facilitation of a meeting, or lack thereof, can result in voices disappearing. Members may feel they do not fit or belong, or they experience feelings of distrust and insecurity. In the face of this, the complexities of facilitating safe spaces for vulnerable people to contribute require innovation and reflection. Even innocent behaviour can marginalize and exclude a whole community, while reinforcing feelings of fear and distrust. For example, before a meeting begins, people may sit around talking about their recent holiday or trip. For those who can only dream of the opportunity to travel (owing to restricted ability or finances, for example), this type of conversation can generate feelings of inadequacy and not belonging. For these individuals, it shuts the meeting down before it has even begun. The meeting hosts must learn to be sensitive to such factors and to be conscious and aware and thus create an environment where sharing is centred on something that can include everyone. It calls on them to step in and "hold" that space even before the official agenda begins.

Recommendations for the Path Going Forward
Essential Dialogue for Community Resiliency

Our greatest learning in this work has been the importance of creating space—both physical and relational—because this strengthens the community through dialogue, learning, and action. It is in these spaces of community that long-term change can happen because community members (who are not in the public sector or in elected positions) can develop connections to each other and build relationships to support their work.

At the grassroots level, community members who deal on the front lines with the most difficult issues are working and committed to long-term change. Unfortunately they often take the most abuse because they highlight challenging or unpleasant issues, such as injustice and systemic inequity. In my years with the centre I have seen many such front-liners excluded from important conversations because they were perhaps too honest with the issues and expressed concerns with great passion. Clearly, agitators are not always welcome, but we fail to recognize that their passion comes from their deep connection to the issues. They have the necessary longevity, legitimacy, and commitment to work in the community, which demands our urgent support; thus, they need not be seen as a threat. Indeed, not listening to these experiences costs the public purse more than addressing the issues and creating more effective and efficient responses.

When we consider how to support the vulnerable, marginalized, and excluded in our cities, more successful outcomes could be achieved if we truly acted on the maxim of "No one left behind," or "Nothing about us, without us." This is what it means to take a human rights–based approach, but it is not an easy thing to negotiate because those who are affected by injustice often carry trauma. This undoubtedly influences the delivery of their message when they speak out, potentially resulting in closed doors.

Investment in Facilitation and Participation

One tangible way in which cities can contribute to dialogic spaces is to invest in facilitation. This might entail supporting skill development and inclusivity among staff or bringing external facilitators from the community to help shepherd processes that value the voice and perspective of all. Cities must also shift their perspective, inviting to the table people with relevant lived experiences and honouring their time and commitment.

A common public sector engagement strategy is to invite community members to participate in committees or consultations; in this way, their voices and perspectives can be brought forward into policy- or decision-making. This practice, however, carries intrinsic limitations: communities that are most marginalized from their rights typically have many complex barriers, which impede their ability to participate in or access these consultation and administrative spaces. We cannot build solutions that meet the needs of those at the margins if it is mostly privileged voices that are heard by those policy- and decision-makers.

Those most marginalized in a community will often also face financial barriers to participation. Consider that giving up unvalued or unpaid time to participate in committees is a great privilege, for example. Frequently, those representing the public sector or non-governmental organizations are present as part of their job; thus, they are being compensated for their time. When applying a rights-based approach, participation calls us to recognize the participation of marginalized and excluded voices as essential. This perspective requires a mindset of investment, as opposed to one of burden, which means recognizing and valuing someone's time, while providing an opportunity for participation. This grants those individuals a sense of belonging and the confidence to engage—in contrast to encountering an attitude of annoyance, for example, when asking to be compensated for their time. For marginalized persons, this may be the way they can justify the time they spend in the meetings or space, time that would otherwise be better spent earning extra money or taking care of family responsibilities.

Spaces to Achieve Remedy
Achieving human rights also depends on access to established and reliable means to seek remedy for violations or abuse. Importantly, we do not have rights if we have no vehicle for remedy. Thus, if such avenues do not exist, we need to create them; if they do exist, they must evolve to

ensure they are truly available, accessible, affordable, and acceptable to all. Civil society must be part of this process because governments have a critical responsibility to invest resources and energy in creating neutral, independent pathways for people to bring forward concerns related to human rights for resolution. Resolution should not necessarily rely on legal systems because such spaces are inaccessible to many and do not offer short-term resolution.

We do currently have tools in place in Canada to seek remedy for human rights violations. The test is whether they are open and accessible to those who need them most. The federal, provincial, and territorial commissions are important avenues for people to access and to document and file issues related to discrimination. At the provincial level we also have numerous advocacy offices available to support people who are seeking remedy or support, such as the health advocate, disability advocate, and children's advocate. These systems provide both access and important feedback loops to the government; nevertheless, they could go further to engage with communities. In fact, our experience shows an inability to connect to the grassroots.

Finding alternative routes to remedy requires that all levels of government therefore act to (a) equip and empower community-based advocates; (b) support localized and responsive capacity that ripples out into the community; and (c) create neutral, safe, and informal spaces in which people can pursue solutions. Such actions will alleviate the pressures on more formal legal mechanisms, while modelling right relations through healthy and restorative opportunities to resolve grievances. Thus, current offices also must provide adequate resources and offices in rural and remote areas of our province. This can be done through partnership with local agencies to enhance transfer of knowledge to community-based advocates. Indigenous Friendship Centres could be one such agency type, presently an under-used resource in our communities.

Conclusion

I suggest that we currently have a crisis in our legal system: it is blocked up, it is inaccessible, and it is unaffordable. We thus must make shifts in how we work and resolve our conflicts to remedy human rights concerns. If we can confront the issues at a localized level where they have urgency and impact, we can create spaces of healing and growth, rather than of hurt and frustration. When we shift to alternative solutions for remedy, we also take pressure off the growing burden on the public dollar that comes from investment in inefficient systems.

Unfortunately the multiple pathways that are currently available to pursue remedy are not always pursued by groups with grievances. For example, they have not traditionally been accessed by Indigenous Peoples due to the lack of trust related to the ongoing erosion of treaty relationships. This can also be said of other communities such as the 2SLGTBQ+ and Black communities. In the last three to four years, however, an increasing number of Indigenous Peoples have been pursuing information on how to seek remedy for issues within their bands, for example. Remedy spaces within nations and settlements are thus critically needed. While the Canadian Human Rights Commission is an option, an important call is underway for more localized and Indigenous-led spaces for remedy, which are accessible and safe. The imposition of a colonial model of governance on First Nations reserves has disconnected many Indigenous Peoples from natural laws and traditional ways and resulted in disjointed action.

Given our history and experiences of colonization in Canada, it is presently quite challenging to host conversations based on the notion of equity, but this we urgently need. When we recognize the manifestations of this colonial history and how it plays out in our communities, municipalities, and other levels of government, we are better positioned to create safe situations within communities, opportunities for intersection and growth, and deeper connections and collaborations. These historical relationships shape how each of us enter into a space—whether we feel confident, valued, heard, or safe.

Within the City of Edmonton we lack spaces for remedy and for concerns to be brought forward for consideration. Over the years, I have heard numerous concerns about workplace culture and harassment within the city and that no place is available to address these conflicts effectively. While unions exist, not everyone feels that they stand for all members, and some consider that they speak for the larger institution rather than their unique members. This is one area in need of innovation and evolution within the city, to create spaces of safety, disclosure, and conflict resolution. Ultimately, to build a human rights city is to commit to a lifelong journey to bring human rights into public discourse for both learning and growth.

This has been the experience in Edmonton; however, cities around the world have made this movement their own at the local level. In the United States a strong movement for human rights cities has generated an alliance across the country, evident in groups such as the UN Human Rights City Alliance (US Human Rights Network, n.d.). Dialogue has been a major part of their work, but the practice of using human rights standards to actively analyze and hold their governments to account has also emerged as an important contributing factor. This practice is not yet deeply embedded here in Edmonton, but the work continues to evolve, and we retain a commitment to the progressive realization of the dignity of all in our community. The human rights city should become a space for ongoing review and audit of our local governments to ensure policies, budgets, and programs are equitably benefiting and supporting all Edmontonians. We strive to leave no one behind.

NOTES

1. For more information on the People's Movement for Human Rights Education and the Human Rights Cities Movement, see https://www.pdhre.org/projects/hrcommun.html.
2. Excerpt from Eleanor Roosevelt's famous speech at the presentation of "In Your Hands: A Guide for Community Action for the Tenth Anniversary of the *Universal Declaration of Human Rights*," on March 27, 1958, at the United Nations in New York.
3. Turtle Island is the name that many Indigenous groups use to refer to North America. For more about the beliefs and legends that give rise to this name, see https://www.thecanadianencyclopedia.ca/en/article/turtle-island.
4. For example, the Canadian Bar Association has reported to UN committees on the

crisis of access to justice as early as 2006. See Canadian Bar Association (2006). In October 2017 the Edmonton Social Planning Council confirmed that these challenges are still deeply embedded in our communities (Jenkins, 2017).

5. For more information on the Catherine Donnelly Foundation, see http://www.catherinedonnellyfoundation.org/.

REFERENCES

Canadian Bar Association. (2006). *Canada's crisis in access to justice.* http://socialrightscura.ca/documents/CESCR-Submissions/canadianbarassociation.pdf

Elden, S. (2009). Space I. In *International Encyclopedia of Human Geography* (pp. 262–267).

Freire, Paolo. (n.d.). *Pedagogy of the oppressed* [Chapter 1 online]. http://www.historyisaweapon.com/defcon2/pedagogy/pedagogychapter1.html

Hunter, D. (2015). *Building a movement to end the new Jim Crow: An organizing guide.* Veterans of Hope.

Jenkins, M. (2017). *Access to justice: The great gap in Canada's justice system.* Edmonton Social Planning Council. https://www.edmontonsocialplanning.ca/wp-content/uploads/2017/10/edmontonsocialplanning.ca_joomlatools-files_docman-files_ESPC-Documents_PUBLICATIONS_A.06.G-REPORTS_ESPC-REPORT_ACCESS-TO-JUSTICE_20170930.pdf

John Humphreys Centre for Peace and Human Rights. (2015). *Youth action project on poverty.* https://drive.google.com/file/d/1wKl4Tl4xWCiIYw4yATEsP4dWIAOUtyHz/view

King, M.L. (1963, April 16). *Letter from a Birmingham jail.* https://www.africa.upenn.edu/Articles_Gen/Letter_Birmingham.html

Kitchen, R. (2009). Space II. In *International Encyclopedia of Human Geography.* (pp. 268–275).

Lefebvre, H. (1992). *The production of space* (D. Nicholson-Smith, Trans.). Wiley-Blackwell.

UN Development Programme. (2013). *Strengthening judicial integrity through enhanced access to justice.* https://www.google.com/search?q=Strengthening+judicial+intregity+through+enhanced+access+to+justice&rlz=1C1CHBF_enCA858CA858&oq=Strengthening+judicial+intregity+through+enhanced+access+to+justice&aqs=chrome..69i57.35998j1j7&sourceid=chrome&ie=UTF-8

UN General Assembly (2000, August 11). *Committee on economic, social, and cultural rights* [Doc. E/C.12/2000/4].

UN General Assembly (2015, October 21). *Transforming our world: The 2003 agenda for sustainable development* [UN Doc. A/RES/70/1]. https://sustainabledevelopment.un.org/post2015/transformingourworld

United Nations. (2004). *Secretary-General in message to mark International Human Rights Day* [Press Release SG/SM/9632-HR/4800-OBV/460].

US Human Rights Network. (n.d.). *National human rights city alliance.* https://ushrnetwork.org/membership/miats/national-human-rights-city-alliance

Zdeb, C. (2014, August 28): Racism colours the opening of two new city swimming pools. *Edmonton Journal*. https://edmontonjournal.com/news/local-news/aug-28-1924-racism-colours-the-opening-of-two-new-city-swimming-pools

III
OTHER RIGHTS IN THE CITY

7
THE RIGHT TO ADEQUATE HOUSING AROUND THE GLOBE
Analysis and Evaluation of National Constitutions

MICHELLE L. OREN & RACHELLE ALTERMAN
—

Introduction

Housing is an essential component of the social and personal life of every individual. With over 1.6 billion people inadequately housed—and given current urban growth trends—the issue of access to adequate housing is of concern to many international and national bodies, who are urging governments to act. Homelessness marks the extreme end of inadequate housing; even Canada has homeless people, although it is one of the world's richest nations. In Toronto alone, according to the City's 2018 *Street Needs Assessment*, the homelessness count was estimated at 8,715 people. Of these, 94 per cent of people experiencing homelessness were staying indoors, and 6 per cent were rough sleeping outdoors. Staying in city-administered sites were 82 per cent, and 12 per cent were living in health and treatment facilities, violence against woman shelters, and correctional facilities. As well, an additional 100,000 households were on the social housing wait-list (although they had some current shelter), which has an average wait time of 10 to 12 years (McIsaac,

2019). Importantly, the *Canada Budget Implementation Act* of 2019 allocated funding for the *National Housing Strategy Act*, marking a significant milestone towards enshrining the right to housing in Canadian legislation.[1] According to Agrawal (2020), Canada has been gradually enhancing its citizens' rights to address housing issues at the city level through constitutional and quasi-constitutional protections, with evolving jurisprudence on housing rights.

The Human Right to Housing

The right to adequate housing goes beyond the right to just having some shelter. In 2016, "ensuring access for all to adequate, safe and affordable housing" (SDG 11.1) was included as a Global Sustainable Development Goal of the United Nations.

The purpose of this chapter is to delve into housing rights as expressed in national constitutions. We report on all 189 constitutions of UN member states, describing and evaluating them in terms of what they say about the right to housing. As a benchmark for evaluation we turn to the UN's main interpretation on adequate housing, known as General Comment No. 4 to the *International Covenant on Economic, Social and Cultural Rights* of 1966 (ICESCR) (UN General Assembly, 1966). This document stipulates seven criteria of adequate housing.

The next section deals with current knowledge about the comparative right to housing, followed by our own contribution. We then expand on each of the seven criteria of adequate housing: legal security of tenure, availability of services and infrastructure, affordability, habitability, accessibility, location, and cultural adequacy. These criteria serve as our benchmarks for evaluating the constitutional right to housing (CRtH) in the wording of all the national constitutions we examine. Next, we report on our empirical research and its method. Many of our findings are counterintuitive and lead to further questions. We conclude with some policy implications.

Comparative Constitutional Right to Housing

There is an immense body of scholarship about the right to housing, too large to survey here. It includes single-country studies and some comparative work. The most comprehensive publication, by Leckie (2003), is a compilation of several country-level cases reporting on the implementation of housing rights that are recognized under international human rights law in 10 countries. Leckie concluded that a disproportionate emphasis had been placed on the international legal dimensions of human rights, at the expense of efforts involving the national level. His pioneering work called for several national level studies in the years to come.

In the United States, Bratt, Stone, and Hartman (2006) encompassed various aspects of housing from a social justice and pragmatic perspective, which orients to the central role that housing plays in people's lives. The right to housing is discussed as a principle of fairness rather than a fundamental legal (constitutional) right. The authors call to de-commodify housing and at the same time achieve the national housing goal declared in the US 1949 *Housing Act*: "A decent home and a suitable living environment for every American family" (p. 8).

Hohmann (2013) offers a theoretical and normative analysis of the right to housing, describing various international and regional covenants in Europe, Inter-America, and Africa and the Arab charter on human rights. She focuses on India (which has no explicit CRtH) and South Africa (which has explicit CRtH), concluding that it is not the rehearsal of legal arguments that fosters the possibility of the right to housing, but the creativity of those who seek to realize the right. The potential of the right to housing is thus in the claims made under it; therefore, the law plays an important role.

Additional publications on housing present compilations of international housing rights legislation delivered as tool kits for public use and reflections on their justiciability (Kenna, 2010b; Leckie, 2000); themed papers and monographs about housing law (Sidoli del Ceno & Vols, 2017); and numerous descriptive country case studies and academic reports on violations of human rights in several countries, such as South Africa and Kenya (De Vos, 2001; Huchzermeyer, 2004), Belgium (Moons, 2018), Ireland (Kenna, 2011), India (Mukherjee, 2019), the United Kingdom,

Spain, and France (Ball, 2012; Wells, 2019). In Canada a recent analysis looked at "Housing First" in Alberta, Canada, a human service and social program promoting an approach that prioritizes permanent housing provision to people experiencing homelessness (Collins & Stout, 2019).

Only scant research, however, is available that takes up comparative analysis of the CRtH. Jung, Hirschl, and Rosevear (2014) survey the world's constitutions for general mention of all types of human rights, among them housing rights. Another contribution is our own earlier paper also based on our survey of housing rights in all the national constitutions (Oren, Alterman, & Zilbershats, 2016). In that paper we present a classification of the format of housing rights, revealing three major types of formats whereby countries have incorporated housing into their constitutions: (a) the explicit (direct) right to housing; (b) embedded rights, that is, rights included in articles referring to housing as a component of some other right; and (c) indirect or implied rights.

Next, we report on additional aspects of housing rights in the world's national constitutions. The database is up to date to 2020. The findings highlight the need for a nuanced understanding of the many aspects of housing rights, and show directions for further research.

Right to Housing in International Treaties and Documents
At the international level, housing has been recognized as a human right by the *Universal Declaration on Human Rights* approved by the United Nations General Assembly in 1948, in which Article 25(1) states: "Everyone has the right to a standard of living adequate for the health and well-being of himself and of his family, including food, clothing, housing and medical care and necessary social services."

The right to housing was later elaborated by the UN's Committee on Economic Social and Cultural Rights (CESCR) in Article 11(1) of the *ICESCR* (1966). General Comment No. 4 to the *ICESCR* (henceforth, UN criteria) takes a big step forward by defining the concept of "housing adequacy" through seven socio-legal components. The intention of the UN was to make the task of compulsory national reporting on the achievement of housing rights more uniform and universally applicable.

These criteria will serve as our standard for evaluation, which we will present and expand on.

Preparation of "General Comments" is one of the three distinct ICESCR activities, the other two being periodic reporting and running a complaints system.[2] General Comments have been conferred considerable weight by national courts throughout the world. They can be used to universalize the ICESCR decisions through the mechanisms of national periodic reporting and through the feedback provided by complaints from the public. Importantly, General Comments may promote domestic legislation to implement housing rights and could influence specific national decisions. They also function as a means of providing authoritative guidance to a broader group of states. Indeed, the CESCR could legitimately look to General Comments as guidance for its activities in states that are not parties to the ICESCR, and in setting the minimum conditions for assistance to such states. Finally, General Comments can be used to reinforce the necessary linkages to other international human rights organs and the international legal system.

Between 1989 and 2020, the CESCR issued 24 General Comments ranging from those that spell out internal procedures of the committee to others that interpret the substantive provisions in their respective covenant.

Several CESCR comments address housing affairs. General Comment No. 5 deals with the accessibility to housing by persons with disabilities, and General Comment No. 7 deals with forced evictions and protections against arbitrary or unlawful interference with one's home. The most widely considered authoritative legal interpretation of "adequate" housing is in General Comment No. 4, issued in 1991. This comment accentuated the central importance of housing to the enjoyment of all other economic, social, and cultural rights, described in these terms: "the right to live somewhere in security, peace and dignity" (Leckie, 2003, p. ix).

With state reports as a starting point, the UN criteria are not legally binding, though General Comment No. 4 has a highly authoritative character with a legal basis in its own right: still, it is not a treaty and does not need ratification by treaty parties. It provides orientation for the practical implementation of this human right to adequate housing and forms a set of criteria for evaluating the progress of states in their implementation of this right.

The most important contribution of General Comment No. 4 is that it approaches housing in an integrative form:

> The right to housing should not be interpreted in a narrow or restrictive sense which equates it with, for example, the shelter provided by merely having a roof over one's head or views shelter exclusively as a commodity. Rather it should be seen as the right to live somewhere in security, peace and dignity...Adequate shelter means...adequate privacy, adequate space, adequate security, adequate lighting and ventilation, adequate basic infrastructure and adequate location with regard to work and basic facilities—all at a reasonable cost.[3]

The UN criteria are divided into three parts. The introductory part describes the efforts of the CESCR to gather information, including many country reports made since 1979. The third part is operative, in which the committee stresses that a request be made to state parties to take immediate steps, including asking governments to abstain from certain practices and calling for international co-operation. These measures might include prioritizing social groups living in unfavourable conditions, encouraging the preparation of a national housing strategy, establishing legislative and administrative measures, and implementing effective monitoring that enables governments to show that maximum efforts have been made to satisfy the obligations.

It is the second part of the General Comment No. 4 that is most relevant to our purpose here because it presents the definition of the right to adequate housing. The concept of adequacy is particularly significant in relation to the right to housing; it serves to underline a number of factors that must be considered in determining whether particular forms of shelter can be assessed as constituting "adequate housing." This second part thus underlines the seven criteria presented below.

The Seven Criteria of Housing Rights in the *ICESCR*

The following criteria presumably reflect a global consensus about the desirable norms of the CRtH. Fifteen years after they were enunciated, a similar set of criteria, or norms, was declaratively adopted as part of the UN's Sustainable Development Goals (SDGs), which were approved by the Habitat III Conference in 2016. In our research we applied the seven criteria of General Comment No. 4 to evaluate the CRtH of each of the UN member states. We wanted to see whether and to what extent their wording reflected these criteria.

Legal Security of Tenure

The term *security of tenure* is the protection provided to a landholder, indicating that the state or a private entity cannot interfere with the land's use or possession. Without regard to the length of the tenure (short or long), security of tenure implies confidence in the legal system and a lack of worry about loss of rights (Durand-Lasserve & Royston, 2012; Thiele, 2002; UN-Habitat, 2003).

General Comment No. 4 states that tenure applies to various contexts: rental (public and private), co-operative, lease, owner-occupation, emergency housing, and informal settlements, including occupation of land or property. All persons should possess a degree of security of tenure that guarantees legal protection against forced eviction or harassment, and states should take immediate measures to confer legal security of tenure.

Availability of Services, Materials, and Infrastructure

Basic infrastructure creates the enabling environment for the overall development of urbanization. It also implies increased public spending, policy interventions, and enabling conditions. In most urban areas local authorities or utility companies have the mandate and responsibility to deliver services to everyone. Infrastructure often involves services (such as water supply, sewage, energy, solid waste, roads, and communications) and assets that accommodate social services, including schools, universities, hospitals, prisons, and community housing. As the world is becoming increasingly urban, and the numbers living in urban slums are growing, affordability of basic services has been a concern for all sectors (Dubnoff, 1985). General Comment No. 4 states the following:

> An adequate house must contain certain facilities essential for health, security, comfort and nutrition. All beneficiaries of the right to adequate housing should have sustainable access to natural and common resources, safe drinking water, energy for cooking, heating and lighting, sanitation and washing facilities, means of food storage, refuse disposal, site drainage and emergency services.[4]

Affordability

Affordability is concerned with securing given standards of housing at a price or a rent that does not impose an unreasonable burden on household incomes, in the eyes of some third party, which usually means the government (Monk & Whitehead, 2010). In the last three decades, housing affordability has climbed to the top of national housing policy agendas, often replacing other traditional housing issues such as neighbourhood decay, substandard housing, and racial discrimination (Evans et al., 2016; Zhang & Ball, 2016). Today housing affordability issues are widespread throughout international housing literature (Aalbers, 2015; Wetzstein, 2017).

General Comment No. 4 states that costs associated with housing should be at such a level that other basic needs are not compromised. The percentage of housing-related costs should be commensurate with income levels. Accordingly, state parties should establish housing subsidies, as well as forms of housing finance. Tenants should be protected against unreasonable rent levels or rent increases. Where natural materials constitute the chief building materials, states parties should ensure their availability.

Habitability

Habitable means fit for habitation or to be lived in. Like many of the other concepts, it has much evolved in the 30 years since its widespread adoption. Whether housing is habitable also depends on geographic variations such as weather, terrain, and location. In climates with severe winters, storm windows may be considered as basic; in rainy areas, protection from damp needs to include waterproofing.

As General Comment No. 4 indicates, adequate housing must provide inhabitants with adequate space and protect them from threats related to their health, structural hazards, and disease vectors. The CESCR encourages state parties to apply the health principles of housing, prepared by the World Health Organization (1989), which shows that inadequate and deficient housing and living conditions are invariably associated with higher mortality and morbidity rates.

Accessibility

Accessibility is the degree to which housing is available to as many people as possible. Based on principles of social cohesion (Wong & Solomon, 2002), all citizens with incapacities, including the homeless and the poorly housed, should have proper accommodation and supportive independent housing, coupled with the provision of community support services. People access housing through "channels of acquirement" that sometimes fail to ensure access to all. They are defective in terms of housing standards and social justice, and they manifest exclusion (Sen, 1999). General Comment No. 4 makes clear the following: Housing policy and law should accord disadvantaged groups full and sustainable access to adequate housing resources, including for the elderly, children, the physically disabled, the terminally ill, HIV-positive individuals, persons with persistent medical problems, the mentally ill, victims of natural disasters, people living in disaster-prone areas, and other groups. They should be ensured some degree of priority consideration in the housing sphere.[5]

Location

Location is crucial in any choice of dwelling, although preferences and patterns may change from region to region and over time (Kemeny, 1992). A combinations of models with variables such as proximity to work, transport networks, local amenities or quality of life, life-cycle, return to human capital accumulation, and real costs of living determine most household location decisions (Schneider, 2004).

According to General Comment No. 4, adequate housing must be in a location—whether urban or rural—that allows access to employment options, health-care services, schools, childcare centres, and other social facilities. Housing should not be built on or near polluted sites that threaten the inhabitants' right to health.

Cultural Adequacy

Housing is a system of settings within which activities take place (Rapoport, 1991). In unpacking the concept of *culture*, Rapoport distinguishes two dimensions: a social one, including kinship, family structure, social networks, identity, status, and so forth; and an ideological dimension that encompasses values, ideals, images, norms, standards, expectations, rules, and so forth (Rapoport, 2000). Chiu (2004) classifies the settings into three major aspects: popular culture, religious and ideological, and anthropological human behaviour. Interestingly, this criterion is not mentioned in the SDGs.

General Comment No. 4 states that the way in which housing is constructed, including the building materials used, must enable the expression of cultural identity and diversity of housing. Development or modernization activities should ensure that the cultural dimensions of housing are not sacrificed, but that appropriate modern technological facilities are also ensured.

Research Findings: The World's Constitutional Right to Housing

Having introduced the UN criteria, we now present our factual global analysis of the constitutional clauses. Our analysis is restricted to the language of these documents. Note that in this research we do not address the legal status of the various clauses as interpreted by further court decisions, nor the de facto polices of governments. Our premise is that language matters.

Rationale and Method

Our key research question is this: To what extent does the wording of the national constitutions of UN member states refer to the right to housing?[6] And do they refer to any of the seven criteria proposed in General Comment No. 4? To conclude, we also look at whether the CRtH clause was adopted before or after the release of General Comment No. 4, to estimate its impact on the wording of the legislation.

To pass the threshold of recognition as a CRtH, the constitution had to state more than the term *housing*; it also had to imply some duty, responsibility, action, or procedure. After analysis of a pilot sample of constitutions, we developed the following threshold list, in which at least one of these actions is included in the constitution:

- Recognize housing as a right
- Protect individuals against deprivation of housing
- Empower private persons to defend their homes
- Establish a duty of the state to create a housing plan, a housing policy, or a housing fund
- Establish a duty of the state to provide the means to achieve housing by supplementing private initiatives
- Establish a duty of the state to provide housing or re-distribute public estates (public/social housing)
- Oblige the state to assure access to housing by minorities and vulnerable or dependent persons

Only constitutions that mentioned housing explicitly, along with at least one of the actions list, would enter our count. It was not necessary to mention any of the seven UN criteria explicitly. The population for analysis were 189 national constitutions of UN member states that possessed full-fledged constitutions. Our method used a version of manual content analysis. We preferred not to use software in order to capture the nuances. In law, such nuances can be all important.

The seven UN criteria served as the base line for evaluation, with scores on an ordinal scale. Mention of only one of the criteria would score 1 and mentions of seven would score 7. Since our population included only constitutions with some reference to housing, if none of the criteria were mentioned explicitly, the score would be zero.

In scanning the body of constitutions for housing rights, we did not differentiate according to the placement of the relevant clause within the structure of the constitution. Any mention of housing rights was included in our dataset. Indeed, our findings reported elsewhere (Oren et al., 2016) showed that the CRtH was distributed among a variety of topic sections within the constitutions, often in more than one spot. These sections included social and economic rights, general provisions, fundamental rights, fiscal policy, local authorities, civil rights, agrarian reform, or urban policies. Rarely were full chapters dedicated to housing.

An obvious question lies in the kinship between housing rights and related human rights. The latter may include property rights, privacy or inviolability of the home, freedom of domicile, general adequate standard of living, right to life, or other social rights. Initially we assumed that we would find overlaps between housing rights and property rights, with difficulties in separating them. However, our findings indicate that explicit references to housing are rarely found within clauses or chapters dedicated to property rights (Oren et al., 2016). We did not address other linkages, leaving them to further research.

Findings

Out of the 189 national constitutions surveyed (valid in 2020), we discovered that only 84 (44%) mentioned a CRtH explicitly somewhere in their wording. Neither the Canadian nor the American constitution has explicit mention of the right to adequate housing. In this they are not alone: most English-speaking countries do not have a CRtH, even though nothing in their legal structure (common law) prevents this. As the numbers show, many other countries have elected not to incorporate a CRtH in their constitutions, but the reasons for this remain unresearched.

In reporting our findings, we first address the database descriptively, to report on the geographic and temporal distributions of constitutions with housing rights. We then undertake to evaluate how multifaceted

FIGURE 7.1: Percentage of constitutions with a CRtH by each UN criterion; N=84

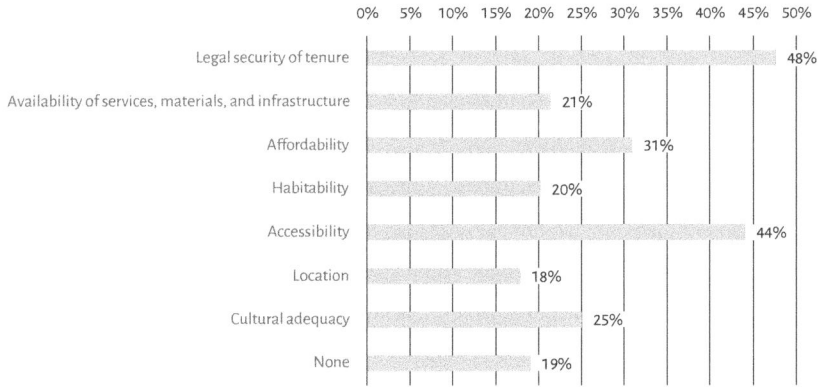

the approach is to the right to housing; specifically, we revisit the seven UN criteria to assess the extent to which each national constitution has incorporated one or more of these criteria.

Global Geographic Distribution over Time
The geographic distribution of the 84 countries with constitutional housing rights shows a good spread across continents: 20 countries in the Americas, 16 in Europe, 24 in Asia, and 24 in Africa. Regardless of size, South America (10 out of 12 sovereign countries) is the continent with the most coverage for a CRtH. North America is the continent with the least "coverage" by housing rights as only Mexico has them. This geographical distribution has implications for the evaluation according to the seven criteria.

References to the UN Criteria of "Adequate Housing"
The UN criteria do indeed appear in the texts of 81% of the constitutions (68/84). The findings are presented in figure 7.1. The criterion most frequently applied is legal security of tenure. It appears in 48% of the constitutions in a variety of forms, which we will detail via several subcategories. This finding resonates with the emphasis on security of tenure in the 2017 SDGs. Next in prevalence are accessibility (44%), affordability (31%), and cultural adequacy (25%). We were surprised and satisfied

to see this last criterion included. These three criteria have an important role in the conception of adequate housing. The remaining three criteria—availability of services, habitability, and location—are apparently less commonly used (ranging between 18% and 21%).

Distribution by Criteria and Scores

Figure 7.2 shows the distribution of countries with a CRtH by number of UN criteria mentioned (scores). Countries were classified by continents to present both their wide geographic distribution and the variety of scores attained within them. (As noted, number of criteria is also viewed as scores for the comparative evaluation.) Countries in the Americas attained the highest score, ranging from one to seven, led by Venezuela, Ecuador, Mexico, Bolivia, and Brazil. European countries attained low scores of zero to two, with the exception of Portugal (7) and Switzerland (4). Asia and Africa attained scores from zero to three, with the Asian countries of Philippines (6) and Iran (4) as exceptions.

Another hypothesis pertains to a possible relationship with the cultural (often language-bound) group to which a country belongs. South and Central America have the highest rate of coverage of a CRtH. These geographic areas also share the Spanish-Portuguese culture. The findings confirm that countries belonging to Spanish, French, and Portuguese cultural heritages have a stronger propensity to adopt housing rights, as they constitute 42% (36/84) of the total number of countries with a CRtH. This group of countries encompasses not only countries in South and Central American countries, but also former Spanish, French, and Portuguese colonies in Asia and Africa (Philippines and Angola), as well as Portugal and Spain in Europe.

We now turn to a deeper look at each of the seven criteria.

First Criterion: Definitions or Perceptions of Legal Security of Tenure

Although none of the constitutions uses the term *security of tenure* explicitly, 39 (48%) of them do refer to specific forms of tenure. We classified them into 13 categories; Table 7.1 presents the various formulations and the number of cases found in each category.

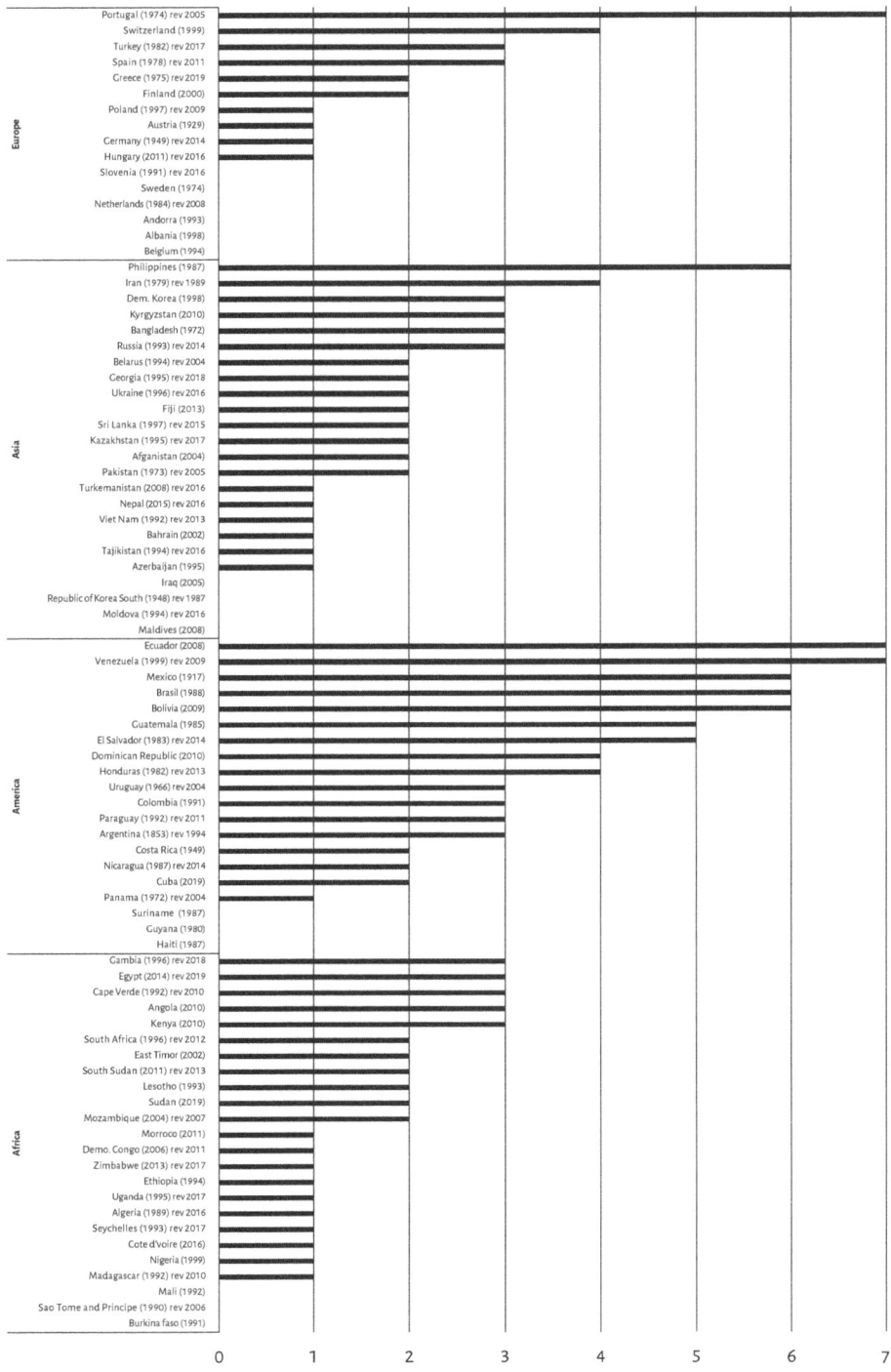

FIGURE 7.2: Number of UN criteria mentioned "scores" total, in each county's constitution, arranged by continent

Public housing is the most widespread type of tenure mentioned (23/39), the responsibility being delegated completely to the state. Various degrees of commitment to housing by the state were found: to provide, to support and encourage, to promote, to control and regulate, to protect. In countries such as Afghanistan, Kyrgyzstan, Ukraine, and Russia, the state commits to the provision of public housing to deserving citizens. In countries like Ecuador, Guatemala, and Switzerland the state commits to support and encourage the construction or planning of public housing. In Bolivia, Colombia, Costa Rica, Dominican Republic, Paraguay, Portugal, and Venezuela the state commits to promote the construction of public housing.

Several countries encourage home ownership (17/39), while only few explicitly encourage rental (6/39), protection against deprivation of housing (7/39), or protection against forced eviction (5/39), or protection against abuse in matters of tenancy (4/39). This is surprising, given the heightened attention to protection from eviction. Sometimes tension and contradictions occur between housing rights and other constitutionally protected norms, such as private property rights. Another interesting finding was references to housing co-operatives (7/39), identified with wording like *communal possession*, seen in Bolivia, Portugal, Colombia, Guatemala, and Mexico.

Unlike the attention given to recognitions of informal settlements in SDGs, our findings show that only a few countries have included this aspect in their national constitution. Recognition of informalities had poor presence (see Table 7.1), such as in informal settlements and squatters (3/39), nomadism (1/39, Afghanistan), resettlement of displaced populations (2/39), and homelessness (3/39).

Second Criterion: Availability of Services, Materials, Facilities, and Infrastructure
References to availability of services, materials, and infrastructure in the context of the right to housing were found in 21% of the CRtHs (18/84) in a range of countries (11 of them Latin). For example, the Greek constitution mentions the "construction of roads, squares and public utility areas,"[7] and Hungary mentions "decent housing and access to public

TABLE 7.1: Number of constitutions that mention security of tenure by subcategory

Subcategory	Findings	No. of CRtH
Tenure/title/ registry	• Have access to titled property • Receive domain and title over property for living purposes • Have different systems of land tenure under co-operative housing	1
Rent and leases (private/public)	• Provide rental housing (private/public) • Promote the access to rental housing • Regulate rental housing, as a governmental duty • Have a system of rents that is compatible with family incomes	6
Ownership	• Enable the greatest possible number of citizens to become homeowners • Create a system for housing ownership that is compatible with incomes • Establish a financing system that grants sufficient cheap credit for people to become house owners • Support activities aimed at acquisition of a home by each citizen • Encourage the construction of housing, and the acquisition and ownership of apartments and houses for the personal use of private individuals	16
Communal possession	• Promote housing co-operatives	7
Social/Public housing	• Adopt the necessary measures for the provision of housing and distribution of public estates • Promote housing projects of social interest	22
Care institutions	• Dependent populations will have access to caregiving centres or institutions	3
Protection against abuse in tenancy matters	• Protect privately owned dwellings • Protect against unfair rents • Assure that every person has the right to subscribe to rental contracts at a just price without abuse • Implement the Protection of Tenants Act and the Rent Act within a province • Legislate against abuses in tenancy matters, and, in particular, against unfair rents, as well as on the procedure for challenging unlawfully terminated leases and the limited extension of leases	4
Protection from deprivation	• No one can be deprived of their living accommodation except on the grounds established by law • Abolish all forms of deprivation of housing • Protect against arbitrary deprivation of housing	7
Protection from forced/arbitrary eviction	• Dwellers shall not be evicted, nor their dwellings demolished, except in accordance with law and in a just and humane manner	5
Informal settlements/ squatters	• Improve living conditions of settlers/squatters (precarious housing) • Pursue a policy with special provision for squatters	3
Nomadism	• Improve the living conditions of nomads' livelihood	1
Resettlement	• Set a program of urban land reform and housing that will make decent housing and basic services available to underprivileged and homeless citizens in urban centres and resettlement areas at an affordable cost	2
Homelessness	• Pursue policies conducive to satisfying citizens' housing needs, particularly combatting homelessness • Establish a program of urban land reform and housing that will make decent housing and basic services available to underprivileged and homeless citizens at an affordable cost	5

services."[8] Other examples mention facilities essential for health, security, comfort, and nutrition, as in Ecuador, which names "a secure and healthy habitat,"[9] and Portugal, which asks for satisfactory standards of hygiene.[10] Examples in which sustainable access to natural and common resources, safe drinking water, energy, heating, and lighting were mentioned include Bolivia, which states that "every person has the right to universal and equitable access to basic services of potable water, sewer systems, electricity, gas services in their domicile,"[11] and Democratic Congo, which states that "the right to decent housing, the right of access to drinking water and to electric energy are guaranteed."[12]

Third Criterion: Affordability
Affordability is mentioned in various forms in 31% of national constitutions with a CRtH. Aside from explicit mentions of affordability, additional clauses assure the percentage of housing-related costs is commensurate with income levels (e.g., using the translated term *low-income persons*), establish housing subsidies and finance programs, or refer to assurances about the availability of building materials where natural materials constitute the chief source of building materials. One example is the constitution of Suriname: "A housing plan shall be determined by law, aimed at the procurement of a sufficient number of affordable houses and state control of the use of real estate for public housing."[13] Another example is Kyrgyzstan, whose constitution states that "housing for low-income persons and other persons in need shall be provided free of charge or for affordable payment funded by the state, municipal or other social institutions in accordance with criteria and the procedures established by law."[14]

Fourth Criterion: Habitability
The CRtH refers to sanitary conditions or adequate size in 20% of the sample. Examples of such clauses are found in El Salvador's comments to "provide a sanitary and comfortable home,"[15] Guatemala's wording of "meet health requirements," and Seychelles' phrasing of "conducive to health and well-being."[16] Portugal's constitution refers to both size and

hygiene (as do East Timor and Brazil), which states: "Everyone has the right, both personally and for his or her family, to a dwelling of adequate size that meets satisfactory standards of hygiene and preserves personal and family privacy."[17]

Fifth Criterion: Accessibility

Of the national CRtHs, 44% refer to accessibility. According to General Comment No. 4, accessibility means that a house must be accessible to those entitled to it, and disadvantaged groups must be accorded full and sustainable access to adequate housing resources. Examples that guarantee access to disadvantaged groups specifically include the constitutions of Brazil, which names "needy children"; Ecuador, which mentions "priority groups"; and Iran, which states that first consideration is given to those who are in need, in particular villagers and labourers.[18]

Sixth Criterion: Location

Location was mentioned in 18% of the CRtHs. We did not find a CRtH that referred specifically to the proximity of the home to work or services, or to distance from environmental hazards. From today's perspective, the absence of references to proximity to work counters the current understanding of the importance of employment opportunities for households. Housing is (or should be) no longer perceived as a stand-alone service or commodity, but, rather, as linked to urban services.

We did find a few references to proximity to transport networks: for example, in Ecuador, "housing, services, public space and transportation"[19]; and in Portugal, "to support plans for urban areas that guarantee an adequate network of transport and social facilities."[20] Some constitutions emphasize access to rural housing, such as in Afghanistan, with "farmers, herders and settlers,"[21] and in El Salvador, which notes that "it shall undertake to see that every farm owner shall provide a sanitary and comfortable home for his workers."[22] Bangladesh emphasizes the need "to remove the disparity in the standards of living between the urban and the rural areas."[23]

Seventh Criterion: Cultural Adequacy

References to some form of cultural adequacy were found in 25% of CRtHs. Sometimes the expression is explicit, as in Bangladesh, which names the "material and cultural standard of living."[24] Protection of culture in the case of development or modernization activities was referenced in the constitutions of the Democratic People's Republic of Korea, which identifies "modern houses in the countryside."[25] Some countries refer to the family, such as in Angola, where "housing and a family and community life"[26] are named, while others (mostly in Latin countries) are like Costa Rica, which specifies that "the State shall promote the construction of low-cost housing and create a family homestead for workers."[27]

Differences between CRtHs Adopted before and after the Release of General Comment No. 4

Logically, for General Comment No. 4 to have the potential to influence a specific national constitution, the adoption of the comment must precede revisions to the constitution. However, no uniform chronological pattern is evident in the trajectory to adoption of housing rights. It could be assumed that most countries would first declare independence, draft a constitution regulating the structure of the state, sign the ICESCR, and then draft a human rights bill. In reality, national systems are dynamic and vulnerable to geopolitical changes. Regained independence, coups d'état, state transitions, and recognition of autonomous territories are among the many factors that affect the trajectory of how constitutions are established. The majority of states that are parties to the ICESCR joined between the late 1970s and the 1980s. We cannot infer that the inclusion of housing rights in constitutions was a direct consequence of adoption of the ICESCR. Moreover, General Comment No. 4 was not published until the early 1990s. Therefore, we examined the language of each of the constitutions adopted post-1991 and compared these with pre-1991 constitutions. We could thus discern whether the language of the CRtH was affected by General Comment No. 4.

The findings show that the insertion of CRtH components, later to be known as the UN housing criteria, started before General Comment No. 4

was published. Overall, we observed an increase since 1991 in the number of constitutions incorporating adequate housing components: pre-1991, only 31 had these provisions; post-1991, 56 did. The increase includes new states that were declared during the third wave of democratization in the 1990s.[28] However, where new constitutions are concerned, it is not easy to single out the direct influence of General Comment No. 4, unless its exact wording is used, because housing rights have been "in the air" for some time.

A more distinctive expression of the influence of General Comment No. 4 can be seen in the revision of previous constitutions, where we can compare the exact wording before and after the emergence of General Comment No. 4. During the last decade, between 2011 and 2020, 20 countries that drafted new constitutions inserted a CRtH in their revised version. These include Algeria (revised in 2016), Côte d'Ivoire (2016), Cuba (2019), Dominican Republic (2015), and Egypt (2014, revised in 2019). All these countries have at least one UN criterion in their CRtH.

So, we leave the readers with this conundrum: do these findings show a high or a low impact of the UN promoted criteria set out in General Comment No. 4? Has the world made significant progress in adopting constitutional housing rights?

Conclusion

In this chapter we have reported on our findings from a content analysis of the language used in all 189 national constitutions of UN member states. It is not easy to conclude whether our findings harbour "bad news" or "good news" for global housing rights.

We first looked at the sheer number and distribution of national constitutions with some form of housing rights. We found a significant presence of such constitutions—84 out of 189, with a broad geographic spread across the globe. Still, many countries and groups of countries have not yet seen merit in incorporating housing rights into their constitutions.

On the positive side, we saw a general increase in constitutions with housing rights over the years. This is especially significant because in the last decade, since 2010, many new constitutions have been adopted, mostly in developing countries. We assume that the involvement in their constitution-making process by international agencies, such as the United Nations Development Programme, may have contributed to the anchoring and a larger presence of economic, social, and cultural rights, including a CRtH.

To coordinate expectations, we must clarify that constitutions can teach us little about the quality and availability of housing in practice. From the analysis of constitutional texts, we can only learn about the texts themselves because there is a large gap between constitutional declarations and implementation de facto. Moreover, a textual analysis does not tell us about any possible interpretation by courts or any other possible regulations and laws that may further elaborate the terminology used by the constitution.

At a deeper level, we sought to evaluate the depth and scope of the housing rights through the prism of a landmark UN document, with international treaty status. This is General Comment No. 4 on "the right to adequate housing." It is appended to the *International Covenant on Economic, Social and Cultural Rights*, prepared in 1966 by the UN Human Rights Committee. General Comment No. 4 refers to seven key socio-legal criteria: legal security of tenure, availability of services and infrastructure, affordability, habitability, accessibility, location, and cultural adequacy. Although these were phrased many decades ago, generally they still resonate well with current conceptions of housing rights, at least as a reasonable minimal standard.

The research analyzed the text of each of the constitutions through the prism of the seven criteria. The findings show major disparities across countries in the number of criteria addressed and in their detailed interpretation. The most prevalent criterion is the right to security of tenure. It fits well with current conceptions, as expressed in the UN Sustainable Development Goals. However, some of the other criteria are not well addressed, leaving housing rights up in the air and thus wide open to almost any interpretation. Some components of housing are distributed better than others, especially among countries sharing a linguistic heritage. Despite the passage of many decades since the approval of the latest international treaty to address housing rights, few signs of convergence are evident in the substance of constitutional housing rights. Of course, the scope of this research cannot rule out a convergence created through court decisions that interpret each of the constitutions.

In the Canadian context, on June 21, 2019, Bill C-97 was enacted, containing the *National Housing Strategy Act* and the federal right-to-housing legislation. This legislation is historic, marking the first legally explicit recognition of the right to housing by the Canadian government and setting a new overall direction for the federal government in terms of its housing programs, policies, and budgets. The Act states the following:

> It is declared to be the housing policy of the Government of Canada to recognize that the right to adequate housing is a fundamental human right affirmed in international law; and to recognize that housing is essential to the inherent dignity and well-being of the person and to building sustainable and inclusive communities.[29]

Although this legal recognition clearly sets out the policy objectives of the federal government, the legislation does not contain any specific mechanisms for individuals seeking access to adequate housing. In other words, the *National Housing Strategy Act* is not a constitutional provision; therefore, in theory it could be repealed by future legislation without constitutional barriers.

Perhaps our findings are an indication that not enough effort has been invested by formal international bodies, civil society, and scholars in attempting to reach a greater consensus on the importance of housing rights and what they should comprise. We must also raise the possibility that, today, initiatives such as the SDGs and the worldwide activities surrounding them may hold a more important place than do formal international treaties. At the national level, however, constitutional rights are likely to remain important in a globalizing world. Our mixed-news findings may represent an alert about deeper issues underlying ideologies and geopolitics. These findings accord with previous arguments

(Kenna, 2010a) on the major obstacles hindering the adoption of international human rights by national laws.

The reality check presented in this chapter is intended to stimulate fresh thinking by scholars, practitioners, and legislators about the right to housing around the globe. The knowledge terrain is still rudimentary and calls for more systematic comparative research. At the same time, more country-specific analysis is needed of the historic and political trajectories whereby specific nations adopt the constitutional right to housing.

NOTES

1. Bill C-97 (Royal Assent) June 21, 2019, https://www.parl.ca/DocumentViewer/en/42-1/bill/C-97/royal-assent
2. Kolocek (2017) presents the findings of a global discourse analysis of periodic reports submitted by countries to the United Nations with regard to their implementation of the right to housing.
3. General Comment No. 4: The right to adequate housing (art. 11 (1) of the Covenant), Section 8, *The concept of adequacy*.
4. General Comment No. 4: The right to adequate housing (art. 11 (1) of the Covenant), Section 8 (b), *Availability of services, materials, facilities and infrastructure*.
5. General Comment No. 4: The right to adequate housing (art. 11 (1) of the Covenant), Section 8 (e), *Accessibility*.
6. There may be a few non-member states with constitutions. They are not analyzed here.
7. *Constitution of Greece*, 1975 (rev 2019), Part II, art 24.3. The text of the constitutions in this and the following examples has been translated into English. We occasionally paraphrased the wording.
8. *Fundamental Law of Hungary*, 2011 (rev 2016), art XXII.
9. *Constitution of the Republic of Ecuador*, 2008 (rev 2021), c 2, s 6, art 30.
10. *Constitution of the Portuguese Republic*, 1976 (rev 2005), Title III, c II, art 65.1.
11. *Political Constitution of the Plurinational State of Bolivia*, 2009, c II, art 20.1.
12. *Constitution of the Democratic Republic of the Congo*, 2005 (rev 2011), c 2, art 48.
13. *Constitution of the Republic of Suriname*, 1987 (rev 1992), c VIII, art 49.
14. *Constitution of the Kyrgyz Republic*, 2010 (rev 2016), s 2, c 1, art 46.4.
15. *Constitution of the Republic of El Salvador*, 1983 (rev 2014), Title V, art 119.
16. *Constitution of the Republic of Seychelles*, 1993 (rev 2017), c III, Part I, art 34.
17. *Constitution of the Portuguese Republic*, 1976 (rev 2005), Title III, c II, art 65.1.

18. *Constitution of the Islamic Republic of Iran*, 1979 (rev 1989), c III, art. 31.
19. *Constitution of the Republic of Ecuador*, 2008 (rev 2021), Title VII, s 4, art 375.1.
20. *Constitution of the Portuguese Republic*, 1976 (rev 2005), Title III, c II, art 65.2(a).
21. *Constitution of the Islamic Republic of Afghanistan*, 2004, c 1. art 14.
22. *Constitution of the Republic of El Salvador*, 1983 (rev 2014), Title V, art 119.
23. *Constitution of the People's Republic of Bangladesh*, 1972 (rev 2014), Part II, art 16.
24. *Constitution of the People's Republic of Bangladesh*, 1972 (rev 2014), Part II, art 15.
25. *Constitution of the Democratic People's Republic of Korea*, 1998, c II, art 28.
26. *Constitution of the Republic of Angola*, 2010, c III, art 82.1.
27. *Constitution of the Republic of Costa Rica*, 1949 (rev 2020), Title V, art 65.
28. The third wave of democratization refers to the global trend that has seen more than 60 countries throughout Europe, Latin America, Asia, and Africa undergo some form of democratic transition. See Huntington (1991).
29. Statues of Canada, *National Housing Strategy Act* (S.C. 2019, c. 29, s. 313), *Housing Policy Declaration Marginal Note: Declaration Section 4*.

REFERENCES

Aalbers, M.B. (2015). The great moderation, the great excess and the global housing crisis. *International Journal of Housing Policy, 15*(1), 43–60.

Agrawal, S. (2020). Human rights and the city: A view from Canada. *Journal of the American Planning Association, 87*(1), 3–10. doi:10.1080/01944363.2020.1775680

Ball, J. (2012). *Housing disadvantaged people? Insiders and outsiders in French social housing*. Routledge.

Bratt, R.G., Stone, M.E., & Hartman, C.W. (Eds.). (2006). *A right to housing: Foundation for a new social agenda*. Temple University Press.

Chiu, R.L. (2004). Socio cultural sustainability of housing: A conceptual exploration. *Housing, Theory and Society, 21*(2), 65–76.

City of Toronto. (2018). *Street Needs Assessment 2018*. https://www.toronto.ca

Collins, D., & Stout, M. (2019). Does Housing First policy seek to fulfil the right to housing? The case of Alberta, Canada. *Housing Studies, 36*(3), 1-23.

De Vos, P. (2001). *Grootboom*, the right of access to housing and substantive equality as contextual fairness. *South African Journal on Human Rights, 17*(2), 258–276.

Dubnoff, S. (1985). How much income is enough? Measuring public judgments. *Public Opinion Quarterly, 49*(3) 285–299.

Durand-Lasserve, A., & Royston, L. (2012). International trends and country contexts—from tenure regularization to tenure security. In A. Durand-Lasserve & L. Royston (Eds.), *Holding their ground* (pp. 17–50). Routledge.

Evans, B., Elisei, P., Rosenfeld, O., Roll, G., Figueiredo, A., & Keiner, M. (2016). Habitat III– Toward a new urban agenda. *disP—the Planning Review, 52*(1), 86–91.

Hohmann, J. (2013). *The right to housing: Law, concepts, possibilities*. Bloomsbury Publishing.

Huchzermeyer, M. (2004). From "contravention of laws" to "lack of rights": Redefining the problem of informal settlements in South Africa. *Habitat International*, 28(3), 333–347.

Huntington, S.P. (1991). Democracy's third wave. *Journal of Democracy*, 2(2), 12–15.

Jung, C., Hirschl, R., & Rosevear, E. (2014). Economic and social rights in national constitutions. *American Journal of Comparative Law*, 62(4), 1043–1098. doi:10.2139/ssrn.2349680

Kemeny, J. (1992). *Housing and social theory*. London and New York: Routledge.

Kenna, P. (2010a). *Can international housing rights based on public international law really impact on contemporary housing systems?* Ashgate.

Kenna, P. (2010b). International instruments on housing rights. *Journal of Legal Affairs and Dispute Resolution in Engineering and Construction*, 2(1), 11–20.

Kenna, P. (2011). *Housing law, rights, and policy*. Clarus Press.

Kolocek, M. (2017). *The human right to housing in the face of land policy and social citizenship*. Palgrave Macmillan. doi:10.1007/978-3-319-53489-3.

Leckie, S. (Ed.). (2000). *Legal resources for housing rights: International and national standards*. Centre on Housing Rights and Evictions.

Leckie, S. (2003). *National perspectives on housing rights*. Springer Netherlands.

McIsaac, E. (2019). Opinion: Why we need cities to fully realize the right to housing in Canada. *Maytree*, https://maytree.com/publications/why-we-need-cities-to-fully-realize-the-right-to-housing-in-canada/

Monk, S., & Whitehead, C. (2010). *Making housing more affordable*. Wiley Online Library. doi:10.1002/9781444327854

Moons, N. (2018). *The right to housing in law and society*. Routledge.

Mukherjee, A. (2019). *The legal right to housing in India*. Cambridge University Press.

Oren, M., Alterman, R., & Zilbershats, Y. (2016). Housing rights in constitutional legislation: A conceptual classification. In P. Kenna, *Contemporary housing issues in a globalized world* (pp. 141–158). Routledge.

Rapoport, A. (1991). Housing and culture. In L. Taylor (Ed.), *Housing: Symbol, Structure, Site* (pp. 14–15). Rizzoli.

Rapoport, A. (2000). Theory, culture and housing. *Housing, theory and society*, 17(4), 145–165

Schneider, D. (2004). The constitutional right to housing in South Africa: *The Government of the Republic of South Africa v. Irene Grootboom*. *International Journal of Civil Society Law*, (2), 45.

Sen, A. (1999). *Development as freedom*. Oxford University Press.

Sidoli del Ceno, J., & Vols, M. (Eds.). (2017). *Regulating the city: Contemporary urban housing law*. (Studies in Housing Law, vol. 1). Eleven International Publishing.

Thiele, B. (2002). The human right to adequate housing: A tool for promoting and protecting individual and community health. *American Journal of Public Health*, 92(5), 712–715.

UN General Assembly. (1966, December 16). *International covenant on economic, social and cultural rights*. https://www.ohchr.org/Documents/ProfessionalInterest/cescr.pdf

UN-Habitat. (2003). *The challenge of slums: Global report on human settlements*. Earthscan. https://www.un.org/ruleoflaw/files/Challenge%20of%20Slums.pdf

Wells, K. (2019). The right to housing. *Political Studies, 67*(2), 406–421.

Wetzstein, S. (2017). The global urban housing affordability crisis. *Urban Studies, 54*(14), 3159–3177.

Wong, Y.L.I., & Solomon, P.L. (2002). Community integration of persons with psychiatric disabilities in supportive independent housing: A conceptual model and methodological considerations. *Mental Health Services Research, 4*(1), 13–28.

World Health Organization. (1989). *Health principles of housing*. https://apps.who.int/iris/handle/10665/39847

Zhang, X.Q., & Ball, M. (2016). Housing the planet: Evolution of global housing policies. *Habitat International, 54*(3), 161–165.

LEGISLATION

Canadian Parliament, *Government Bill C-97, An Act to Implement Certain Provisions of the budget tabled in Parliament on March 19, 2019 and other measures*, Part 4, Division 19, 1st Session, 42nd Parliament (SC 2019, c. 29).

Constitution of the Democratic People's Republic of Korea, 1998, c II, art 28.

Constitution of the Democratic Republic of the Congo, 2005 (rev 2011), c 2, art 48.

Constitution of Greece, 1975 (rev 2019), Part II, art 24.3.

Constitution of the Islamic Republic of Afghanistan, 2004, c 1. art 14.

Constitution of the Islamic Republic of Iran, 1979 (rev 1989), c III, art 31.

Constitution of the Kyrgyz Republic, 2010 (rev 2016), s 2, c 1, art 46.4.

Constitution of the People's Republic of Bangladesh, 1972 (rev 2014), Part II, art 16.

Constitution of the Portuguese Republic, 1976 (rev 2005), Title III, c II, art 65.1.

Constitution of the Republic of Angola, 2010, c III, art 82.1.

Constitution of the Republic of Costa Rica, 1949 (rev 2020), Title V, art 65.

Constitution of the Republic of Ecuador, 2008 (rev 2021), c 2, s 6, art 30.

Constitution of the Republic of El Salvador, 1983 (rev 2014), Title V, art 119.

Constitution of the Republic of Seychelles, 1993 (rev 2017), c III, Part I, art 34.

Constitution of the Republic of Suriname, 1987 (rev 1992), c VIII, art 49.

Fundamental Law of Hungary, 2011 (rev 2016), art XXII.

Political Constitution of the Plurinational State of Bolivia, 2009, c II, art 20.1.

UN Committee on Economic, Social and Cultural Rights (CESCR), *General Comment No. 4: The Right to Adequate Housing (Art. 11 (1) of the Covenant)*, 13 December 1991, E/1992/23.

UN General Assembly, *International Covenant on Economic, Social and Cultural Rights*, 16 December 1966, United Nations, Treaty Series, vol. 993, p. 3.

UN General Assembly, *Universal Declaration of Human Rights*, 10 December 1948, 217 A (III).

8
PROPERTY RIGHTS AND THE CANADIAN CITY

ERAN S. KAPLINSKY
—

Introduction

Property, as described by Bentham (1843), is often understood as legally protected expectations regarding valuable things. Given this broad definition, the various rights exercised in Canadian cities related to the physical environment can be characterized as property. Such rights range from a homeowner's immunity from trespass to a homeless person's privilege to use a bench in a city park. The institution of property establishes complex networks of legal relationships between individuals with respect to buildings, open spaces, and municipal infrastructure and amenities. These relationships are shaped and enforced, in turn, by informal norms and local customs developed over time, and by laws, regulations, and other formal institutions. The property rights of landowners in particular are formally governed in Canada by a patchwork of common-law rules pertaining to land tenure, acquisition and disposition, lateral and vertical boundaries, domestic and other sharing, possessory and equitable interests, and servitudes, as modified by provincial legislation. Nowadays, municipal and planning legislation has supplanted the doctrine of nuisance as the primary means of regulating relationships between neighbours and prescribing the uses that may be made of private land.

The focus of this chapter is *property rights*, a term used colloquially to describe the rights of a private property "owner" to resist, or receive compensation for, expropriation, regulation, or other government action. Notably, the owner is the one who owns full title, but the person could actually be anyone who holds a legal interest in the property. Property rights in Canada are also defined by common law and statute. The chapter begins by situating property rights within the Canadian legal framework. It proceeds to review the principles that govern various interferences with property, including expropriation, injurious affection where no land is taken, and land use regulation. As will be shown, while planning legislation can be hindered by doctrinal ambiguity and inconsistency that invites litigation and makes compensation contingent on arbitrary circumstances, the courts' inclination to balance private and public interests, to be animated by policy concerns, and to spread the burdens and benefits of public projects varies greatly depending on the context.

Property and the City

In many parts of the world, property rights are enshrined in a constitution. The effect of constitutionalizing property rights is to demarcate certain proprietary entitlements outside the reach of the political majority. Canada remains, however, one of the jurisdictions in which private property is not afforded constitutional protection directly (Alterman, 2010).[1] Instead, private property rights in Canada are delineated by common law and legislation. An act by the government that impinges on common-law private rights must be authorized by a valid statute. Legislative authority in Canada is divided in the *Constitution Act, 1867*,[2] between Parliament and the provincial legislatures. Specifically, exclusive jurisdiction over property is conferred on the provinces (with a few important exceptions, such as authority over aeronautics, telecommunications, and Indian reserves). In turn, substantial powers over the use of land are delegated to municipal authorities (which are similarly subject to exclusive provincial jurisdiction) by enabling statutes such as Ontario's *Planning Act*, 1990,[3] and Alberta's *Municipal Government Act*, 2000.[4]

During the past century the political discourse, and in particular the legal discourse, that surrounds property rights in many parts of the world has been heavily influenced by debates in the United States (Alexander, 2006), where the fifth amendment to the Constitution famously provides: "nor shall private property be taken for public use, without just compensation." This framing of property rights focuses on the characterization of the government action as a "taking." The taxonomy of takings in the United States consists of acts of eminent domain (i.e., expropriation) and regulatory takings. The latter category is further divided into per se takings (regulatory actions that deprive the affected owner of all viable economic uses of the property, or compel the owner to endure permanent physical occupation of the property) and ad hoc takings (regulatory acts that are found by the courts to go too far, considering the character of the impugned action, the extent of its economic impact, and the owner's investment-backed expectations).

The Canadian law of expropriation and compensation was developed in the English legal tradition and for the most part remains unaffected by American jurisprudence. Illustrative of the Canadian approach is the decision of the Court of Appeal of Nova Scotia in *Mariner Real Estate Ltd. v Nova Scotia (Attorney General).*[5] There, pursuant to a provincial enactment, the plaintiffs' lands were designated as protected beaches under ministerial control. The minister subsequently denied the plaintiffs' applications to develop their property. The plaintiffs argued that the Crown's actions amounted to expropriation and that they were entitled to compensation. In support of their position, the plaintiffs cited the US Supreme Court's decision in *Lucas v South Carolina Coastal Council*,[6] which held that substantially similar restrictions were unconstitutional in the absence of fair compensation to the owner. Justice Cromwell (as he then was) noted that the US takings case law concerned constitutional limits on legislative authority over private property that were inapplicable in Canada:

As O'Connor, J. said in the United States Supreme Court case of *Eastern Enterprises v Apfel*, the purpose of the U.S. constitutional provision (referred to as the "takings clause") is to prevent the government from "...forcing some people alone to bear public burdens which, in all fairness and justice, should be borne by the public as a whole." Canadian courts have no similar broad mandate to review and vary legislative judgments about the appropriate distribution of burdens and benefits flowing from environmental or other land use controls. In Canada, the courts' task is to determine whether the regulation in question entitles the respondents to compensation...not to pass judgment on the way the Legislature apportions the burdens flowing from land use regulation.[7]

Under the Canadian approach, the protection of property rights does not hinge on the characterization of the government action as a taking, as it does in the United States. Any infringement may be authorized by statute, and whether or not the affected owner is entitled to compensation or other relief is a matter of statutory interpretation.[8] Nevertheless, as the next sections show, the distinction between expropriation and lesser interferences with private property (notably, restrictions on the use and development of land) remains important because of expropriation legislation across Canada. Such legislation provides landowners with express compensation rights and procedural guarantees that apply whenever an expropriation authority compulsorily acquires an interest in private property. Where no interest is formally acquired, the rights of the property owner depend on the interpretation of the legislative scheme authorizing the interference, or a finding of constructive (de facto) expropriation.

Expropriation and the City
The power of expropriation inheres in the Crown's ultimate ownership of all land in Canada and may be traced to the ancient royal prerogative to take the property of the Crown's subjects for the purpose of defending the realm or in the public interest: *salus populi suprema lex esto*. Canadian municipalities are delegated expropriation powers for municipal

purposes. The City of Vancouver's *Charter*,[9] for example, provides that "if, in the exercise of any of its powers of acquiring real property, the city fails to come to an agreement with its owner as to the terms of acquisition, the city may, by bylaw or resolution of the Council, expropriate such real property."[10] Typical municipal purposes include acquisition of land for municipal buildings or infrastructure, road widenings, provision of building sites, or land development or redevelopment. Councils in Nova Scotia may expropriate land for any purpose for which they may spend money.[11] Private property in the city is also subject to the expropriation powers granted to school boards, utilities, transit authorities, hospitals, and other local and provincial agencies.

All expropriations are subject to the applicable provincial enactment (e.g., Ontario's *Expropriations Act*),[12] or, if the expropriation is carried out pursuant to federal legislation, the Canada *Expropriation Act*, 1985, is the relevant legislation.[13] The legislative scheme is substantially similar in the various jurisdictions.[14] The expropriation agency must serve notice on every owner whose interest is proposed to be acquired. Any interested person may object to the expropriation, but the objection must relate to the fairness and necessity of the expropriation and not to the undertaking proposed by the authority. If the expropriation is duly approved, the owner of the expropriated property is entitled to compensation as provided in the legislation. The compensation awarded in Canada generally consists of the market value of the interest acquired, along with additional compensation such as disturbance or relocation expenses designed to make the owner as whole as possible.[15] In principle, a valid enactment may authorize a local government to expropriate private property without compensation or with partial compensation, but this has never been done in Canada.[16] Furthermore, Canadian courts follow the principle laid out by the House of Lords in *Attorney General v De Keyser's Royal Hotel Ltd.*[17] that a statute is not to be interpreted to allow private property to be taken for public purposes without compensation, unless the words of the statute clearly indicate an intention to do so.[18]

Compensation for Injurious Affection Where No Land Is Taken

Property owners may be entitled to compensation for "injurious affection" resulting from municipal projects or public works even where no land is taken. Such rights are provided in lieu of a common-law action in nuisance that public authorities can often answer with a defence of statutory authority. In Alberta, for example, a municipality must compensate landowners for losses sustained due to the closing of roads or for any permanent net reduction in value to land that arises from the existence of public works.[19]

Similar compensation is provided by the expropriation statutes of the various provinces. The *Expropriation Act*, 1990, of Ontario provides for compensation where land is devalued due to an action taken under statutory authority, which but for that statutory authority would give rise to liability if the loss resulted from the construction and not the use of the works. In *Antrim Truck Centre Ltd. v Ontario (Transportation)*,[20] the Supreme Court of Canada (SCC) ordered that compensation be awarded to the appellant, who was effectively put out of business as a result of a highway project that restricted access to the appellant's property. The SCC clarified that an owner claiming injurious affection whose land is not expropriated must demonstrate that the interference with the property is substantial and that it would be unreasonable, in all of the circumstances, to require the owner to suffer it without compensation. In determining the reasonableness of the interference, both the utility of the project and the magnitude of the harm must be considered, but the greater public good cannot in itself trump the private interest; the question is whether in the absence of compensation the owner would be required to bear a disproportionate share of the burden of the works.

Land Use Regulation

Canadian municipalities and planning authorities are delegated extensive powers over the use and development of land.[21] The enabling legislation in the various provinces provides for zoning bylaws, subdivision controls, development charges and obligations, and other regulations. "In this country extensive and restrictive land use regulation is the norm," observed Justice Cromwell in *Mariner Real Estate Ltd. v*

Nova Scotia (Attorney General).[22] In the Canadian city, property rights are defined by the ambit of such regulation. Zoning and property rights are intimately linked in two ways. Not only do zoning restrictions curtail common-law rights of use and enjoyment, but zoning itself has been characterized as a collective property right—one that consists of the pooled rights to prospective use of landowners in the community and entrusted to local decision-makers (Tarlock, 1972). As the Chief Justice of the Manitoba Court of Appeal remarked, ratepayers "are entitled to expect that only similar homes will be built in their vicinity, and that the integrity of that particular zoned area of the community will not be interfered with."[23] In this conception then, property is none other than legally protected expectations.

Public authority over private property exists only insofar as it is granted expressly or by implication in the legislation. The general modern rule of statutory interpretation is that "the words of an Act are to be read in their entire context in their grammatical and ordinary sense harmoniously with the scheme of the Act, the object of the Act and the intention of [the legislator]."[24] Over the years, different principles have guided the courts in interpreting municipal and planning legislation. Some early decisions held that the legislation should be construed strictly when property or other common-law rights are affected.[25] That approach has shifted in favour of a more generous and deferential approach, especially to elected councils and expert bodies.[26] As a result, planning authorities are granted considerable latitude in balancing the public interest against private property rights.[27]

Zoning in Good Faith and in the Public Interest

The courts have held that municipalities are granted zoning powers so they may "organize a municipality's territory so as to protect citizens' interests and maintain order"[28] and "establish a rational and fair basis upon which land users may predicate their behaviour...for the benefit of the general populace."[29] To ensure that this mandate is fulfilled, zoning is subject to statutory requirements of procedure, notice, and public participation. In addition, principles for judicial review of zoning have been developed in the case law (Kong, 2010). For example, on an application by an interested party, the courts may quash a zoning bylaw on the grounds that it was not adopted in good faith and in the public interest.[30] Greater scrutiny is paid when the impugned regulations appear to target specific parcels or owners. While zoning assumes, by definition, that different parts of the municipality will be subject to different regulations, it also assumes uniformity within each area.[31] This is consistent with the argument put forward by Tarlock (1972) and others in the property rights approach to zoning (Fischel, 1978, 2015; Nelson, 1977) that zoning tends to be most equitable and economically efficient when applied homogenously.[32]

A striking example of judicial review of zoning is provided by the Ontario Divisional Court's judgment in *H.G. Winton Ltd. v North York (Borough)*.[33] In that case, residents of a suburban enclave learned that a house in their neighbourhood had been sold to a Zoroastrian society, which intended to use the house as a temple. The municipality's zoning permitted religious uses in residentially zoned parts of the borough, and this was confirmed by the municipality in writing prior to the purchase. A petition to stop the Zoroastrians' plans was circulated and signed by 250 residents and submitted to the mayor's office. North York council responded to the neighbours' petition by adopting a zoning amendment bylaw that limited the use of the property for residential uses and precluded its use as a temple.

The amendment was marked by two remarkable features. First, it was hastily adopted in a single council meeting, with the usual two-week notice period and public hearing waived at the request of the mayor. No planning report or other evidence was presented in support of the amendment. Importantly, the buyers were not informed of the meeting or invited to make their submission before the council. Second, the amendment did not apply to all similarly zoned residential areas of the borough but only to a part of the municipality comprising a few streets. The court found that as a matter of fact, the bylaw targeted only the Zoroastrian's intended purchase, and the addition of other properties was meant to disguise the amendment's true purpose.

The circumstances of the case tested the limits of the zoning power and the court's role in balancing the property interests of new and existing users (Kaplinsky, 2012b). The court held that the municipality abused and exceeded the powers granted to it by statute. It found that the amending bylaw was tainted by bad faith in that the council had acted "unreasonably and arbitrarily and without the degree of fairness, openness, and impartiality required of a municipal government."[34] The fault lay not only in the procedural irregularities in the adoption of the bylaw (albeit not in contradiction of the formal statutory requirements) but also in the absence of substantive justifications, other than the petitioners' demands, for restricting only the lands described in the bylaw. This was in contrast to all similarly situated land in the municipality and thus constituted impermissible discrimination.[35]

The Right to an Existing Use and the Right to a Development Permit

If the notion of property lies in expectation, the right to a development permit (or "building permit," depending on the province) is not a protected property right. According to the case law, an application for a development permit may be defeated by new regulations that come into force after the application has been made but before the permit is granted. For example, new zoning restrictions can defeat an application for a permit for a use that was permitted at the time the permit was requested.[36] However, zoning changes normally do not affect existing lawful ("non-conforming") uses or development.[37]

Oppressive Zoning

Municipalities are delegated broad powers to regulate the use and development of land. And while the exercise of such powers, even in good faith and in the public interest, can inflict significant hardship and loss of economic value on private owners, the checks on these powers in Canada are largely political. The general legal rule is that "compensation does not follow zoning either up or down,"[38] but some exceptions to the rule against compensation do exist. A long-standing policy of the Ontario Municipal Board, now the Ontario Land Tribunal, when it was tasked with reviewing zoning bylaws, was that "if lands in private ownership are to be zoned for conservation or recreational purposes for the benefit of the public as whole, then the appropriate authority must be prepared to acquire the lands within a reasonable time otherwise the zoning will not be approved."[39] Similar limits are implemented by legislation in Alberta[40] and in Nova Scotia.[41] Outside these limited exceptions, the courts consistently denied compensation. This was the case even for imposing the most stringent restrictions on the use and development of private property, or for placing it in limbo in a holding category, so long as the restrictions were authorized by legislation.[42]

A drastic example is the landmark ruling of the SCC in *Canadian Pacific Railway Co. [CPR] v Vancouver (City)*.[43] The plaintiff railway company owned a stretch of land in Vancouver known as the Arbutus corridor. CPR operated a rail line along the corridor for many years, but as industrial demands declined, the company prepared to decommission the line and redevelop the lands. By then, the Arbutus corridor had become surrounded by urban uses and was very valuable for development. The city and other public bodies expressed their interest in converting the lands for public transit and other community uses, but they were unwilling to meet the company's price or expropriate the lands for market value. After negotiations between the parties proved unsuccessful, CPR proposed detailed plans to redevelop the corridor for residential and commercial uses in keeping with the extant land use regulations. Before these plans could be approved, however, the city adopted a development plan bylaw designating the Arbutus corridor as a public thoroughfare for transportation and greenways, including pedestrian and cycling paths, to the exclusion of any other development. The purpose and effect of the regulation was, as the court put it, to halt the redevelopment of the corridor and confine CPR to economically nonviable uses of its property.

CPR challenged the development plan bylaw on the grounds that the designation of the entirety of the property as a public thoroughfare constituted a taking of its private property for a public purpose without compensation. The City of Vancouver denied that a compensable taking had occurred, relying in its defence inter alia on Section 569 of the *Vancouver Charter*. This defence provided that upon the exercise of the city's land use regulation powers,

> any property thereby affected shall be deemed as against the city not to have been taken or injuriously affected by reason of the exercise of any such powers or by reason of such zoning and no compensation shall be payable by the city or any inspector or official thereof.[44]

At trial, the court characterized the issue as one of statutory interpretation—that is, whether the bylaw was within the powers granted to the city by its enabling legislation, the *Vancouver Charter*. The court relied on the principle that legislation should not be presumed to authorize the taking of private property without compensation in the absence of clear words to that effect. Justice Brown cited case law that extended the presumption not only to cases involving expropriation de jure but to all "potentially confiscatory legislation."[45] She then reviewed the various provisions of the *Vancouver Charter* and observed that the city was authorized to acquire any land for a public thoroughfare by consent or by expropriation. Justice Brown reasoned that Section 569 should not be construed to contemplate the use of zoning to achieve the same objectives without compensation:

> The Vancouver Charter does not give the City the power to use the vehicle of an official development plan to denude a private property of all use, except as a public thoroughfare, without acquiring title to the property, or reaching some other agreement with the land owner. Such a power would be an extraordinary power and would require very specific language in the enabling statute. I am satisfied that, had the Legislature intended such a result, it would have used much clearer language than that of s. 569.[46]

In the court's view, the city was guilty not only of overreaching but also of taking land from CPR. Although the city did not acquire formal title to the property, the bylaw had the effect of appropriating the amenity of the land in its undeveloped state for the benefit of the public. The only right left to CPR was the right to exclude the public, which would be a "futile exercise" given the circumstances.

On the court's interpretation of the legislative scheme, "where the City proposes to designate a property of an owner for use only as a public park or street, it must acquire that property or reach an agreement with the property owner...To do otherwise...would deprive the owner of the use and enjoyment of its property, to appropriate it to the public without compensation."[47] The *Vancouver Charter* stated clearly that no compensation was payable, but the bylaw was set aside.

The Court of Appeal overturned the trial judge's decision, taking a far more generous interpretation of the city's powers under the *Vancouver Charter* and finding that the bylaw was authorized without directly engaging the argument that such an exercise of power would require clear language. All members of the panel agreed that even if the outcome was unfair to CPR, this provided no legal grounds to quash the bylaw. In a separate concurring opinion Justice Southin called the city to acquire the Arbutus corridor or for the province to force a settlement.

The case was appealed one final time to the SCC, which agreed with the Court of Appeal's conclusion that the city did not exceed its statutory powers. Chief Justice McLachlin noted in her determination that the section immunizing the city from having to pay compensation to the owners of land affected by land use regulations was added to the enabling legislation when it was amended, to allow the designation of public thoroughfares by a development plan. However, like the Court of Appeal, the SCC did not directly address the question of the sufficiency and clarity of the wording necessary to authorize the designation of private lands for public purposes without compensation. The only remaining matter was the purported taking, which was rendered moot in this instance by the express provisions of Section 569.

According to Chief Justice McLachlin, a finding of constructive (de facto) expropriation requiring compensation in Canada requires both (1) an acquisition of a beneficial interest in the property or that flows from it, and (2) a removal of all reasonable uses of the property.[48] The SCC found that the development plan bylaw did not amount to an acquisition of a beneficial interest in CPR's property. All that the city obtained was "some assurance that the land will be used or developed in accordance with its vision,"[49] while CPR remained entitled to exclude anyone from accessing or using its land. Moreover, the bylaw did not preclude the existing use of the lands, nor did it extinguish other private uses even if those were uneconomic.

The ruling in this case has been criticized for its doctrinal requirements and as a missed opportunity to make sense of the Canadian position on compensation for regulatory restrictions, which previous case law had failed to articulate cogently (Brown, 2007, 2009; Kaplinsky & Percy, 2015). Others view the ruling as a confirmation of the Canadian courts' reluctance to mediate the conflicting interests of planning agencies and private property owners (Harris, 2012). The case establishes a stringent test for constructive expropriation that is difficult to satisfy (Kaplinsky, 2012a). As long as a landowner is allowed even to walk across their property, no finding of an expropriation can arise even if the land is effectively sterilized.

Since the SCC's ruling in *CPR v Vancouver*, land use regulation has been recognized as constructive expropriation only once. In *Lynch v St John's (City)*,[50] the owners' application for subdivision approval was denied by the municipality; the owners were informed that the land must be kept in its natural, undeveloped state to protect the watershed of the city. The facts of the case resembled those in *CPR v Vancouver* and *Mariner Real Estate v Nova Scotia* in that all development was prohibited. Nonetheless, the Court of Appeal of Newfoundland and Labrador found that the requirements for de facto expropriation laid out by the SCC had been met. The court relied on the original grant of the land by the Crown, which included all "appurtenances," part of which, according to the court, was the water percolating through the property. In the court's analysis, the effect of the city's actions was to appropriate the groundwater and thus acquire a beneficial interest in the property. The court acknowledged that some agricultural uses could be accommodated in principle;

however, it pointed out that the city's position was that the best course of action was prohibiting all activity on the property, leading to the conclusion that all reasonable private uses of the property were denied. Accordingly, the court issued a declaration that the lands were constructively expropriated and that the owners were entitled to compensation under the *Expropriation Act*.[51] The SCC denied the city's application for leave to appeal.

Discussion

Municipalities and planning authorities face a daunting task of balancing private rights and the public interest, and the competing private interests of residents and developers. The supremacy of legislative bodies, unfettered by constitutional protection of property rights, ensures that public authorities can be vested with statutory authority to pursue a broad range of objectives. For example, whereas the US *Constitution* limits the purposes for which property may be taken to "public" uses,[52] Canadian legislation can authorize a taking for any purpose. By the same token, legislation can empower local authorities to infringe on private property rights or extinguish them altogether with or without compensation.

Compelling policy arguments exist for compensation. Compensation promotes an equitable allocation of the costs and the benefits of public endeavours and prevents the community from imposing disproportionate burdens on some of its members. Compensation also promotes efficient use of social resources by requiring public authorities to confront the full range of costs—private and public—of projects and by providing landowners with the assurances necessary to incentivize investment. Finally, compensation ensures that land use policy is used for land use objectives and not as a blunt and ineffective tool for wealth redistribution.[53] Of these policy concerns, the Canadian law of expropriation and compensation seems to take notice only of equity, but inconsistently so. It is not without good reason that law has been described as "incoherent" (Brown, 2009).

The oft-cited rule in *De Keyser's Royal Hotel* states that "unless the words of the statute clearly so demand, a statute is not to be construed so as to take away the property of a subject without compensation."[54] The courts impute to the legislature, by default, an intention to compensate because the legislature "cannot fairly be supposed to intend...that one man's property shall be confiscated for the benefit of others, or of the public, without any compensation being provided."[55] The court's premise is that an uncompensated deprivation in the name of the public interest is unjust. In view of this notion, it is difficult to see why the presumption of compensation should not apply in cases of oppressive land use regulations such as *Mariner Real Estate* and *CPR v Vancouver*, where the total deprivation is equally unfair.

Despite the court's assertion in *Mariner Real Estate*—that Canadian courts have no "broad mandate" (referring to the absence of constitutional protection of private property) to set aside legislative judgments about "the appropriate distribution of burdens and benefits flowing from...land use controls"[56]—the rule in *De Keyser's Royal Hotel* demonstrates that the courts do have an important role in protecting property rights, to uphold deeply held notions of fairness. Notions of fairness are surprisingly central to the courts' application of statutory provisions pertaining to injurious affection. In such cases (where no land is taken), the affected owner's entitlement to compensation turns on the reasonableness of the harm: in other words, whether in the court's assessment, it would be unjust for the owner to bear the impact of the project.

To summarize the state of the law in Canada, an owner whose land is expropriated is effectively guaranteed the procedural safeguards and predictable compensation offered by legislation. In contrast, an owner whose land is restricted, no matter how severely, will rarely be entitled to compensation unless the legislation expressly requires it. Ordinarily, zoning and other land use controls are subject only to process requirements, and judicial review is limited to clear cases of excess or abuse. Finally, an owner whose land is not taken, but injuriously affected by public works, may receive compensation, but only if the court determines that the injury was significant and unreasonable. The courts' willingness to balance private and public interests, to apportion burdens and benefits, and to be animated by policy concerns varies greatly depending on the context. Legislatures, too, are guilty sometimes of doctrinal ambiguity and inconsistency that invite litigation and make compensation contingent on arbitrary circumstances.

NOTES

1. The *Canadian Charter of Rights of Freedoms* protects certain proprietary interests indirectly—for example, by prohibiting unreasonable search and seizure or discriminatory government allocations based on protected categories such as race or religion. For a discussion of constitutional and quasi-constitutional protections of property in Canada, see Ziff (2005). The right to life, liberty, and security of the person, which is protected in Section 7 of the *Charter*, was invoked in *Victoria (City) v Adams*, 2008 BCSC 1363, 299 DLR (4th) 193, to strike down a bylaw prohibiting homeless persons from erecting overnight shelter in city parks in the absence of alternative accommodations in the city. The point is that the right to use a public space is a form of property.
2. *Constitution Act*, 1867, 30 & 31 Vict, c 3.
3. *Planning Act*, RSO 1990, c P.13.
4. *Municipal Government Act*, RSA 2000, c M-26 (Alberta).
5. *Mariner Real Estate Ltd. v Nova Scotia (Attorney General)*, (1999), 99 NSCA 98, 177 DLR (4th) 696.
6. *Lucas v South Carolina Coastal Council*, (1992), 505 US 1003.
7. *Ibid.*, at para 41.
8. *R v Sisters of Charity of Rockingham*, [1922] 2 AC 315, (UKJCPC).
9. *Vancouver Charter*, SBC 1953, c 55 (British Columbia).
10. *Ibid.*, at s 532.
11. *Municipal Government Act*, SNS 1998, c 18 (Nova Scotia), at s 52(1).
12. *Expropriations Act*, RSO 1990, c E.26 (Ontario).
13. *Expropriation Act*, RSC 1985, c E-21 (Canada).
14. For a detailed explanation of expropriation procedures and the rules pertaining to the calculation of compensation, see Todd (1992).
15. *Dell Holdings Limited v Toronto Area Transit Operating Authority*, 1997 SCC 400, [1997] 1 SCR 32.
16. That is not to say that expropriation without compensation has never been authorized in Canada. In 2010 the *Mines and Minerals Act*, RSA 2000, c M-17, of Alberta was amended to vest title to all "pore space" under all the land in Alberta in the provincial Crown, expressly denying any right to compensation.
17. *Attorney General v De Keyser's Royal Hotel Ltd.*, [1920] AC 508 (UKHL).
18. *Manitoba Fisheries v R.*, [1979] 1 SCR 101, 88 DLR (3d) 462.

19. *Municipal Government Act* RSA 2000, c M-26 (Alberta). For a detailed analysis of the Alberta provisions and their counterparts in other provinces, see Marion (2010).
20. *Antrim Truck Centre Ltd. v Ontario (Transportation)*, 2013 SCC 13, [2013] 1 SCR 594.
21. The first comprehensive zoning scheme in Canada was adopted in 1924, but modern land use controls can be traced to building and land use regulations that we adopted in the nineteenth century or earlier. See, for example, Fischler (2007).
22. *Mariner Real Estate Ltd. v Nova Scotia (Attorney General)*, at para 42.
23. *Alcoholism Foundation of Manitoba v Winnipeg (City)*, (1990), 69 DLR (4th) 697, at para 41.
24. *Verdun v Toronto Dominion Bank*, [1996] 3 SCR 550, 139 DLR (4th) 415, at para 22.
25. *Merritt v Toronto (City)*, (1895), 22 OAR 205 (CA); *Re Corporation of the District of Surrey*, (1959), 20 DLR (2d), at 174.
26. *Nanaimo (City) v Rascal Trucking Ltd.*, 2000 SCC 13, [2000] 1 SCR 342.
27. Alberta's *Municipal Government Act*, RSA 2000, c M-26 provides expressly in Section 617 that the purpose of its planning provisions and all bylaws and regulations passed under such provisions is "(a) to achieve the orderly, economical and beneficial development, use of land and patterns of human settlement, and (b) to maintain and improve the quality of the physical environment within which patterns of human settlement are situated in Alberta, without infringing on the rights of individuals for any public interest except to the extent that is necessary for the overall greater public interest." On several occasions the courts of Alberta declined to set aside planning decisions on the grounds that they encroached too far on private interest: see, for example, *Stantec Consulting Ltd. v Edmonton (City)*, 2004 ABCA 241, 47 Alta. LR (4th) 219, as well as *Canada Lands Company CLC Limited v Edmonton (City)*, 2005 ABCA 218.
28. *Congrégation des témoins de Jéhovah de St-Jérôme-Lafontaine v. Lafontaine (Village)*, 2004 SCC 48, [2004] 2 SCR 650, at para 81.
29. *Quebec (Attorney General) v Lacombe*, 2010 SCC 38, [2010] 2 SC. 453, at para 50.
30. *Scarborough (Township) v Bondi*, [1959] SCR 444, 18 DLR (2d) 161.
31. *Johannesson v West St. Paul (Rural Municipality)*, [1952] 1 SCR 292.
32. See, for example, *Love v Flagstaff (County) Subdivision and Development Appeal Board*, 2002 ABCA 292, where the Alberta Court of Appeal held that planning laws should be interpreted in keeping with the "underlying rationale," namely, "to avoid pitting neighbour against neighbour by imposing on all parties clearly defined reciprocal rights and obligations."
33. *H.G. Winton Ltd. v North York (Borough)*, [1978] 20 OR (2d) 737, 88 DL. (3d) 733 (Div. Ct.).
34. *Ibid.*, at para. 741.
35. Whether or not discrimination is permissible is undoubtedly a question of statutory authority. The Alberta *Municipal Government Act*, 2000, s 641, expressly authorizes a council to designate any part of the municipality as a direct control district and, subject to any applicable statutory plan, regulate and control the use or development of land or buildings in the district in any manner it considers necessary.

36. *Toronto Roman Catholic Separate School Board*, [1926] AC 81, [1925] 3 DLR 880 (UKJCPC).
37. *Saint-Romuald (City) v Olivier*, 2001 SCC 57, [2001] 2 SCR 898.
38. *R v Tener*, [1985] 1 SCR 533, at para 10.
39. *Re Nepean Restricted Area By-law 73-76*, (1978), 9 OMBR 36, at p. 55, cited in *Russell v Toronto (City)*, (2000), 196 DLR (4th) 558 (ONCA), at para 6.
40. *Municipal Government Act*, RSA 2000, c M-26 (Alberta), s 644.
41. *Municipal Government Act*, SNS 1998, c 18 (Nova Scotia), at s 222.
42. In this case, *Hartel Holdings Co. Ltd. v City of Calgary*, [1984] 1 SCR 337, 8 DLR (4th) 321, the City of Calgary was able to avoid compensation payable when private land was designated for public uses under a *land use bylaw*, by designating the appellant's land for a public park in a *statutory plan* instead.
43. *Canadian Pacific Railway [CPR] v Vancouver (City)*, 2006 SCC 5, [2006] 1 SCR 227.
44. *Vancouver Charter*, SBC 1953, c 55 (British Columbia) at 569(1).
45. *New Brunswick v Estabrooks Pontiac Buick Ltd.*, (1982), 144 DLR (3d) 21 (NB CA); *Pacific National Investments Ltd. v Victoria (City)*, 2000 SCC 64, [2000] 2 SCR 919.
46. *Canadian Pacific Railway [CPR] v Vancouver (City)*, 2006 SCC 5, [2006] 1 SCR 227, at para 76.
47. *Ibid.*, at para 80.
48. *Ibid.*, at para 30.
49. *Ibid.*
50. *Lynch v St John's (City)*, 2016 NLCA 35, 400 DLR (4th) 62, leave to appeal the SCC refused [2016] SCCA No. 390.
51. *Expropriation Act*, RSNL 1990, c E-19 (Newfoundland and Labrador).
52. *Kelo v City of New London*, 545 US 469 (2005).
53. For select authorities reflecting the debate over compensation see Michelman (1967), Sax (1971), Blume and Rubinfeld (1984), Epstein (1985), and Dagan (2000).
54. *Attorney General v De Keyser's Royal Hotel Ltd.*, [1920] AC 508 (UKHL)., at p. 542 (citing *London and North Western Ry. Co. v Evans*, [1893] 1 Ch. 16, p. 28).
55. *Ibid.*
56. *Mariner Real Estate Ltd. v Nova Scotia (Attorney General)*, (1999), 99 NSCA 98, 177 DLR (4th) 696, at para 41.

REFERENCES

Alexander, G.S. (2006). *The global debate over constitutional property: Lessons for American takings jurisprudence*. University of Chicago Press.

Alterman, R. (2010). *Takings international: A comparative perspective on land use regulation and compensation rights*. American Bar Association.

Bentham, J. (1843). Principles of the civil code. In J. Bowring (Ed.), *The works of Jeremy Bentham* (Vol. 1). https://oll.libertyfund.org/titles/bentham-works-of-jeremy-bentham-11-vols

Blume, L., & Rubinfeld, D.L. (1984). Compensation for takings: An economic analysis. *California Law Review, 72*, 569–628.

Brown, R. (2007). The constructive taking at the Supreme Court of Canada: Once more, without feeling. *University of British Columbia Law Review, 40*, 315–342.

Brown, R. (2009). Legal incoherence and the extra-constitutional law of regulatory takings: The Canadian experience. *International Journal of Law in the Built Environment, 1*(3), 179–193.

Dagan, H. (2000). Just compensation, incentives, and social meanings. *Michigan Law Review, 99*(1), 134–156.

Epstein, R.A. (1985). *Takings: Private property and the power of eminent domain*. Harvard University Press.

Fischel, W.A. (1978). A property rights approach to municipal zoning. *Land Economics, 54*(1), 64–81.

Fischel, W.A. (2015). *Zoning rules! The economics of land use regulation*. Lincoln Institute of Land Policy.

Fischler, R. (2007). Development controls in Toronto in the nineteenth century. *Urban History Review, 36*(1), 16–31.

Harris, D.C. (2012). A railway, a city, and the public regulation of private property. In E. Tucker, B.H. Ziff, & J. Muir (Eds.), *Property on trial: Canadian cases in context* (pp. 455–486). Irwin Law.

Kaplinsky, E. (2012a). Property rights, politics, and community in Canada, and the Alberta Land Stewardship Act. *Hōsei Riron, Journal of Law and Politics, 45*(1), 78–111.

Kaplinsky, E. (2012b). The Zoroastrian temple in Toronto: A case study in land-use regulation, Canadian style. In E. Tucker, B.H. Ziff, & J. Muir (Eds.), *Property on trial: Canadian cases in context* (pp. 233–257). Irwin Law.

Kaplinsky, E., & Percy, D.R. (2015). The impairment of subsurface resource rights by government as a "taking" of property: A Canadian perspective. In B. Hoops, E.J. Marais, H. Mostert, J.A.M.A. Sluysmans, & L.C.A. Verstappen (Eds.), *Rethinking expropriation law II: Context, criteria, and consequences of expropriation* (pp. 224–262). Eleven International Publishing.

Kong, H. (2010). Something to talk about: Regulation and justification in Canadian municipal law. *Osgoode Hall Law Journal, 3–4*, 499.

Marion, M.A. (2010). Compensation where no land is taken: Update of the law in Alberta. *Alberta Law Review, 48*(1), 127–166.

Michelman, F.I. (1967). Property, utility, and fairness: Comments on the ethical foundations of "just compensation" law. *Harvard Law Review, 80*(6), 1165.

Nelson, R.H. (1977). *Zoning and property rights: An analysis of the American system of land-use regulation*. MIT Press.

Sax, J.L. (1971). Takings, private property and public rights. *Yale Law Journal, 81*(2), 149.

Tarlock, A.D. (1972). Toward a revised theory of zoning. *Land Use Controls Annual*, 141.

Todd, E.C.E. (1992). *The law of expropriation and compensation in Canada* (2nd ed.). Carswell.

Ziff, B. (2005). "Taking" liberties: Protections for private property in Canada. In E. Cooke (Ed.), *Modern studies in property law* (Vol. 3, pp. 341–360). Hart Publishing.

LEGISLATION

Canadian Charter of Rights and Freedoms, Part I of the *Constitution Act*, 1982, being Schedule B to the *Canada Act 1982* (UK), 1982, c 11.

Constitution Act, 1867, 30 & 31 Vict, c 3.

Expropriation Act, RSC 1985, c E-21 (Canada).

Expropriation Act, RSNL 1990, c E-19 (Newfoundland and Labrador).

Expropriations Act, RSO 1990, c E.26 (Ontario).

Mines and Minerals Act, RSA 2000, c M-17.

Municipal Government Act, RSA 2000, c M-26 (Alberta).

Municipal Government Act, SNS 1998, c 18 (Nova Scotia).

Planning Act, RSO 1990, c P.13 (Ontario).

Vancouver Charter, SBC 1953, c 55 (British Columbia).

JURISPRUDENCE

Alcoholism Foundation of Manitoba v Winnipeg (City), (1990), 69 DLR (4th) 697.

Antrim Truck Centre Ltd. v Ontario (Transportation), 2013 SCC 13, [2013] 1 SCR 594.

Attorney General v De Keyser's Royal Hotel Ltd., [1920] AC 508 (UKHL).

Canada Lands Company CLC Limited v Edmonton (City), 2005 ABCA 218.

Canadian Pacific Railway [CPR] v Vancouver (City), 2006 SCC 5, [2006] 1 SCR 227.

Congrégation des témoins de Jéhovah de St-Jérôme-Lafontaine v Lafontaine (Village), 2004 SCC 48, [2004] 2 SCR 650.

Dell Holdings Limited v Toronto Area Transit Operating Authority, 1997 SCC 400, [1997] 1 SCR 32.

Hartel Holdings Co. Ltd. v City of Calgary, [1984] 1 SCR 337, 8 DLR (4th) 321.

H.G. Winton Ltd. v North York (Borough), [1978] 20 OR (2d) 737, 88 DLR (3d) 733 (Div. Ct.).

Johannesson v West St. Paul (Rural Municipality), [1952] 1 SCR 292.

Kelo v City of New London, 545 US 469 (2005).

London and North Western Ry. Co. v Evans, [1893] 1 Ch. 16.

Love v Flagstaff (County) Subdivision and Development Appeal Board, 2002 ABCA 292.

Lucas v South Carolina Coastal Council (1992), 505 US 1003.

Lynch v St John's (City), 2016 NLCA 35, 400 DLR (4th) 62, leave to appeal the SCC refused [2016] SCCA No. 390.

Manitoba Fisheries v R, [1979] 1 SCR 101, 88 DLR (3d) 462.

Mariner Real Estate Ltd. v Nova Scotia (Attorney General), (1999), 99 NSCA 98, 177 DLR (4th) 696.

Merritt v Toronto (City), (1895), 22 OAR 205 (CA).

Nanaimo (City) v Rascal Trucking Ltd., 2000 SCC 13, [2000] 1 SCR 342.

New Brunswick v Estabrooks Pontiac Buick Ltd., (1982), 144 DLR (3d) 21 (NB CA).

Pacific National Investments Ltd. v Victoria (City), 2000 SCC 64, [2000] 2 SCR 919.

Quebec (Attorney General) v Lacombe, 2010 SCC 38, [2010] 2 SCR 453.

Re Corporation of the District of Surrey, (1959), 20 DLR (2d) 174.

Re Nepean Restricted Area By-law 73-76, (1978), 9 OMBR 36.

Russell v Toronto (City), (2000), 196 DLR (4th) 558 (ONCA).

R v Sisters of Charity of Rockingham, [1922] 2 AC 315, (UKJCPC).

R v Tener, [1985] 1 SCR 533.

Saint-Romuald (City) v Olivier, 2001 SCC 57, [2001] 2 SCR 898.

Scarborough (Township) v Bondi, [1959] SCR 444, 18 DLR (2d) 161.

Stantec Consulting Ltd. v Edmonton (City), 2004 ABCA 241, 47 Alta. LR (4th) 219.

Toronto Roman Catholic Separate School Board, [1926] AC 81, [1925] 3 DLR 880 (UKJCPC).

Verdun v Toronto Dominion Bank, [1996] 3 SCR 550, 139 DLR (4th) 415.

Victoria (City) v Adams, 2008 BCSC 1363, 299 DLR (4th) 193.

9
THE DANGERS OF ALLOWING "OTHERING" SPEECH IN A CITY'S PUBLIC SPACES

OLA P. MALIK & SASHA BEST

Introduction

Managing a city's public space presents a challenging dilemma.[1] Municipalities in Alberta and elsewhere are legislatively mandated[2] to provide their citizens good government,[3] safe and viable communities,[4] and bylaws that protect the safety, health, and welfare of their citizens.[5] In a diverse country like Canada, providing safe communities includes "a commitment to equality and respect for group identity and the inherent dignity owed to all human beings,"[6] a recognition of "the importance of civility in public debate,"[7] and the preservation and enhancement of multicultural values.[8] At the same time, an important purpose of a city's public space is to provide citizens with a spontaneous, democratizing environment in which to meet one another, share and disseminate opinions, express themselves, and engage in public advocacy. Fulfilling this purpose involves fostering expressive activities that are protected by Section 2(b) of the *Canadian Charter of Rights and Freedoms*.[9]

The public square is more crowded and divisive than ever before.[10] The rise of well-funded and sophisticated public interest advocacy groups has complicated how we negotiate the intersection of inflammatory advocacy in public spaces with the maintenance of inclusive, civil society. Cities' public spaces, whether they be town halls, public libraries, downtown squares, plazas, or parks, have become battlegrounds for public interest advocacy. These public spaces tend to be situated in a city's downtown core, at the heart of business, cultural, and government centres. These locations are often symbolic seats of civil society that attract a captive audience comprising citizens and visitors who cannot avoid these places while going about their business.

What we see increasingly from fringe advocacy groups is the rise of "othering" speech, speech that draws normative distinctions between "us" and "them." This type of speech is perpetuated through stigmatizing, discriminatory, demeaning, and stereotyping messaging that undermines its target group's legitimacy, moral worthiness, and reputation in the eyes of the larger community. This othering form of speech does not foster meaningful debate or conversations between "us" and "them," because any sort of collaborative discourse would require acknowledging that the other's perspective has value worth discussing. Instead, othering is a process by which advocacy groups normalize the gradual devaluation of the "other" so that they are viewed as "less-than" in all respects and unentitled to protection under the law.[11]

In this chapter we argue that othering advocacy messaging, particularly when it is communicated to a captive audience in a city's most public spaces, undermines the very values that our society seeks to foster by protecting free speech. These values include the promotion of liberty, human dignity, equality, the enhancement of democracy, and the pursuit of truth through inclusive public debate. It is therefore our view that while othering advocacy messaging is a protected form of expression pursuant to Section 2(b) of the *Charter*, it can nonetheless be subject to reasonable restrictions in appropriate cases, and such restrictions should be upheld by our courts.

Why Protect Freedom of Expression at All?

A fundamental question to ask is why freedom of expression is so jealously protected in the first place. It is an important question because Section 2(b) of the *Charter* protects virtually *all* forms of expressive activity that convey meaning, irrespective of content, "however unpopular, distasteful or contrary to the mainstream."[12] The only exempted form of expressive activity that is not protected by Section 2(b) is *actual violence*. Consequently, expression that is protected by Section 2(b) of the *Charter* includes the criminal offences of hate speech and defamatory libel.[13] Pornography (including child pornography) and obscenity are also protected pursuant to Section 2(b).[14]

Three prevalent rationales have been advanced for protecting freedom of expression:[15]

- Freedom of expression is essential in a free and democratic society.
- The free exchange of and competition between ideas allows society to achieve consensus on what is viewed as just and right.
- Allowing people to freely express themselves goes to their individual growth, self-development, and fulfillment.

The rationale for protecting free speech has been considered at length in several Supreme Court of Canada (SCC) decisions,[16] including *Irwin Toy Ltd. v Quebec (Attorney General)*,[17] where the court identified the values underlying the rationale for constitutionally protecting free speech, as follows:

(1) ...seeking and attaining the truth is an inherently good activity; (2) participation in social and political decision-making is to be fostered and encouraged; and (3) the diversity in forms of individual self-fulfillment and human flourishing ought to be cultivated in an essentially tolerant, indeed welcoming, environment not only for the sake of those who convey a meaning, but also for the sake of those to whom it is conveyed.[18]

Protecting free speech satisfies both the individualist's aspiration to achieve fulfillment through self-expression and the communitarian's belief that a civil society that is fully participatory, pluralistic, and democratic provides the right environment for individual flourishing. In either case, everyone must be able to participate as equals in the free exchange and advocacy of ideas, no matter how outlandish and outrageous those ideas might be.

The *Charter*'s protection of expressive activity, however, like any other *Charter*-protected freedom, is not absolute and may be limited pursuant to Section 1 of the *Charter* by "a reasonable limit prescribed by law as can be demonstrably justified in a free and democratic society."[19] In the SCC's decision of *R v Oakes*,[20] the court articulated the test that the government must meet to justify a restriction on a *Charter* freedom pursuant to Section 1 of the *Charter*. Chief Justice Dickson held that the core values and principles that underlie a free and democratic society are "respect for the inherent dignity of the human person, commitment to social justice and equality, accommodation of a wide variety of beliefs, respect for cultural and group identity, and faith in social and political institutions which enhance the participation of individuals and groups in society."[21] Not only do these core values serve as the basis for justifying these guaranteed rights; they serve as the rationale for limiting them.

Consequently, while hate speech, defamation, and the dissemination of child pornography are protected forms of expressive activity pursuant to Section 2(b) of the *Charter*, they can be restricted pursuant to Section 1 as they are forms of expression that cannot be reconciled with Chief Justice Dickson's articulation of the values and principles underlying a free and democratic society. This was illustrated by the SCC, which concluded that hate speech

> opposes the targeted group's ability to find self-fulfillment by articulating their thoughts and ideas. It impacts on [the targeted] group's ability to respond to the substantive ideas under debate, thereby placing a serious barrier to their full participation in our democracy. Indeed, a particularly insidious aspect of hate speech is that it acts

to cut off any path of reply by the group under attack. It does this not only by attempting to marginalize the group so that their reply will be ignored, it also forces the group to argue for their basic humanity or social standing, as a precondition to participating in the deliberative aspects of our democracy.[22]

In another SCC case dealing with the criminal offence of libel, the court held that defamatory statements do not benefit from *Charter* protection as they do not further the values underlying the rationale for protecting free speech:

> Defamatory statements are…inimical to the search for truth. False and injurious statements cannot enhance self-development. Nor can it ever be said that they lead to healthy participation in the affairs of the community. Indeed, they are detrimental to the advancement of these values and harmful to the interests of a free and democratic society.
>
> Most certainly defamatory libel is far from and indeed inimical to the core values of freedom of expression. It would trivialize and demean the magnificent panoply of rights guaranteed by the *Charter* if a significant value was attached to the deliberate recounting of defamatory lies that are likely to expose a person to hatred, ridicule or contempt.[23]

In Canada a person's freedom to achieve self-fulfillment through expression is ultimately subject to reasonable and justifiable limits that underlie a free and democratic society. The idea that free speech can be restricted to the extent necessary to ensure those values are upheld should not be viewed as irreconcilable with the protection of free speech generally. The search for truth through individual self-expression can only occur if others, *indeed everyone*, has that same opportunity. Othering speech—especially by powerful, well-funded advocacy groups—that is directed towards minority communities robs these communities of their opportunity to participate as equals in the free exchange of ideas and thereby detracts from the very purpose that protecting free speech is intended to serve.

In our view, othering speech is a form of expression that should properly be subject to reasonable restrictions because its content and its impact are inconsistent with the values and principles underlying a free and democratic society, which justify the safeguarding of free speech. Othering speech does not respect the dignity of the other and does not accommodate the other's cultural values, identity, faith, or desire to participate as an equal in political and social discourse. Othering speech is nullifying speech from the perspective of the target it seeks to silence.

Hate Speech

The SCC's decision in *Saskatchewan (Human Rights Commission) v Whatcott*[24] is the leading decision on hate speech in Canada and sets out a high threshold for establishing "hate speech," as follows.

The speech must *objectively* expose a protected group to hatred. The subjective emotions of the communicator of hate speech and the individual feelings of hurt felt by the target(s) of the expression are not the focus.[25] The test is objective and asks "whether a reasonable person aware of the context and circumstances surrounding the expression, would view it as exposing the protected group to hatred."[26]

The words *hatred* and *contempt* are, in their application to expression, restricted to those most extreme forms of the emotion described as "detestation" and "vilification."[27] Prohibiting language that is merely offensive, is humiliating, impugns individual dignity, or causes hurt feelings is impermissibly overbroad and falls outside the objectives of human rights legislation.[28] This sets a high threshold for what constitutes hate speech. Only speech that has the effect of subjecting a person or group to detestation, vilification, or contempt qualifies as hate speech. This captures speech that, in respect of a target person or group, "seek[s] to abuse, denigrate or delegitimize them, to render them lawless, dangerous, unworthy, or unacceptable,"[29] or "accus[es] them of disgusting characteristics, inherent deficiencies or immoral propensities which are too vile in nature"[30] to be shared by others in society. The category of hate speech, the Supreme Court noted, may not capture expression "belittling a minority group or attacking its dignity through jokes, ridicule or insults...[howsoever] hurtful and offensive,"[31] because this type of expression does not expose the target group to *hatred*.

The focus of a hate-speech inquiry must be the *likely effect of the speech*. To qualify as hate speech, expression must be likely to expose a person or group to hatred by others.[32] Hateful or offensive expression must rise beyond the level of individual harm and must "marginalize the group by affecting its social status and acceptance in the eyes of the majority."[33] For the court, "it is the need to protect the societal standing of vulnerable groups that is the objective of legislation restricting hate speech."[34]

The threshold for proving hate speech is onerous. Courts have recognized that "the public must accept a certain amount of unpleasant, disagreeable, and even repugnant speech."[35] The SCC has held that derogatory and insensitive words that criticize, insult, belittle, ridicule, offend, or affront the dignity of a vulnerable group are not, in themselves, synonymous with hatred, although the dividing line may at times be unclear:

> Expression criticizing or creating humour at the expense of others can be derogatory to the extent of being repugnant. Representations belittling a minority group or attacking its dignity through jokes, ridicule or insults may be hurtful and offensive. However, offensive ideas are not sufficient to ground a justification for infringing on freedom of expression. While such expression may inspire feelings of disdain or superiority, it does not expose the targeted group to hatred.
>
> There may be circumstances where expression that "ridicules" members of a protected group goes beyond humour or satire and risks exposing the person to detestation and vilification on the basis of a prohibited ground of discrimination. In such circumstances, however, the risk results from the intensity of the ridicule reaching a level where the target becomes exposed to hatred. While ridicule, taken to the extreme, can conceivably lead to exposure to hatred, in my view, "ridicule" in its ordinary sense would not typically have the potential to lead to the discrimination that the legislature seeks to address.[36]

It is difficult to draw a line for when speech intended to ridicule or belittle a group does or does not subject a group to hatred, particularly when the ridicule becomes normalized, and the target group so othered or diminished in public estimation that it cannot defend itself. At what point does othering speech, intended to hurt, shame, or marginalize a targeted group, cross the threshold into what the courts would consider hate speech and cease to be a constitutionally protected form of expression?

Herein lie the practical challenges posed by othering advocacy speech from a public policy perspective: advocacy messaging that seeks to foster harmful stereotypes against a group often masquerades as public information intended to educate the public on a "legitimate" public policy issue. While it may at first appear benign, this type of speech often serves as a cover for its sponsor's more sinister objective—that of normalizing hateful and exclusionary rhetoric that others the targeted group, advances harmful stereotypes, and creates insidious tropes that, over time, diminish the group's legitimacy to the point that the group simply ceases to be visible.

Othering Speech

Othering speech can, perhaps unhelpfully, be defined as speech that does not meet the threshold for hate speech but that nevertheless refers to a group in a manner that is intended to ridicule, demean, marginalize, or place them outside of the mainstream. This type of speech is intended to other its target with hateful, stereotypical rhetoric that invites the viewer to make moral judgments about the target group's legitimacy and sense of worth. As one writer described it, "everything turns on who counts as a fellow human being, as a rational agent in the only relevant sense—the sense in which rational agency is synonymous with membership of *our* moral community" (Rorty, 1993, p. 124). To be successfully depicted as the other is to be silenced, or deprived, to a certain extent or entirely, of "counting" as a human being, and therefore deprived of a valid justification for others listening to one's voice.

A helpful standard for evaluating whether, for example, an advertisement constitutes othering expression is the *Canadian Code of Advertising Standards* (Advertising Standards Canada, n.d.; henceforth, the *Code*). The *Code* was created and is administered by Advertising Standards Canada, a self-regulating group of private advertisers and various other media agencies. It is used as a guide by many Canadian municipalities to determine acceptable advertising content. The *Code* defines advertising as "any message...the content of which message is controlled directly or indirectly by the advertiser expressed in any language and communicated in any medium...to Canadians with the intent to influence their choice, opinion or behaviour." The *Code* expressly excludes from its application what it defines as "political advertising" and "election advertising," but it applies to all other advertising by "entities seeking to improve their public image or advance a point of view whether the advertising is for a commercial purpose."[37]

Provision 14 of the *Code* addresses "unacceptable depictions and portrayals" as follows (Advertising Standards Canada, Clause 14):

> It is recognized that advertisements may be distasteful without necessarily conflicting with the provisions of this Clause 14; and the fact that a particular product or service may be offensive to some people is not sufficient grounds for objecting to an advertisement for that product or service.
>
> Advertisements shall not:
> a) condone any form of personal discrimination, including discrimination based upon race, national or ethnic origin, religion, gender identity, sex or sexual orientation, age or disability;
> b) appear in a realistic manner to exploit, condone or incite violence; nor appear to condone, or directly encourage, bullying; nor directly encourage, or exhibit obvious indifference to, unlawful behaviour;
> c) demean, denigrate or disparage one or more identifiable persons, group of persons, firms, organizations, industrial or commercial activities, professions, entities, products or services, or attempt to bring it or them into public contempt or ridicule;

d) undermine human dignity; or display obvious indifference to, or encourage, gratuitously and without merit, conduct or attitudes that offend the standards of public decency prevailing among a significant segment of the population.

Importantly, Canadian courts, including the SCC, have held that the *Code* may be used to establish reasonable limits that may be upheld under Section 1 of the *Charter*, with respect to unacceptable speech.[38] The *Code* has therefore become a very helpful tool for courts when assessing the limits of controversial advertising, and it is worth briefly examining how the courts have interpreted the *Code* in light of a number of recent challenges.

Harmful Advertising on the Sides of City Buses

The *Code*'s application to advocacy speech has been considered in a series of decisions by Canadian courts, particularly with respect to advertising on the sides of city buses and in other city transit facilities.[39] Here, we will focus on two decisions: *American Freedom Defence Initiative v Edmonton (City)* (hereafter AFDI), in which Muslim immigrants were the subject of the othering messaging;[40] and *Canadian Centre for Bio-Ethical Reform v The City of Grande Prairie (City)* (hereafter CCBR Queen's Bench), where the othering messaging was directed towards women who had undergone abortions.[41]

In the case of AFDI, the American Freedom Defense Initiative (AFDI)[42] applied for a declaration that the City of Edmonton's removal of its advertisement from the exterior of Edmonton Transit System buses constituted an infringement on its freedom of expression. AFDI describes itself as "an American non-profit, non-partisan human rights activist and advocacy group based in New York, USA, whose objectives include the promotion and defence of freedom of speech, freedom of conscience, individual rights and the equality of all people before the law."[43] The organization publicly calls for surveilling and carefully scrutinizing Muslims, as well as barring Muslim immigration generally.[44] AFDI submitted an advertisement for display on Edmonton buses, depicting photographs of seven Muslim women indicated as having been murdered by honour killings. The AFDI advertisement included the logo for AFDI and the logo for its sister organization, Stop Islamization of America (SIOA).[45] The Alberta Court of Queen's Bench held that the City of Edmonton's objective of providing a safe and welcoming public transit system was a sufficiently important objective to warrant placing a limit on AFDI's freedom of expression.[46] It was found that the City of Edmonton had acted reasonably in its decision to restrict advertising, which was designed to stigmatize Muslims,[47] and that ultimately the infringement upon AFDI's freedom of expression was justified under Section 1 of the *Charter*.[48]

In the case of *CCBR* Queen's Bench, the Canadian Centre for Bio-Ethical Reform (CCBR),[49] an "educational" "pro-life" activist organization, applied to post a graphic advertisement on the side of City of Grande Prairie buses that featured the fully capitalized words "ABORTION KILLS CHILDREN." The advertisement provided the online address for the CCBR website and a link to its EndtheKilling campaign.[50] The City of Grande Prairie rejected the CCBR's advertisement, which brought an application for judicial review. The Alberta Court of Queen's Bench took a similar contextual approach as was applied in *AFDI* and examined the content of the CCBR website, concluding that the various statements on the website "vilify women who have chosen…to have an abortion."[51] The court further concluded that the advertisements, because of their proximity and visibility to other users of the road and the public, created a captive audience, as viewing could not reasonably be avoided.[52] Exposure to the CCBR advertisement was said to be psychologically harmful, especially to women who had, or were seeking to have, an abortion, and to the young, unprepared viewer.[53] In the result, the court found that the city's decision to reject the CCBR advertisement was reasonable.[54] The case was appealed to the Alberta Court of Appeal, which, in a majority decision, upheld the lower court's decision and provided useful additional commentary.[55]

Are the Advertisements in *AFDI* and *CCBR* Othering Messages?

In *AFDI*, the Alberta Court of Queen's Bench found that the AFDI advertisement was not intended to provide help for victims of religious extremism but rather was designed to

> bring the Muslim population of Edmonton, including Muslim/Islamic Faith in general into public contempt or ridicule. This purpose is clear from a review of the AFDI website as well as the SIOA's website. The aim is to encourage Muslim individuals to leave Islam and convert from their Muslim faith, or alternatively to advocate special treatment of Muslims and their exclusion from non-majority Muslim countries.[56]

The court noted that by including the AFDI and SIOA logos in the advertising and by suggesting that viewers of the advertisement "go to FightforFreedom.us," the advertisement was directing viewers to discriminatory and unacceptable content without explicitly referencing that content in the advertisement itself:

> In fact, the AFDI's advertisement might reasonably be viewed as a ruse to further what appears to be one of its true objectives, which is to target Muslims. The phrase "dog whistle politics" comes to mind, whereby coded messaging is understood by a portion of the population who might support the objectives of the advertiser, in this case AFDI and SIOA.[57]

In *CCBR* Queen's Bench, the Alberta Court of Queen's Bench concluded that the various statements on the CCBR's website, which characterized abortion as killing, vilified women who had chosen to have an abortion, and were not "merely informative and educational."[58] While the Alberta Court of Queen's Bench declined to determine whether the CCBR advertisement constituted the *Criminal Code* offence of hate speech, the majority in the Alberta Court of Appeal decision concluded that the advertisement was in fact hate speech:

The advertisement clearly portrays women who terminate pregnancies, and medical professionals and facilities that assist, as "killers of children." On any reasonable view, the advertisement is likely to promote hatred against identifiable groups of "women" and their doctors.[59]

In our view, both the AFDI and the CCBR advertisements constitute othering speech. The sponsor behind the AFDI advertisements advocates for the profiling of Muslims at airports, the surveillance of mosques, and the immediate halting of Muslim immigration into North America,[60] and the CCBR characterizes women who have had abortions as murderers. The sponsors of these advertisements would likely claim that they are engaging the public on "legitimate" policy issues of public interest and are merely exercising their right to free speech. However, closer examination of the advertisements, including the sponsors' motivations and the content they actively promote through various other advertising channels, reveals their true purpose: marginalizing, demeaning, and ultimately othering their respective target groups in a way that undermines their legitimacy and minimizes their ability to respond to these attacks. This sort of objective is not one that the *Charter* right to free speech was contemplated to protect.

Creating a Captive Audience for Othering Messages

Under the captive-audience doctrine widely discussed in American literature and commentary,[61] a listener's right to privacy from unwanted speech, which they find offensive, may in some cases trump the speaker's freedom to express it. This doctrine allows government to regulate speech delivered to the unwilling listener who finds the message antagonistic, hurtful, offensive, or profane.[62] In the United States the freedom to speak that is enshrined in the First Amendment right of the US *Constitution* can therefore be restricted by the captive-audience doctrine if "substantial privacy interests are being invaded in an essentially intolerable manner" (Corbin, 2009, p. 943).

Although this doctrine has been the subject of extensive academic discussion and jurisprudence in the United States, it has not yet been widely applied in Canada.⁶³ However, in the British Columbia Court of Appeal case of *R v Breeden*,⁶⁴ the court confirmed that political protest in the lobby of a courthouse, municipal hall, or a fire station did not attract *Charter* protection. In this case, an aggrieved firefighter, unhappy with his union's declining to take up grievance action on his behalf and with the actions of various provincial court officials, carried sandwich boards protesting the corruption of union and government in the lobby of a courthouse, the foyer of a city hall, and the reception area of a fire station.

The court held that the values that underlie freedom of expression, namely democratic discourse, truth finding, and self-fulfillment, are undermined when observers are not given the practical choice of avoiding the message:

> When an audience is forced to observe material at close range, this can be at odds with the interplay and competition between ideas, and as such it could tend to undermine truth seeking and democratic discourse, basic *Charter* values. Being faced with these signboards inside a relatively confined building envelope such as the foyers of the premises in this case is qualitatively different from the observation of same in a sidewalk setting or concourse area. The discomfiting of staff and members of the public going about necessary business in these places is an unwarranted interference with the proper function of these premises. The usage argued for is without historical foundation.⁶⁵

This approach was adopted in CCBR Queen's Bench, where the court agreed that "forced listening is antithetical to the principles underlying freedom of expression, since it denies the competition of ideas that is assumed to be the foundation of free communication."⁶⁶

The captive-audience doctrine recognizes that freedom *from* unwanted speech is a necessary corollary to freedom *to* speak. If the purpose of freedom of expression is to foster a civil society in which everyone can freely participate as equals in the exchange of ideas, without being made to feel marginalized, then a listener's freedom *from* unwanted speech balances the careful equilibrium between the freedoms of *both* the speaker and the listener.

A review of American commentary (Black, 1953) indicates that a listener may be considered a captive audience to another's unwanted speech if two factors are present. First, the method of communicating the unwanted speech must thrust the message upon the audience in such a manner that the listener cannot reasonably avoid it. Consequently, a listener who can take reasonable steps to avoid the offending speech cannot be said to be harmed and therefore does not require legal protection. Second, the unwanted speech must be received in a location where the listener has some expectation of privacy. Forcing the unwanted recipient to be exposed to the speech where they have a right to quiet enjoyment and privacy intrudes upon the listener's privacy interest in an "essentially intolerable manner."

In CCBR Queen's Bench, the court endorsed the captive-audience doctrine and cited with approval a passage from an earlier case that explains the captive-audience doctrine in the following terms:

> If we are to turn a bus or streetcar into either a newspaper or a park, we take great liberties with people who because of necessity become commuters and at the same time captive viewers or listeners.
>
> In asking us to force the system to accept his message as a vindication of his constitutional rights, the petitioner overlooks the constitutional rights of the commuters. While [the] petitioner clearly has a right to express his views to those who wish to listen, he has no right to force his message upon an audience incapable of declining to receive it. In my view the right of the commuters to be free from forced intrusions on their privacy precludes the city from transforming its vehicles of public transportation into forums for the dissemination of ideas upon this captive audience.[67]

One of the hallmark characteristics of a captive audience is that the message must be forced on an audience in such a manner that the listener cannot reasonably avoid it. Consequently, a listener who can take reasonable steps to avoid the offending speech cannot be said to be harmed and therefore does not require the use of the doctrine for protection. It is unlikely that a captive audience exists if the listener can avoid the message by averting their eyes, turning away, or crossing the street. In *Breeden* the court distinguished the case of a truly captive viewer who is confronted with a signboard in a confined building space such as a foyer, as contrasted with someone on a sidewalk or in a concourse area.[68] The argument was that sidewalks and concourses allow an unwilling listener to take evasive action and avoid the unwanted message. One might have thought that this reasoning would similarly have applied to members of the public of Grande Prairie who happened to see the CCBR advertisement—they could just have averted their eyes or turned away from the bus.

However, in CCBR Queen's Bench, the court was not prepared to recognize this distinction as meaningful:

> Ads on city buses are viewed in very close proximity by those who have no other means of transportation. They are also viewed in close proximity by other users of the road, be they drivers or passengers in their own private vehicles or taxis, cyclists, or pedestrians, etc. City bus ads can also be seen from inside homes, while playing at playgrounds, or simply walking on city sidewalks...[69]

> Everyone sees a city bus, from the youngest to the oldest citizens of a municipality. Consequently, the messages carried on city buses must be appropriate for such a diverse audience.[70]

The Alberta Court of Queen's Bench concluded and the Alberta Court of Appeal affirmed that the advertising of othering messaging when communicated on municipal buses created a "captive audience," thereby amplifying the harmful impact of the hateful content:

> If it is acceptable and justifiable to restrict the audience for certain types of content, then the corollary is that it must be acceptable and

justifiable to restrict the content when it is impossible to restrict the audience, to protect the same vulnerable groups. Children should not be forced to view potentially upsetting images and phrases in a public place.[71]

I find the ad is likely to cause psychological harm to women who have had an abortion or who are considering an abortion. It is also likely to cause fear and confusion among children who may not fully understand what the ad is trying to express. They may not be familiar with the word abortion, but they can read and understand that "something" kills children. Expression of this kind may lead to emotional responses from the various people who make use of public transit and other users of the road, creating a hostile and uncomfortable environment. The creation of such an environment is antithetical to the statutory objective of providing a safe and, in particular, a welcoming transit system, within the greater context of providing services and developing and maintaining a safe and viable community.[72]

It is this intersection between othering messaging and a captive audience that is particularly troubling. Subjecting unwilling passers-by to hateful, othering messaging in public places, which passers-by cannot in their daily routine avoid, places the passers-by in an environment where they are subjected to shaming and ostracizing speech directed towards the othered subject.

Of course, the impact of harm on a captive audience may differ depending on the extent to which its members can avoid the othering messaging, and every case will require a contextual analysis. For example, the harm associated with the handing out of pamphlets is narrow because only those who voluntarily choose to take the pamphlet and read it are affected; even then, that is because of the reader's choice to engage with the material being proffered. The smaller the images and text used on signage, posters, or placards to communicate the message, the more limited the audience. Likewise, placards that only contain text may be less alluring to the passer-by's eyes than those that include graphic imagery. Placards, posters, and signs may be easier to avoid than auditory messaging that is communicated through loudspeakers at high volume. Advocacy messaging that is timed to coincide with public events, such as civic celebrations, street parades, or other large public gatherings, are more likely to create a captive audience. Similarly, large signage placed on the exterior of vehicles being driven during rush hour thereby forces exposure of the imagery upon anyone stuck in a nearby vehicle.

Conclusion

Othering advocacy speech that is imposed on a captive audience of unwilling viewers, particularly when it occurs in cities' most public and visible places, poses significant challenges from a public policy perspective for the following reasons:

- Othering advocacy messaging disseminated in municipal public spaces can lead to confusion as to whether a city has granted the advocacy organization permission to engage in hateful expression; it also forces municipal officials to explain whether the messaging represents the city's views.
- Othering advocacy can be interpreted as the permission needed for fringe extremists to take violent measures against the targeted group.
- Othering advocacy messaging that is consistently directed towards a group may attract a response by the targeted group, thereby increasing the likelihood of counter protests and violent confrontation.
- Othering advocacy messaging in prominent public city spaces undermines the perception that these spaces are "safe," inclusive places for anyone to be.
- Othering advocacy messaging displayed in a city's public spaces erodes the targeted group's confidence that their interests will be defended, while also undermining efforts by city officials to build trust with the group's members.

In this chapter we have argued that some circumstances exist in which othering advocacy messaging can properly be regulated in compliance with a municipality's *Charter* obligations. Our intention is not to stifle free speech or deny the vital importance that the free exchange of ideas has to the flourishing of our civic communities. Rather, we recognize that, as with any *Charter*-protected freedom, the aim is to achieve a balance between the person's freedom *of* speech and the unwilling listener's freedom *from* speech. And is that not always the challenge that arises when mediating between competing rights and freedoms—that of finding the right balance?

AUTHORS' NOTE

The views expressed in this chapter are solely those of the authors and do not reflect the views of any organization or employer with which the authors may be associated.

NOTES

1. On this issue we have found Blomley (1994, 2004, 2011) to be useful.
2. Municipalities are subject to statutes and can only exercise those powers specifically delegated to them legislatively. In Alberta, municipalities derive their statutory powers from the *Municipal Government Act*, RSA 2000, c M-26.
3. *Ibid.*, s 3(a).
4. *Ibid.*, s 3(c).
5. *Ibid.*, s 7(a).
6. *Saskatchewan (Human Rights Commission) v Whatcott*, [2013] 1 SCR 467, 2013 CanLII 11, at para 66 [*Whatcott*].
7. *Canadian Centre for Bio-Ethical Reform v Grande Prairie (City)*, 2018 ABCA 154, at para 80.
8. *American Freedom Defence Initiative v Edmonton (City)*, 2016 ABQB 555, at para 90 [*AFDI*].
9. *Canadian Charter of Rights and Freedoms*, s 2(b), Part I of the *Constitution Act, 1982*, being Schedule B to the *Canada Act 1982* (UK), 1982, c 11 [*Charter*].
10. See, for example, Casey (2019), CBC (2019), Hudes (2019), Junker (2017), and Wilson (2017).
11. For further discussion of the concept of othering, see, for example, Powell and Menendian (2016), Staszak (2009), and Vinkenburg (2014).
12. *R v Keegstra*, [1990] 3 SCR 697, 1990 CanLII 24, at 826 [*Keegstra*].
13. *Criminal Code*, RSC 1985, c C-46, ss 298, 318, 319.
14. For a general discussion, see Hogg (2016), ch 43 at 43-38–43-44.
15. *Ibid.*, at 43-7–43-10.

16. See these cases, for example: *Reference re Alberta Legislation*, [1983] SCR 100, 1938 CanLII 1, at 133, 147; *R v Boucher*, [1951] SCR 265, 1950 CanLII 2, at 277, 288, 290, 308, 344; *Switzman v Elbling*, [1957] SCR 285, 1957 CanLII 2, at 304–306, 326–328; *Ford v Québec (Procureur général)*, [1988] 2 SCR 712, 1988 CanLII 19, at 716–718, 764–767; *Edmonton Journal v Alberta (Attorney General)*, [1989] 2 SCR 1326, 1989 CanLII 20, at 1327, 1336–1337, 1373–1375; *R v Keegstra*, [1990] 3 SCR 697, 1990 CanLII 24, at 826, at 725–732, 760–767; *Canada (Human Rights Commission) v Taylor*, [1990] 3 SCR 892, 1990 CanLII 26, at 894–895, 916, 918–923; *Committee for the Commonwealth of Canada v Canada*, [1991] 1 SCR 139, 1991 CanLII 119, at 156–158, 166, 169–177, 178–185, 227; *R v Butler*, [1992] 1 SCR 452, 1992 CanLII 124 (SCC), at 488–491, 496–498; *R v Zundel*, [1992] 2 SCR 731, 1992 CanLII 75 (SCC), at 752–759; and *R v Sharpe*, [2001] 1 SCR 45, 2001 SCC 2 (CanLII), at 70–72, 123–127.

17. *Irwin Toy Ltd. v Québec (Procureur général)*, [1989] 1 SCR 927, 1989 CanLII 87, at 931, 967–977.

18. *Ibid.*, at 976.

19. *Canadian Charter of Rights and Freedoms*, s 2(b), Part I of the *Constitution Act, 1982*, being Schedule B to the *Canada Act 1982* (UK), 1982, c 11. Section 1 reads: "The *Canadian Charter of Rights and Freedoms* guarantees the rights and freedoms set out in it subject only to such reasonable limits prescribed by law as can be demonstrably justified in a free and democratic society."

20. *R v Oakes*, [1986] 1 SCR 103, 1986 CanLII 46.

21. *Ibid.*, at 136.

22. *Saskatchewan (Human Rights Commission) v Whatcott*, [2013] 1 SCR 467, 2013 CanLII 11, at para 75.

23. *Hill v Church of Scientology of Toronto*, [1995] 2 SCR 1130, 1995 CanLII 59, at 1174.

24. *Saskatchewan (Human Rights Commision) v Whatcott*, [2013] 1 SCR 467, 2013 CanLII 11, at para 66.

25. *Ibid.*, at para 35.

26. *Ibid.*, at para 56.

27. *Ibid.*, at paras 37–48.

28. *Ibid.*, at para 57.

29. *Ibid.*, at para 41.

30. *Ibid.*, at para 43.

31. *Ibid.*, at para 90.

32. *Ibid.*, at paras 52–54, 58.

33. *Ibid.*, at para 80.

34. *Ibid.*, at para 82.

35. *Canadian Centre for Bio-Ethical Reform v Grande Prairie (City)*, 2018 ABCA 154, at para 79.

36. *Saskatchewan (Human Rights Commission) v Whatcott*, [2013] 1 SCR 467, 2013 CanLII 11, at paras 90–91.

37. Curiously, in its interpretation guidelines the *Code* excludes from its definition of political advertising "any issue that is not currently the subject of debate at any level of government. For example: (a) pro-life/pro-choice advertising, (b) animal rights advocacy; or (c) climate change advertising (a message for or against the fact of climate change as distinct from an ad about a specific program to combat climate change)." This means that advocacy messaging that raises these issues generally when they are not the subject of a specific legislative proposal or debate at any level of government is captured by the *Code*.
38. See, for example, *Greater Vancouver Transportation Authority v Canadian Federation of Students*, [2009] 2 SCR 295, 2009 CanLII 31, at para 70 [*GVTA*]; *American Freedom Defence Initiative v Edmonton (City)*, 2016 ABQB 555, at para 69; *Canadian Centre for Bio-Ethical Reform v Grande Prairie (City)*, 2018 ABCA 154, at para 75.
39. *Greater Vancouver Transportation Authority v Canadian Federation of Students*, [2009] 2 SCR 295, 2009 CanLII 31, at para 70; *American Freedom Defence Initiative v Edmonton (City)*, 2016 ABQB 555, at para 90; *Canadian Centre for Bio-Ethical Reform v Grande Prairie (City)*, 2016 ABQB 734 [*CCBR* Queen's Bench]; *Canadian Centre for Bio-Ethical Reform v Grande Prairie (City)*, 2018 ABCA 154, at para 80; *The Canadian Centre for Bio-Ethical Reform v South Coast British Columbia Transportation Authority*, 2017 BCSC 1388; *Canadian Centre for Bio-Ethical Reform v South Coast British Columbia Transportation Authority*, 2018 BCCA 344; *Christian Heritage Party of Canada v City of Hamilton*, 2018 ONSC 3690. For commentary, see, for example, Malik, Best, and Watson (2018), Malik and Burton (2015), and Malik and Watson (2017).
40. *American Freedom Defence Initiative v Edmonton (City)*, 2016 ABQB 555, at para 90.
41. *Canadian Centre for Bio-Ethical Reform v Grande Prairie (City)*, 2016 ABQB 734.
42. American Freedom Defense Initiative, https://afdi.us.
43. *American Freedom Defence Initiative v Edmonton (City)*, 2016 ABQB 555, at para 11.
44. *Ibid.*, at para 12.
45. Stop Islamization of America, https://freedomdefense.typepad.com.
46. *American Freedom Defence Initiative v Edmonton (City)*, 2016 ABQB 555, at paras 83–86.
47. *Ibid.*, at para 88.
48. *Ibid.*, at para 116.
49. Canadian Centre for Bio-Ethical Reform, https://www.endthekilling.ca.
50. *Ibid.*
51. *Canadian Centre for Bio-Ethical Reform v Grande Prairie (City)*, 2016 ABQB 734, at para 80.
52. *Ibid.*, at paras 68–69.
53. *Ibid.*, at para 72.
54. *Ibid.*, at para 84.
55. *Canadian Centre for Bio-Ethical Reform v Grande Prairie (City)*, 2018 ABCA 154, at para 80.
56. *American Freedom Defence Initiative v Edmonton (City)*, 2016 ABQB 555, at para 94.
57. *Ibid.*, at para 100.

58. *Canadian Centre for Bio-Ethical Reform v Grande Prairie (City)*, 2016 ABQB 734, at para 80.
59. *Canadian Centre for Bio-Ethical Reform v Grande Prairie* (City), 2018 ABCA 154, at para 71. Had the Alberta Court of Appeal not found that the CCBR advertisement constituted hate speech, we would have argued that the advertisement would have met the lower threshold of proving othering speech.
60. *American Freedom Defence Initiative v Edmonton* (City), 2016 ABQB 555, at para 12.
61. For American academic commentary see, for example, Black (1953), Corbin (2009), Crocker (2007), Flynn (1994–1995), Haiman (1972), Strauss (1991), and Taylor (1983).
62. For a Canadian discussion, see, for example, Malik (2017) and Malik and Yurkewich (2019).
63. See two cases that deal with the captive-audience doctrine in the context of prohibitions on protesting near abortion clinics: *R v Spratt*, 2008 BCCA 340, where the court upheld provisions of the *Access to Abortion Services Act*, which prohibited protest and other interfering activities within a certain distance from abortion clinics; and *R v Von Dehn*, 2013 BCCA 187. For a similar example proposed by a municipality with respect to creating safe zones around schools, see Potkins (2019).
64. *R v Breeden*, 2009 BCCA 463 [*Breeden*].
65. Ibid., at para 34.
66. *Canadian Centre for Bio-Ethical Reform v Grande Prairie (City)*, 2016 ABQB 734, at para 56, citing *R v Breeden*, 2009 BCCA 463.
67. *Canadian Centre for Bio-Ethical Reform v Grande Prairie (City)*, 2016 ABQB 734, at para 57.
68. *R v Breeden*, 2009 BCCA 463, at para 34.
69. *Canadian Centre for Bio-Ethical Reform v Grande Prairie (City)*, 2016 ABQB 734, at para 69.
70. Ibid., at para 70.
71. Ibid., at para 72.
72. Ibid., at para 82.

REFERENCES

Advertising Standards Canada. (n.d.) *Canadian Code of Advertising Standards.* https://adstandards.ca/code/the-code-online/

Black, C.L., Jr. (1953). He cannot choose but hear: The plight of the captive auditor. *Columbia Law Review*, 960–972. https://digitalcommons.law.yale.edu/cgi/viewcontent.cgi?referer=&httpsredir=1&article=3591&context=fss_papers

Blomley, N.K. (1994). *Law, space, and the geographies of power.* Guilford Press.

Blomley, N. (2004). *Unsettling the city: Urban land and the politics of property.* Routledge.

Blomley, N. (2011). *Rights of passage: Sidewalks and the regulation of public flow.* Routledge.

Casey, L. (2019, October 29). Hundreds protest controversial Toronto library event featuring Meghan Murphy. *Global News.* https://globalnews.ca/news/6098974/toronto-public-library-meghan-murphy-event/

CBC. (2019, November 6). Staffers stage protest as Chiarelli returns to city hall. *CBC News*. https://www.cbc.ca/news/canada/ottawa/rick-chiarelli-ottawa-councillor-staff-1.5349935

Corbin, C.M. (2009). The First Amendment right against compelled listening. *Boston University Law Review, 89*, 940–1016. https://ssrn.com/abstract=1353489

Crocker, T.P. (2007). Displacing dissent: The role of "place" in First Amendment jurisprudence. *Fordham Law Review, 75*(5), 2587–2639.

Flynn, P.J. (1994). Street preachers versus merchants: Will the First Amendment be held captive in the balance? [Symposium on the Regulation of Free Expression in the Public Forum]. *St. Louis University Public Law Review, 14*(2), 613–654.

Haiman, F.S. (1972). Speech v privacy: Is there a right not to be spoken to? *Northwest University Law Review, 67*, 153–199.

Hogg, P.W. (2016). *Constitutional Law of Canada* (5th ed.). Carswell.

Hudes, S. (2019, September 27). Climate strike fills plaza outside city hall as protesters demand action. *Calgary Herald*. https://calgaryherald.com/news/local-news/climate-strike-fills-plaza-outside-city-hall-as-protesters-demand-action

Junker, A. (2017, June 26). A weekend of controversial rallies ends with no arrests. *Calgary Herald*. https://calgaryherald.com/news/local-news/a-weekend-of-controversial-rallies-ends-with-no-arrests

Malik, O. (2017, January 19). Lost and found? The captive audience doctrine returns in *Canadian Centre for Bio-Ethical Reform v The City of Grande Prairie (City)* [blog]. *ABLAWG*. https://ablawg.ca/2017/01/19/lost-and-found-the-captive-audience-doctrine-returns/

Malik, O., Best, S., & Watson, J. (2018). Left at the bus stop: How bus advertising cases have redefined the limits of hateful speech in our public places. *Digest of Municipal & Planning Law, 8*(23), 2d.

Malik, O., & Burton, S. (2015). Controversial advertising on city buses: Are municipalities ready for what's to come? *Digest of Municipal & Planning Law, 7*(5), 2d.

Malik, O., & Watson, J. (2017). A trio of bus advertising cases and five useful lessons for municipalities seeking to regulate offensive advertisement messaging. *Digest of Municipal & Planning Law, 8*(2), 2d.

Malik, O., & Yurkewich, T. (2019, December 10). The captive audience doctrine: Protecting the unwilling listener's right to privacy from unwanted speech [blog]. *ABLAWG*. https://ablawg.ca/2013/12/10/the-captive-audience-doctrine-protecting-the-unwilling-listeners-right-to-privacy-from-unwanted-speech

Potkins, M. (2019, November 13). Committee votes in favour of drafting "safe zones" around schools bylaw. *Calgary Sun*. https://calgarysun.com/news/local-news/students-should-be-protected-from-being-blindsided-by-harmful-expression-committee-hears/wcm/8b9d4cad-fd43-43e7-ae5f-f3f5e02f3063

Powell, J.A., & Menendian, S. (2016). The problem of othering: Towards inclusiveness and belonging. *Othering and Belonging: Expanding the Circle of Human Concern, 1*, 14–41.

Rorty, R. (1993). Human rights, rationality, and sentimentality. In S. Shute & S.L. Hurley (Eds.), *On human rights* (pp. 111–134). Basic Books.

Staszak, J.-F. (2009) Other/Otherness. In *International Encyclopedia of Human Geography* (Vol. 8) (pp. 43–47).

Strauss, M. (1991). Redefining the captive audience doctrine. *Hastings Constitutional Law Quarterly*, 19(1), 85–121. https://repository.uchastings.edu/cgi/viewcontent.cgi?article=1 481&context=hastings_constitutional_law_quaterly

Taylor, M. (1983). I'll defend to the death your right to say it...but not to me: The captive audience corollary to the First Amendment. *Southern Illinois University Law Journal*, 8(2), 211–226.

Vinkenburg, C.J. (2014). Titles matter: Addressing the normalization of othering. *Academy of Management Review*, 39(3), 382–386. doi:10.5465/amr.2013.0527

Wilson, J. (2017, March 6). Anti-Islam and anti-Islamophobia protesters clash at Saskatoon city hall. *Global News*. https://globalnews.ca/news/3288381/city-hall-hot-spot-for-debate-as-anti-islam-and-anti-islamophobia-protesters-clash/

LEGISLATION

Access to Abortion Services Act, RSBC 1996, c 1.

Canadian Charter of Rights and Freedoms, s 2(b), Part I of the *Constitution Act, 1982*, being Schedule B to the *Canada Act 1982* (UK), 1982, c 11.

Criminal Code, RSC 1985, c C-46, ss 298, 318, 319.

Municipal Government Act, RSA 2000, c M-26.

JURISPRUDENCE

American Freedom Defence Initiative v Edmonton (City), 2016 ABQB 555.

Canada (Human Rights Commission) v Taylor, [1990] 3 SCR 892, 1990 CanLII 26.

Canadian Centre for Bio-Ethical Reform v Grande Prairie (City), 2018 ABCA 154.

Canadian Centre for Bio-Ethical Reform v Grande Prairie (City), 2016 ABQB 734.

Canadian Centre for Bio-Ethical Reform v South Coast British Columbia Transportation Authority, 2017 BCSC 1388.

Canadian Centre for Bio-Ethical Reform v South Coast British Columbia Transportation Authority, 2018 BCCA 344.

Christian Heritage Party of Canada v City of Hamilton, 2018 ONSC 3690.

Committee for the Commonwealth of Canada v Canada, [1991] 1 SCR 139, 1991 CanLII 119.

Edmonton Journal v Alberta (Attorney General), [1989] 2 SCR 1326, 1989 CanLII 20.

Ford v Québec (Procureur général), [1988] 2 SCR 712, 1988 CanLII 19.

Greater Vancouver Transportation Authority v Canadian Federation of Students, [2009] 2 SCR 295, 2009 CanLII 31.

Hill v Church of Scientology of Toronto, [1995] 2 SCR 1130, 1995 CanLII 59.

Irwin Toy Ltd. v Québec (Procureur général), [1989] 1 SCR 927, 1989 CanLII 87.

Reference re Alberta Legislation, [1983] SCR 100, 1938 CanLII 1.

R v Boucher, [1951] SCR 265, 1950 CanLII 2.

R v Breeden, 2009 BCCA 463.

R v Butler, [1992] 1 SCR 452, 1992 CanLII 124 (SCC).

R v Keegstra, [1990] 3 SCR 697, 1990 CanLII 24, at 826.

R v Oakes, [1986] 1 SCR 103, 1986 CanLII 46.

R v Sharpe, [2001] 1 SCR 45, 2001 SCC 2 (CanLII).

R v Spratt, 2008 BCCA 340.

R v Von Dehn, 2013 BCCA 187.

R v Zundel, [1992] 2 SCR 731, 1992 CanLII 75 (SCC).

Saskatchewan (Human Rights Commission) v Whatcott, [2013] 1 SCR 467, 2013 CanLII 11.

Switzman v Elbling, [1957] SCR 285, 1957 CanLII 2.

AFTERWORD
After Rights?

BENJAMIN DAVY

SHORTLY AFTER Sandeep Agrawal invited me to write an afterword to this book, a discussion erupted on PlanetNew, a listserv for the international community of mostly planning scholars. Sasha Tsenkova had generously shared an open-access link to her newly edited book *Cities and Affordable Housing: Planning, Design and Policy Nexus* with the community.[1] I forwarded the link to my colleague Michael Kolocek, who has published on the human right to housing (Kolocek, 2017). Michael responded quickly that the book paid little attention to housing rights. On a whim I posted this message to Sasha on PlanetNew:

> I forwarded it [the link] to a colleague who is an expert on the human right to housing. He was quite disappointed that the rights aspect of housing has no or little role in your edited volume. I agree. From Vancouver to Berlin, from Wien to London, you cannot discuss cities and housing without looking deeply at the rights of landlords and tenants.

A passionate discussion ensued. Anybody registered with PlanetNew can read what was said.² At one point, Professor Tsenkova responded to the PlanetNew community in a long message that included the following:

> While the housing rights approach is a good point of departure, even in the UN organisations it has been acknowledged that its implementation is very limited. I have worked for a good number of these international entities over the years. It was indeed recognised that many countries do not want to adopt this approach in their housing policies, and even if they do, it is not necessarily implemented.

The message and the entire discussion emphasizes that a number of spatial planners, housing experts, and urbanists believe that the discourse on cities and housing has moved into a space "after rights." Is this a prudent move?

Rights and the City: Problems, Progress, and Practice, the timely book edited by Sandeep Agrawal, proves the notion of "after rights" to be misleading. I agree with the thesis of this book that cities and rights deserve more attention. The thought that rights do not matter is misleading because housing and other aspects of cities are always and everywhere entwined with notions of belonging and appropriation, coordinating various interests in the uses of urban space and the legitimacy of inclusion and exclusion. To put it in a shorter way, housing and other aspects of city life are always and everywhere entwined with rights.

The notion of "after rights" is correct, however, as long as we envision rights to and in the city as flawless, consistent, and uncontested institutions that distribute duties and rights among all stakeholders in a superbly just and efficient fashion. Most of the time and in most places, rights do not work like this. Rights are frames for urban struggles. In many cities, individuals and groups struggle over the use of public spaces, affordable housing, evictions, contested memories, ancient burial grounds, environmental justice, and many other urban conflicts. Such struggles are often framed in rights language even though a resolution cannot always be found in court.

On different levels, each chapter in this collection deals with the ambiguity of the concepts of *city* and *rights*. Is *city* about municipal institutions, the built environment, the community of urban dwellers, opportunities to become rich and famous? Are *rights* about natural rights, legal rights, moral entitlements, cultural expectations, individual or collective claims? And if *rights* mean legal rights, does this mean that rights are grounded in domestic or international law, and constitutional, private, or administrative law (such as statutory law on planning and building)?

The three parts of the book—addressing the right *to* the city, rights *in* the city, and other rights *and* the city—organize a rich discussion of rights and cities. All contributions look at *legal* rights and the city, some from the perspective of human rights (Chapters 3, 5, 6, and to some extent 7), and others from the perspective of Canadian law (Chapters 1, 2, 4, 8, and 9). Henri Lefebvre's famous concept of a *right to the city*, which guides the book's narrative, was not about legal rights in the sense of well-established legal rules that are no longer subject to reasonable dispute. Particularly in Latin America, the right to the city developed as a political and cultural claim of activists. Chapter 2 is a deliberation on how such a claim could transform Canadian law. Nonetheless, several contributions consider rights and cities with regard to legal detail (Chapters 3, 4, and 8).

Chapter 7 demonstrates the value of comparison in understanding better how rights and cities relate to each other. Michelle Oren and Rachelle Alterman examine the right to adequate housing from the perspective of global human rights law and of comparative constitutional law. They find in particular that out of 189 national constitutions surveyed, 84 (44%) mention the right to adequate housing, and that neither the Canadian *Charter* nor the US *Constitution* mention this right. Perhaps this means that more could be done worldwide for the implementation and protection of the right to housing. Surely, however, it does not mean that housing and cities have moved into a space "after rights."

Critical thinking about rights often condemns rights that protect the wealthy and powerful, putting marginalized individuals and communities at a disadvantage. It is easy to illustrate the biased impact of many laws with examples of urban injustice. In 2020 the Black Lives Matter movement protested the disrespect shown by police officers for the rights of Black persons, a disrespect that too often ended with the killing of Black men and women. Cities built with blood money from colonialism and slavery protect the property rights of corporate landlords better than the rights of tenants who cannot pay their rent and are threatened with eviction and homelessness. In many Western cities, cars have the right "to sleep" on the street, but homeless persons are not allowed to sleep rough or "loiter."

But rights can also enable and empower disadvantaged individuals and communities. In Canada, Indigenous rights are essential for the protection of First Nations (see Chapters 1 and 4). Sometimes the rights granted by the *Charter* even protect homeless persons who build a tent village in a public park (see Chapter 8, note 1). Rights, even if fairly weak, help structure the conversation on how urban land could be used. Of course, alternative dispute resolution and mediation would guide conflicting stakeholders more effectively to find acceptable solutions to problems that are too complex for a rights-based solution. Yet, if alternative dispute resolution is unavailable, resorting to rights is better than resorting to violence. The "rights to the city" initiatives—including many variations, from the Occupy movement of 2011 to guerilla gardening—can give active voice to neglected causes.

The discussion on PlanetNew mentioned at the beginning reminded me of the debate on civil, political, and social rights. This debate reflected distrust in the liberal and libertarian ideology of rights that protect the wealthy and powerful elites. If we associate rights with the rights of corporate landlords, distrust is reasonable and even necessary. But rights also can be important instruments in the inclusion of marginalized individuals and groups. Regarding class and citizenship, T.H. Marshall (1950) emphasized the relevance of rights. Nobody really is included unless they have an individual right to belong; nobody really is excluded unless they are denied even the right to claim some space for themselves.

Marshall (1950, pp. 10–27) specified three elements of citizenship—civil, political, and social—which derive from individual rights. Traditionally, citizenship had been associated with civil and political rights. Civil rights (e.g., property rights, freedom of religion) and political rights (e.g., the right to a peaceful assembly, voting rights) have been considered the core of citizenship. Marshall doubted that society, even in the face of abundant natural resources, could "enable every man to be a gentleman" (p. 6). He added a "social element" to citizenship that comprised "the right…to live the life of a civilised being according to the standards prevailing in the society" (p. 11). Social rights, although often considered weak, are important to grant every child, every woman, every man, and every diverse person a social modicum and dignity.

Talking about the right to the city turns attention to the inclusion and appreciation of marginalized individuals and groups. Chapter 6 demonstrates the importance of human dignity as one of four pillars of responsibility in establishing a human rights city. Sadly, town planners often neglect human dignity as a fundamental value of planning urban spaces (Davy 2020, pp. 8–10). However, the right to the protection of and the respect for human dignity must be considered a lodestar for the development and growth of sustainable and attractive cities.

NOTES

1. See https://www.taylorfrancis.com/books/oa-edit/10.4324/9781003172949/cities-affordable-housing-sasha-tsenkova.
2. See https://groups.google.com/forum/#!forum/planetnew/join.

REFERENCES

Davy, B. (2020). Human dignity: Is there a place for it in planning? *Transactions of the Association of European Schools of Planning*, 4(1), 7–21. http://transactions-journal.aesop-planning.eu/volume-4/article-32/

Kolocek, M. (2017). *The human right to housing in the face of land policy and social citizenship: A global discourse analysis*. Palgrave Macmillan.

Marshall, T H. (1950). *Citizenship and social class and other essays*. Cambridge University Press.

CONTRIBUTORS
—

SANDEEP AGRAWAL is a professor and inaugural director of the School of Urban and Regional Planning at the University of Alberta. Dr. Agrawal has a diverse array of research interests that currently encompasses sustainable urban and rural planning, international development, multiculturalism, Indigenous issues, and human rights. His most recent research has focused on human rights and Indigenous rights as they relate to housing and homelessness issues, municipal restructuring, and international development works in countries like India, Sri Lanka, Brazil, and the United Arab Emirates. As an accomplished author with over a hundred articles and professional reports and a book, Dr. Agrawal has also contributed to planning practice and affected city bylaws and planning policies and legislation, with a lens on human rights and equity. He is the recipient of the Canadian Institute of Planners' national academic award for his significant contribution to planning education and research in the country.

RACHELLE ALTERMAN is emeritus professor of Urban Planning and Law at Technion–Israel Institute of Technology where she heads the Lab on Comparative Planning Law and Land Policy. She is also a senior researcher at Technion's Neaman Institute for National Policy Research.

Dr. Alterman is the founding president of the International Academic Association on Planning, Law and Property Rights, and an honorary member of the Association of European Schools of Planning. Her many publications focus on cross-national analysis of planning law, property rights, housing tenure, and housing policy. Dr. Alterman's advice (usually pro bono) is sought by UN Habitat, the Organisation for Economic Co-operation and Development, the World Bank, and Chinese government bodies. In Israel her research is often cited by the courts, and her opinions are sought by the Knesset, government bodies, civil society, and the media.

SASHA BEST completed her juris doctor at the University of Calgary's Faculty of Law, following an undergraduate degree at Memorial University in Newfoundland. During her time at the University of Calgary, Ms. Best became project lead with Pro Bono Students Canada's The Consent Project, a public legal education initiative providing informed consent education to young people. She has worked as a prosecutor with both Alberta Justice and the City of Calgary. Ms. Best is passionate about increasing meaningful access to justice for marginalized individuals and those who face barriers when interacting with the legal system.

BENJAMIN DAVY is visiting professor at the Faculty of Law, University of Johannesburg, South Africa. From 1997 through 2019 he was Professor of Land Policy, Land Management, and Municipal Geoinformation at the School of Spatial Planning, TU Dortmund University in Germany. He is a member of several boards of real estate appraisal. Dr. Davy was vice-president and president of the International Academic Association on Planning, Law, and Property Rights (PLPR), as well as vice-president and president of the Association of European Schools of Planning (AESOP). He is a member of the editorial boards of the *Journal of the American Planning Association* and *Planning Theory and Practice*. Dr. Davy was the essay editor of *Planning Theory* and co-editor of the *Town Planning Review*.

His research interests currently include human dignity and planning, land use ethics, and land reform.

ALEXANDRA FLYNN is an assistant professor at University of British Columbia's Allard School of Law. Her teaching and research focus on municipal law and governance, including Indigenous–municipal legal relationships. Dr. Flynn is currently working on several projects related to precariously housed people in Canadian cities. She has a long history of volunteer work in the areas of homelessness and access to justice, as a TEDx speaker, and as a frequent media commentator.

ERAN S. KAPLINSKY, LL.B., LL.M., SJD, is a professor of Law, and research director of the Alberta Land Institute at the University of Alberta. He teaches and researches in the areas of property, municipal, and planning law. Dr. Kaplinsky has published widely on land use and municipal regulations, development obligations, expropriation and compensation, and property rights. He is a collaborator in Dr. Agrawal's research on human rights and cities, funded by the Social Sciences and Humanities Research Council.

OLA P. MALIK, MA, LL.M., worked as a lawyer with the City of Calgary for over 12 years, writing on cases involving *Charter* issues and municipal bylaw drafting and enforcement. Mr. Malik has been a strong champion of access to justice initiatives and has served on numerous not-for-profit boards and organizations.

JENNIFER A. ORANGE is an assistant professor at the Lincoln Alexander School of Law at Ryerson University. She is a lawyer, adjudicator, and human rights scholar. Dr. Orange is a former member of the Human Rights Tribunal of Ontario and is currently a member of the Canadian Human Rights Tribunal. She is passionate about the potential for partnerships between cultural and legal institutions in the work to prevent and recover from human rights violations. Dr. Orange has also taught at the law faculties of the University of Toronto and the University of Western Ontario and is a frequent speaker on international law, human rights, and the role of museums. All views expressed in this chapter are her own.

MICHELLE L. OREN heads the Urban Futures lab at the Bar-Ilan Center for Smart Cities. She is a lecturer and research fellow at Bar-Ilan University's Graduate School of Business Administration. Dr. Oren earned her doctorate from the Faculty of Architecture and Town Planning at the Technion–Israel Institute of Technology. Her doctoral dissertation, "The Constitutional Right to Housing: A Public Policy Approach," was supervised by Professor Rachelle Alterman. As a practising urban planner, Dr. Oren has contributed to numerous development plans assuming positions in both the private and public sectors (local government). She is the author of the forthcoming UN DESA, UNPOG handbook *Promoting Innovation for Inclusion of Vulnerable Groups and Leaving No One Behind: Innovative Local Governance for the Implementation of the Sustainable Development Goals*.

RENÉE VAUGEOIS is the executive director of the John Humphrey Centre for Peace and Human Rights based in Edmonton. The mission of the centre, named after John Peters Humphrey, a principal drafter of the United Nations' *Universal Declaration of Human Rights*, is to advance dignity, freedom, justice, and security through collaborative relationships and transformative education on peace and human rights. Ms. Vaugeois is a network builder, facilitator, educator, and collaborator and has been a driving force behind the declaration of Edmonton as a human rights city; she is also a facilitator of several human rights education and peace-building programs across Alberta and the country.

Other Titles from University of Alberta Press

The Right to Be Rural
Edited by KAREN R. FOSTER &
JENNIFER JARMAN
The provocative concept of a "right to be rural" illuminates challenges facing rural communities worldwide.

Indigenous Women and Street Gangs
AMBER, BEV, CHANTEL, JAZMYNE, FAITH, JORGINA & ROBERT HENRY
Six Indigenous women demonstrate survivance through photos and narratives about street gangs and street lifestyle.

Power Play
Professional Hockey and the Politics of Urban Development
JAY SCHERER, DAVID MILLS &
LINDA SLOAN MCCULLOCH
Big money and municipal politics collide in the story of Edmonton's Rogers Place hockey arena.

More information at uap.ualberta.ca

www.ingramcontent.com/pod-product-compliance
Ingram Content Group UK Ltd.
Pitfield, Milton Keynes, MK11 3LW, UK
UKHW011605021025
463508UK00002B/136